Mazda GLC Automotive Repair Manual

by Larry Warren and John H Haynes

Member of the Guild of Motoring Writers

Models covered

Front-wheel drive 2- and 4-door hatchback and 4-door sedan with 1.5 liter engine, and 4- or 5-speed manual or 3-speed automatic transaxle

ISBN 85010 284 8

Printed in the USA   *(1V8 - 757)*

AB

Library of Congress

Catalog card number

86-81149

Haynes Publishing Group
Sparkford Nr Yeovil
Somerset BA22 7JJ England

Haynes North America, Inc
861 Lawrence Drive
Newbury Park
California 91320 USA

Acknowledgements

Special thanks are due to Toyo Kogyo Company for their supply of technical information and certain illustrations. Champion Spark Plug Company supplied the illustrations showing the various spark plug conditions. The bodywork repair section photographs were provided by Holt Lloyd Limited.

About this manual

Its purpose

The purpose of this manual is to help you get the best value from your vehicle. It can do so in several ways. It can help you decide what work must be done even if you choose to get it done by a dealer service department or a repair shop; it provides information and procedures for routine maintenance and servicing; and it offers diagnostic and repair procedures to follow when trouble occurs.

It is hoped that you will use the manual to tackle the work yourself. For many simpler jobs, doing it yourself may be quicker than arranging an appointment to get the vehicle into a shop and making the trips to leave it and pick it up. More importantly, a lot of money can be saved by avoiding the expense the shop must pass on to you to cover its labor and overhead costs. An added benefit is the sense of satisfaction and accomplishment that you feel after having done the job yourself.

Using the manual

The manual is divided into Chapters. Each Chapter is divided into numbered Sections, which are headed in bold type between horizontal lines. Each Section consists of consecutively numbered paragraphs.

The two types of illustrations used (figures and photographs) are referenced by a number preceding their captions. Figure reference numbers denote Chapter and numerical sequence in the Chapter; i.e. Fig. 12.4 means Chapter 12, figure number 4. Figure captions are followed by a Section number which ties the figure to a specific portion of the text. All photographs apply to the Chapter in which they appear, and the reference number pinpoints the pertinent Section and paragraph.

Procedures, once described in the text, are not normally repeated. When it is necessary to refer to another Chapter, the reference will be given as Chapter and Section number; i.e. Chapter 1/16. Cross references given without use of the word 'Chapter' apply to Sections and/or paragraphs in the same Chapter. For example, 'see Section 8' means in the same Chapter.

Reference to the left or right of the vehicle is based on the assumption that one is sitting in the driver's seat facing forward.

Even though extreme care has been taken during the preparation of this manual, neither the publisher nor the author can accept responsibility for any errors in, or omissions from, the information given.

Introduction to the Mazda GLC

Available in 2-door hatchback, 4-door hatchback and 4-door sedan body styles, these models feature front drive and 4-wheel independent suspension.

The cross-mounted 4-cylinder engine drives the front wheels through a 4- or 5-speed manual or 3-speed automatic transaxle by way of un-equal length driveshafts. The rack-and-pinion steering gear is mounted behind the engine.

Brakes are disc in the front and self-adjusting drum at the rear with a vacuum servo assist as standard. Information on 1983 through 1986 models can be found in the Supplement starting on page 162.

Contents

Three-quarter front view Mazda GLC

Three-quarter rear view Mazda GLC

General dimensions, capacities and weights

Dimensions
Overall length
    2-door hatchback .... 159.1 in
    4-door sedan and hatchback .... 166.7 in
Overall height .... 54.1 in
Overall width .... 64.2 in
Wheelbase .... 93.1 in

Capacities
Engine oil .... 4.0 US qts
Radiator coolant .... 5.8 US qts
Manual transaxle lubricant .... 3.4 US qts
Automatic transaxle fluid .... 6.0 US qts
Fuel tank .... 11.1 US gallons

Curb weight
2-door hatchback .... 1900 lbs
4-door sedan and hatchback .... 1945 lbs

Buying parts

Buying spare parts

Replacement parts are available from many sources, which generally fall into one of two categories – authorized dealer parts departments and independent retail auto parts stores. Our advice concerning these parts is as follows:

Retail auto parts stores: Good auto parts stores will stock frequently needed components which wear out relatively fast, such as clutch components, exhaust systems, brake parts, tune-up parts, etc. These stores often supply new or reconditioned parts on an exchange basis, which can save a considerable amount of money. Discount auto parts stores are often very good places to buy materials and parts needed for general vehicle maintenance such as oil, grease, filters, spark plugs, belts, touch-up paint, bulbs, etc. They also usually sell tools and general accessories, have convenient hours, charge lower prices and can often be found not far from home.

Authorized dealer parts department: This is the best source for parts which are unique to the vehicle and not generally available elsewhere (such as major engine parts, transmission parts, trim pieces, etc.).

Warranty information: If the vehicle is still covered under warranty, be sure that any replacement parts purchased – regardless of the source – do not invalidate the warranty!

To be sure of obtaining the correct parts, have engine and chassis numbers available and, if possible, take the old parts along for positive identification.

Vehicle identification numbers

Regardless from which source parts are obtained, it is essential to provide correct information concerning the vehicle model and year of manufacture plus the engine serial number and the vehicle identification number (VIN). The accompanying illustrations show where these important numbers can be found.

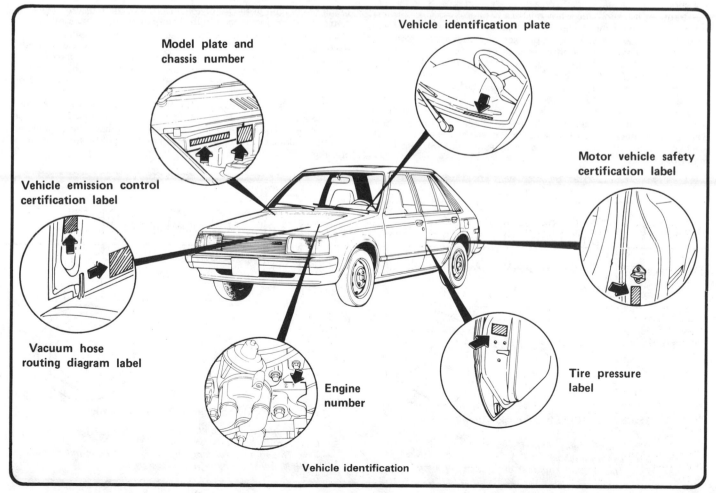

Vehicle identification plate

Model plate and chassis number

Motor vehicle safety certification label

Vehicle emission control certification label

Vacuum hose routing diagram label

Engine number

Tire pressure label

Vehicle identification

Maintenance techniques, tools and working facilities

Basic maintenance techniques

There are a number of techniques involved in maintenance and repair that will be referred to throughout this manual. Application of these techniques will enable the home mechanic to be more efficient, better organized and capable of performing the various tasks properly, which will ensure that the repair job is thorough and complete.

Fasteners

Fasteners, basically, are nuts, bolts, studs and screws used to hold two or more parts together. There are a few things to keep in mind when working with fasteners. Almost all of them use a locking device of some type; either a lock washer, locknut, locking tab or thread adhesive. All threaded fasteners should be clean and straight, with undamaged threads and undamaged corners on the hex head where the wrench fits. Develop the habit of replacing damaged nuts and bolts with new ones. Special locknuts with nylon or fiber inserts can only be used once. If they are removed, they lose their locking ability and must be replaced with new ones.

Rusted nuts and bolts should be treated with a penetrating fluid to ease removal and prevent breakage. Some mechanics use turpentine in a spout-type oil can, which works quite well. After applying the rust penetrant, let it "work" for a few minutes before trying to loosen the nut or bolt. Badly rusted fasteners may have to be chiseled or sawed off or removed with a special nut breaker, available at tool stores.

If a bolt or stud breaks off in an assembly, it can be drilled and removed with a special tool commonly available for this purpose. Most automotive machine shops can perform this task, as well as other repair procedures (such as repair of threaded holes that have been stripped out).

Flat washers and lock washers, when removed from an assembly should always be replaced exactly as removed. Replace damaged washers with new ones. Always use a flat washer between a lock washer and any soft metal surface (such as aluminum), thin sheet metal or plastic.

Fastener sizes

For a number of reasons, automobile manufacturers are making wider and wider use of metric fasteners. Therefore, it is important to be able to tell the difference between standard (sometimes called U.S., English or SAE) and metric hardware, since they cannot be interchanged.

All bolts, whether standard or metric, are sized according to diameter, thread pitch and length. For example, a standard $\frac{1}{2}$ – 13 x 1 bolt is $\frac{1}{2}$ inch in diameter, has 13 threads per inch and is 1 inch long. An M12 – 1.75 x 25 metric bolt is 12 mm in diameter, has a thread pitch of 1.75 mm (the distance between threads) and is 25 mm long. The 2 bolts are nearly identical, and easily confused, but they are not interchangeable.

In addition to the differences in diameter, thread pitch and length, metric and standard bolts can also be distinguished by examining the bolt heads. To begin with, the distance across the flats on a standard bolt head is measured in inches, while the same dimension on a metric bolt is measured in millimeters (the same is true for nuts). As a result, a standard wrench should not be used on a metric bolt and a metric wrench should not be used on a standard bolt. Also, standard bolts have slashes radiating out from the center of the head to denote the grade or strength of the bolt (which is an indication of the amount of torque that can be supplied to it). The greater the number of slashes, the greater the strength of the bolt (grades 0 through 5 are commonly used on automobiles). Metric bolts have a property class (grade) number, rather than a slash, molded into their heads to indicate bolt strength. In this case, the higher the number the stronger the bolt (property class numbers 8.8, 9.8 and 10.9 are commonly used on automobiles).

Strength markings can also be used to distinguish standard hex nuts from metric hex nuts. Standard nuts have dots stamped into one side, while metric nuts are marked with a number. The greater the number of dots, or the higher the number, the greater the strength of the nut.

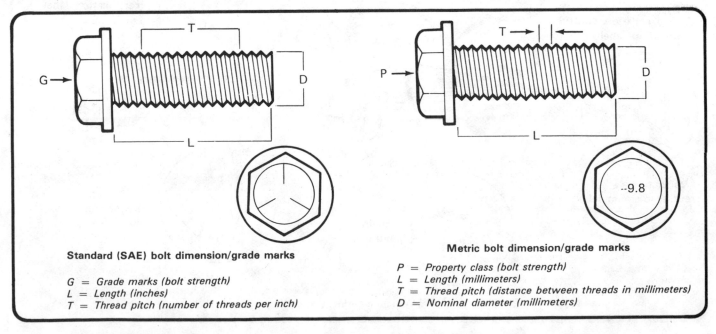

Standard (SAE) bolt dimension/grade marks

G = Grade marks (bolt strength)
L = Length (inches)
T = Thread pitch (number of threads per inch)

Metric bolt dimension/grade marks

P = Property class (bolt strength)
L = Length (millimeters)
T = Thread pitch (distance between threads in millimeters)
D = Nominal diameter (millimeters)

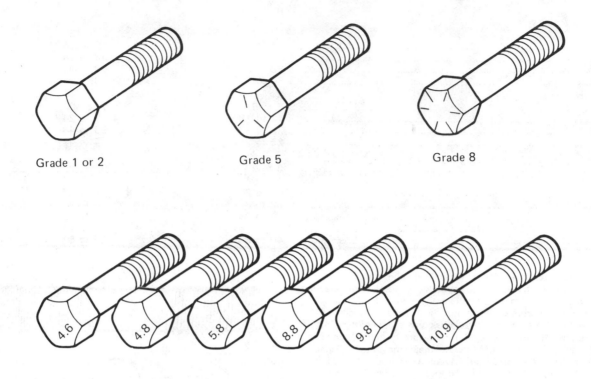

Bolt strength markings (top – standard/SAE, bottom – metric)

Grade	Identification	Class	Identification
Hex Nut Grade 5	3 Dots	Hex Nut Property Class 9	Arabic 9
Hex Nut Grade 8	6 Dots	Hex Nut Property Class 10	Arabic 10

Standard hex nut strength markings   **Metric hex nut strength markings**

Metric studs are also marked on their ends according to property class (grade). Larger studs are numbered (the same as metric bolts), while smaller studs carry a geometric code to denote grade.

It should be noted that many fasteners, especially Grades 0 through 2, have no distinguishing marks on them. When such is the case, the only way to determine whether it is standard or metric is to measure the thread pitch or compare it to a known fastener of the same size.

Since fasteners of the same size (both standard and metric) may have different strength ratings, be sure to reinstall any bolts, studs or nuts removed from your vehicle in their original locations. Also, when replacing a fastener with a new one, make sure that the new one has a strength rating equal to or greater than the original.

Tightening sequences and procedures

Most threaded fasteners should be tightened to a specific torque value (torque is basically a twisting force). Over-tightening the fastener can weaken it and lead to eventual breakage, while under-tightening can cause it to eventually come loose. Bolts, screws and studs, depending on the materials they are made of and their thread diameters, have specific torque values (many of which are noted in the Specifications Section at the beginning of each Chapter). Be sure to follow the torque recommendations closely. For fasteners not assigned a specific torque, a general torque value chart is presented here as a guide. As was previously mentioned, the sizes and grade of a fastener determine the amount of torque that can safely be applied to it. The figures listed here are approximate for Grade 2 and Grade 3 fasteners (higher grades can tolerate higher torque values).

	ft-lb	Nm
Metric thread sizes		
M-6	6 to 9	9 to 12
M-8	14 to 21	19 to 28
M-10	28 to 40	38 to 54
M-12	50 to 71	68 to 96
M-14	80 to 140	109 to 154
Pipe thread sizes		
1/8	5 to 8	7 to 10
1/4	12 to 18	17 to 24
3/8	22 to 33	30 to 44
1/2	25 to 35	34 to 47
U.S. thread sizes		
1/4 - 20	6 to 9	9 to 12
5/16 - 18	12 to 18	17 to 24
5/16 - 24	14 to 20	19 to 27
3/8 - 16	22 to 32	30 to 43
3/8 - 24	27 to 38	37 to 51
7/16 - 14	40 to 55	55 to 74
7/16 - 20	40 to 60	55 to 81
1/2 - 13	55 to 80	75 to 108

Fasteners laid out in a pattern (i.e. cylinder head bolts, oil pan bolts, differential cover bolts, etc.) must be loosened and tightened in a definite sequence to avoid warping the component. Initially, the bolts or nuts should be assembled finger-tight only. Next, they should be tightened one full turn each, in a criss-cross or diagonal pattern. After each one has been tightened one full turn, return to the first one and tighten them all one half turn, following the same pattern. Finally, tighten each of them one-quarter turn at a time until they all have been tightened to the proper torque value. To loosen and remove them the procedure would be reversed.

Component disassembly

Component disassembly should be done with care and purpose to help ensure that the parts go back together properly. Always keep track of the sequence in which parts are removed. Make note of special characteristics or markings on parts that can be installed more than one way (such as a grooved thrust washer on a shaft). It is a good idea to lay the disassembled parts out on a clean surface in the order that they were removed. It may also be helpful to make simple sketches or take instant photos of components before removal.

When removing fasteners from an assembly, keep track of their locations. Sometimes threading a bolt back in a part, or putting the washers and nut back on a stud, can prevent mixups later. If nuts and bolts cannot be returned to their original locations, they should be kept in a compartmented box or a series of small boxes. A cupcake or muffin tin is ideal for this purpose, since each cavity can hold the bolts and nuts from a particular area (i.e. oil pan bolts, valve cover bolts, engine mount bolts, etc.). A pan of this type is especially helpful when working on assemblies with very small parts (such as the carburetor, alternator, valve train or interior dash and trim pieces). The cavities can be marked with paint or tape to identify the contents.

Whenever wiring looms, harnesses or connectors are separated, it's a good idea to identify them with numbered pieces of masking tape so that they can be easily reconnected.

Gasket sealing surfaces

Throughout any vehicle, gaskets are used to seal the mating surfaces between two parts and keep lubricants, fluids, vacuum or pressure contained in an assembly.

Many times these gaskets are coated with a liquid or paste-type gasket sealing compound before assembly. Age, heat and pressure can sometimes cause the two parts to stick together so tightly that they are very difficult to separate. Often the assembly can be loosened by striking it with a soft-faced hammer near the mating surfaces. A regular hammer can be used if a block of wood is placed between the hammer and the part. Do not hammer on cast parts or parts that could be easily damaged. With any particularly stubborn part, always recheck to see that every fastener has been removed.

Avoid using a screwdriver or bar to pry apart an assembly, as they can easily mar the gasket sealing surfaces of the parts (which must remain smooth). If prying is absolutely necessary, use an old broom handle, but keep in mind that extra clean-up will be necessary if the wood splinters.

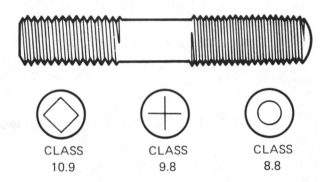

Metric stud strength markings

CLASS 10.9   CLASS 9.8   CLASS 8.8

After the parts are separated, the old gasket must be carefully scraped off and the gasket surfaces cleaned. Stubborn gasket material can be soaked with rust penetrant or treated with a special chemical to soften it so that it can be easily scraped off. A scraper can be fashioned from a piece of copper tubing by flattening and sharpening one end. Copper is recommended because it is usually softer than the surfaces to be scraped, which reduces the chance of gouging the part. Some gaskets can be removed with a wire brush, but regardless of the method used, the mating surfaces must be left clean and smooth. If for some reason the gasket surface is gouged, then a gasket sealer thick enough to fill scratches will have to be used upon reassembly of the components. For most applications, a non-drying (or semi-drying) gasket sealer should be used.

Hose removal tips

Caution: *If equipped with air conditioning, do not ever disconnect any of the a/c hoses without first de-pressurizing the system.*

Hose removal precautions closely parallel gasket removal precautions. Avoid scratching or gouging the surface that the hose mates against or the connection may leak. This is especially true for radiator hoses. Because of various chemical reactions, the rubber in hoses can bond itself to the metal spigot that the hose fits over. To remove a hose, first loosen the hose clamps that secure it to the spigot. Then, with slip joint pliers, grab the hose at the clamp and rotate it around the spigot. Work it back and forth until it is completely free, then pull it off (silicone or other lubricants will ease removal if they can be applied between the hose and the spigot). Apply the same lubricant to the inside of the hose and the outside of the spigot to simplify installation.

If a hose clamp is broken or damaged, do not re-use it. Do not reuse hoses that are cracked, split or torn.

Tools

A selection of good tools is a basic requirement for anyone who plans to maintain and repair his or her own vehicle. For the owner who has few tools, if any, the initial investment might seem high, but when compared to the spiraling costs of professional auto maintenance and repair, it is a wise one.

To help the owner decide which tools are needed to perform the tasks detailed in this manual, the following tool lists are offered: *Maintenance and minor repair, Repair and overhaul* and *Special.* The newcomer to practical mechanics should start off with the *Maintenance and minor repair* tool kit, which is adequate for the simpler jobs performed on a vehicle. Then, as his confidence and experience grow, he can tackle more difficult tasks, buying additional tools as they are needed. Eventually the basic kit will be expanded into the *Repair and overhaul* tool set. Over a period of time, the experienced do-it-yourselfer will assemble a tool set complete enough for most repair and overhaul procedures and will add tools from the *Special* category when he feels the expense is justified by the frequency of use.

Maintenance and minor repair tool kit

The tools in this list should be considered the minimum for performance of routine maintenance, servicing and minor repair work. We recommend the purchase of combination wrenches (box end and open end combined in one wrench); while more expensive than open-ended ones, they offer the advantages of both types of wrench.

> *Combination wrench set ($\frac{1}{4}$ in to 1 in or 6 mm to 19 mm)*
> *Adjustable wrench – 8 in*
> *Spark plug wrench (with rubber insert)*
> *Spark plug gap adjusting tool*
> *Feeler gauge set*
> *Brake bleeder wrench*
> *Standard screwdriver ($\frac{5}{16}$ in x 6 in)*
> *Phillips screwdriver (No.2 x 6 in)*
> *Combination pliers – 6 in*
> *Hacksaw and assortment of blades*
> *Tire pressure gauge*
> *Grease gun*
> *Oil can*
> *Fine emery cloth*
> *Wire brush*
> *Battery post and cable cleaning tool*
> *Oil filter wrench*
> *Funnel (medium size)*
> *Safety goggles*
> *Jack stands (2)*
> *Drain pan*

Note: *If basic tune-ups are going to be a part of routine maintenance, it will be necessary to purchase a good quality stroboscopic timing light and a combination tachometer/dwell meter. Although they are included in the list of Special tools, they are mentioned here because they are absolutely necessary for tuning most vehicles properly.*

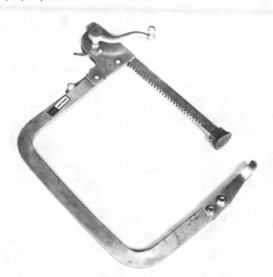

Valve spring compressor

Repair and overhaul tool set

These tools are essential for anyone who plans to perform major repairs and are in addition to those in the *Maintenance and minor repair tool kit.* Included is a comprehensive set of sockets which, though expensive, will be found invaluable because of their versatility (especially when various extensions and drives are available). We recommend the $\frac{1}{2}$ in drive over the $\frac{3}{8}$ in drive. Although the larger drive is bulky and more expensive, it has the capability of accepting a very wide range of large sockets (ideally, the mechanic would have a $\frac{3}{8}$ in drive set and a $\frac{1}{2}$ in drive set).

> *Socket set(s)*
> *Reversible ratchet*
> *Extension – 10 in*
> *Universal joint*
> *Torque wrench (same size drive as sockets)*
> *Ball pein hammer – 8 oz*
> *Soft-faced hammer (plastic/rubber)*
> *Standard screwdriver ($\frac{1}{4}$ in x 6 in)*
> *Standard screwdriver (stubby – $\frac{5}{16}$ in)*
> *Phillips screwdriver (No.3 x 8 in)*
> *Phillips screwdriver (stubby – No.2)*
> *Pliers – vise grip*
> *Pliers – lineman's*
> *Pliers – needle nose*
> *Pliers – spring clip (internal and external)*
> *Cold chisel – $\frac{1}{2}$ in*
> *Scriber*
> *Scraper (made from flattened copper tubing)*
> *Center punch*
> *Pin punches ($\frac{1}{16}$, $\frac{1}{8}$, $\frac{3}{16}$ in)*
> *Steel rule/straight edge – 12 in*
> *Allen wrench set ($\frac{1}{8}$ to $\frac{3}{8}$ in or 4 mm to 10 mm)*
> *A selection of files*
> *Wire brush (large)*
> *Jack stands (second set)*
> *Jack (scissor or hydraulic type)*

Note: *Another tool which is often useful is an electric drill motor with a chuck capacity of $\frac{3}{8}$ in (and a set of good quality drill bits).*

Special tools

The tools in this list include those which are not used regularly, are expensive to buy, or which need to be used in accordance with their manufacturer's instructions. Unless these tools will be used frequently, it is not very economical to purchase many of them. A consideration would be to split the cost and use between yourself and a friend or friends. In addition, most of these tools can be obtained from a tool rental shop on a temporary basis.

This list contains only those tools and instruments widely available to the public, and not those special tools produced by vehicle manufacturers for distribution to dealer service departments. Occasionally, references to the manufacturer's special tools are included in the text of this manual. Generally, an alternative method of doing the job without the special tool is offered. However, sometimes there is no alternative to their use. Where this is the case, and the tool cannot be purchased or borrowed, the work should be turned over to the dealer, a repair shop or an automotive machine shop.

> *Valve spring compressor*
> *Piston ring groove cleaning tool*
> *Piston ring compressor*
> *Piston ring installation tool*
> *Cylinder compression gauge*
> *Cylinder ridge reamer*
> *Cylinder surfacing hone*
> *Cylinder bore gauge*
> *Micrometer(s) and/or dial calipers*
> *Hydraulic lifter removal tool*
> *Balljoint separator*
> *Universal-type puller*
> *Impact screwdriver*
> *Dial indicator set*
> *Stroboscopic timing light (inductive pickup)*
> *Hand-operated vacuum/pressure pump*
> *Tachometer/dwell meter*
> *Universal electrical multi-meter*

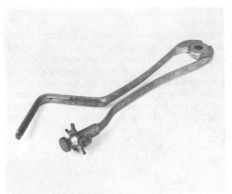

Piston ring groove cleaning tool

Piston ring compressor

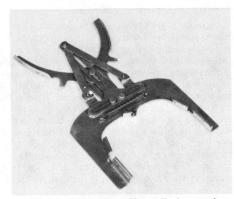

Piston ring removal/installation tool

Cylinder ridge reamer

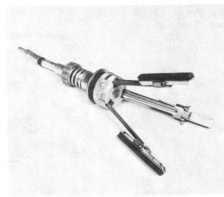

Cylinder bore hone

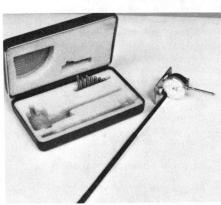

Cylinder bore gauge

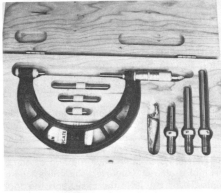

Micrometer set

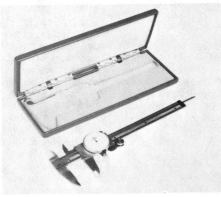

Dial caliper

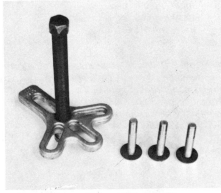

Universal-type hub puller

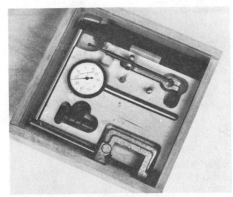

Dial indicator set

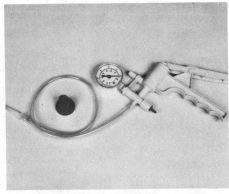

Hand-operated vacuum pump

Brake shoe spring tool

Cable hoist
Brake spring removal and installation tools
Floor jack

Buying tools

For the do-it-yourselfer who is just starting to get involved in vehicle maintenance and repair, there are a couple of options available when purchasing tools. If maintenance and minor repair is the extent of the work to be done, the purchase of individual tools is satisfactory. If, on the other hand, extensive work is planned, it would be a good idea to purchase a modest tool set from one of the large retail chain stores. A set can usually be bought at a substantial savings over the individual tool prices (and they often come with a tool box). As additional tools are needed, add-on sets, individual tools and a larger tool box can be purchased to expand the tool selection. Building a tool set gradually allows the cost of the tools to be spread over a longer period of time and gives the mechanic the freedom to choose only those tools that will actually be used.

Tool stores will often be the only source of some of the special tools that are needed, but regardless of where tools are bought, try to avoid cheap ones (especially when buying screwdrivers and sockets) because they won't last very long. The expense involved in replacing cheap tools will eventually be greater than the initial cost of quality tools.

Care and maintenance of tools

Good tools are expensive, so it makes sense to treat them with respect. Keep them in a clean and usable condition and store them properly when not in use. Always wipe off any dirt, grease or metal chips before putting them away. Never leave tools lying around in the work area. Upon completion of a job, always check closely under the hood for tools that may have been left there (so they don't get lost during a test drive).

Some tools, such as screwdrivers, pliers, wrenches and sockets, can be hung on a panel mounted on the garage or workshop wall, while others should be kept in a tool box or tray. Measuring instruments, gauges, meters, etc. must be carefully stored where they cannot be damaged by weather or impact from other tools.

When tools are used with care and stored properly, they will last a very long time. Even with the best of care, tools will wear out if used frequently. When a tool is damaged or worn out, replace it; subsequent jobs will be safer and more enjoyable if you do.

For those who desire to learn more about tools and their uses, a book entitled *How to Choose and Use Car Tools* is available from the publishers of this manual.

Working facilities

Not to be overlooked when discussing tools is the workshop. If anything more than routine maintenance is to be carried out, some sort of suitable work area is essential.

It is understood, and appreciated, that many home mechanics do not have a good workshop or garage available, and end up removing an engine or doing major repairs outside (it is recommended that the overhaul or repair be completed under the cover of a roof).

A clean, flat workbench or table of suitable working height is an absolute necessity. The workshop should be equipped with a vise that has a jaw opening of at least 4 inches.

As mentioned previously, some clean, dry storage space is also required for tools, as well as the lubricants, fluids, cleaning solvents, etc. which soon become necessary.

Sometimes waste oil and fluids, drained from the engine or transmission during normal maintenance or repairs, present a disposal problem. To avoid pouring oil on the ground or into the sewage system, simply pour the used fluids into large containers, seal them with caps and deliver them to a local recycling center or disposal facility. Plastic jugs (such as old anti-freeze containers) are ideal for this purpose.

Always keep a supply of old newspapers and clean rags available. Old towels are excellent for mopping up spills. Many mechanics use rolls of paper towels for most work because they are readily available and disposable. To keep the area under the vehicle clean, a large cardboard box can be cut open and flattened to protect the garage or shop floor.

Whenever working over a painted surface (such as when leaning over a fender to service something under the hood), always cover it with an old blanket or bedspread to protect the finish. Vinyl covered pads, made especially for this purpose, are available at auto parts stores.

Jacking and towing

Jacking

The jack supplied with the vehicle should only be used for raising the car for changing a tire or placing jackstands under the frame. **Under no circumstances should work be performed beneath the vehicle or the engine started while this jack is being used as the only means of support.**

All vehicles are supplied with a scissors type jack which fits into a notch in the vertical rocker panel flange nearest to the wheel being changed.

The car should be on level ground with the wheels blocked and the transmission in Park (automatic) or Reverse (manual). Pry off the hub cap (if equipped) using the tapered end of the lug wrench. Loosen the wheel nuts one half turn and leave them in place until the wheel is raised off the ground.

Place the jack under the side of the car in the jacking notch. Use the supplied wrench to turn the jackscrew clockwise until the wheel is raised off the ground. Remove the wheel nuts, pull off the wheel and replace it with the spare.

With the beveled side in, replace the wheel nuts and tighten them until snug. Lower the vehicle by turning the jackscrew counter-clockwise. Remove the jack and tighten the nuts in a diagonal fashion. Replace the hubcap by placing it into position and using the heel of your hand or a rubber mallet to seat it.

Towing

The vehicle can be towed with all four wheels on the ground provided speeds do not exceed 35 mph and the distance is not over 50 miles, otherwise transmission damage can result.

Towing equipment specifically designed for this purpose should be used and should be attached to the main structural members of the car and not the bumper or brackets.

Safety is a major consideration when towing and all applicable state and local laws must be obeyed. A safety chain system must be used for all towing.

While towing, the parking brake should be fully released and the transmission should be in Neutral. The steering must be unlocked (ignition switch in the Off position). Remember that power steering and power brakes will not work with the engine off.

Front lift point (arrow)

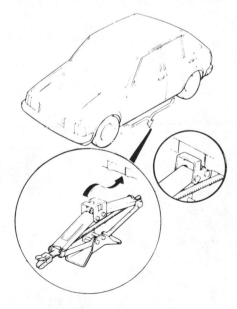

Rear jacking point (arrow)

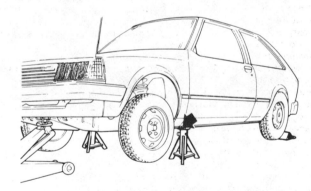

Front end jack stand installation

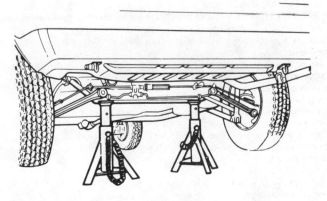

Rear crossmember jack stand installation

Automotive chemicals and lubricants

A number of automotive chemicals and lubricants are available for use in vehicle maintenance and repair. They represent a wide variety of products ranging from cleaning solvents and degreasers to lubricants and protective sprays for rubber, plastic and vinyl.

Contact point/spark plug cleaner is a solvent used to clean oily film and dirt from points, grime from electrical connectors and oil deposits from spark plugs. It is oil free and leaves no residue. It can also be used to remove gum and varnish from carburetor jets and other orifices.

Carburetor cleaner is similar to contact point/spark plug cleaner but it is a stronger solvent and may leave a slight oily residue. It is not recommended for cleaning electrical components or connections.

Brake system cleaner is used to remove grease or brake fluid from brake system components (where clean surfaces are absolutely necessary and petroleum-based solvents cannot be used); it also leaves no residue.

Silicone based lubricants are used to protect rubber parts such as hoses, weatherstripping and grommets, and are used as lubricants for hinges and locks.

Multi-purpose grease is an all purpose lubricant used whenever grease is more practical than a liquid lubricant such as oil. Some multi-purpose grease is colored white and specially formulated to be more resistant to water than ordinary grease.

Bearing grease/wheel bearing grease is a heavy grease used where increased loads and friction are encountered (i.e. wheel bearings, universal joints, etc.).

High temperature wheel bearing grease is designed to withstand the extreme temperatures encountered by wheel bearings in disc brake equipped vehicles. It usually contains molybdenum disulfide, which is a 'dry' type lubricant.

Gear oil (sometimes called gear lube) is a specially designed oil used in differentials, manual transmissions and manual gearboxes, as well as other areas where high friction, high temperature lubrication is required. It is available in a number of viscosities (weights) for various applications.

Motor oil, of course, is the lubricant specially formulated for use in the engine. It normally contains a wide variety of additives to prevent corrosion and reduce foaming and wear. Motor oil comes in various weights (viscosity ratings) of from 5 to 80. The recommended weight of the oil depends on the seasonal temperature and the demands on the engine. Light oil is used in cold climates and under light load conditions; heavy oil is used in hot climates and where high loads are encountered. Multi-viscosity oils are designed to have characteristics of both light and heavy oils and are available in a number of weights from 5W-20 to 20W-50.

Oil additives range from viscosity index improvers to slick chemical treatments that purportedly reduce friction. It should be noted that most oil manufacturers caution against using additives with their oils.

Gas additives perform several functions, depending on their chemical makeup. They usually contain solvents that help dissolve gum and varnish that build up on carburetor and intake parts. They also serve to break down carbon deposits that form on the inside surfaces of the combustion chambers. Some additives contain upper cylinder lubricants for valves and piston rings.

Brake fluid is a specially formulated hydraulic fluid that can withstand the heat and pressure encountered in brake systems. Care must be taken that this fluid does not come in contact with painted surfaces or plastics. An opened container should always be resealed to prevent contamination by water or dirt.

Undercoating is a petroleum-based tar-like substance that is designed to protect metal surfaces on the under-side of a vehicle from corrosion. It also acts as a sound deadening agent by insulating the bottom of the vehicle.

Weatherstrip cement is used to bond weatherstripping around doors, windows and trunk lids. It is sometimes used to attach trim pieces as well.

Degreasers are heavy duty solvents used to remove grease and grime that accumulate on engine and chassis components. They can be sprayed or brushed on and, depending on the type, are rinsed with either water or solvent.

Solvents are used alone or in combination with degreasers to clean parts and assemblies during repair and overhaul. The home mechanic should use only solvents that are non-flammable and that do not produce irritating fumes.

Gasket sealing compounds may be used in conjunction with gaskets, to improve their sealing capabilities, or alone, to seal metal-to-metal joints. Many gaskets can withstand extreme heat, some are impervious to gasoline and lubricants, while others are capable of filling and sealing large cavities. Depending on the intended use, gasket sealers either dry hard or stay relatively soft and pliable. They are usually applied by hand, with a brush, or are sprayed on the gasket sealing surfaces.

Thread cement is an adhesive locking compound that prevents threaded fasteners from loosening because of vibration. It is available in a variety of types for different applications.

Moisture dispersants are usually sprays that can be used to dry out electrical components such as the distributor, fuse block and wiring connectors. Some types can also be used as treatment for rubber and as a lubricant for hinges, cables and locks.

Waxes and polishes are used to help protect painted and plated surfaces from the weather. Different types of paint may require the use of different types of wax or polish. Some polishes utilize a chemical or abrasive cleaner to help remove the top layer of oxidized (dull) paint in older vehicles.

Troubleshooting

Contents

Engine

1 Engine will not rotate when attempting to start

1   Battery terminal connections loose or corroded. Check the cable terminals at the battery; tighten or clean corrosion as necessary.
2   Battery discharged or faulty. If the cable connectors are clean and tight on the battery posts, turn the key to the On position and switch on the headlights and/or windshield wipers. If these fail to function, the battery is discharged.
3   Automatic transmission not fully engaged in Park or manual transmission clutch not fully depressed.
4   Broken, loose or disconnected wiring in the starting circuit. Inspect all wiring and connectors at the battery, starter solenoid (at lower right side of engine) and ignition switch (on steering column).
5   Starter motor pinion jammed on flywheel ring gear. If manual transmission, place gearshift in gear and rock the vehicle to manually turn the engine. Remove starter (Chapter 5) and inspect pinion and flywheel (Chapter 5) at earliest convenience.
6   Starter solenoid faulty (Chapter 5).
7   Starter motor faulty (Chapter 5).
8   Ignition switch faulty (Chapter 5).

2 Engine rotates but will not start

1   Fuel tank empty.
2   Battery discharged (engine rotates slowly). Check the operation of electrical components as described in previous Section (see Chapter 1).
3   Battery terminal connections loose or corroded. See previous Section.
4   Carburetor flooded and/or fuel level in carburetor incorrect. This will usually be accompanied by a strong fuel odor from under the hood. Wait a few minutes, depress the accelerator pedal all the way to the floor and attempt to start the engine.
5   Choke control inoperative (Chapter 4).
6   Fuel not reaching carburetor. With ignition switch in Off position, open hood, remove the top plate of air cleaner assembly and observe the top of the carburetor (manually move choke plate back if necessary). Have an assistant depress accelerator pedal fully and check that fuel spurts into carburetor. If not, check fuel filter (Chapters 1 and 4), fuel lines and fuel pump (Chapter 4).
7   Excessive moisture on, or damage to, ignition components (Chapter 5).
8   Worn, faulty or incorrectly adjusted spark plugs (Chapter 1).
9   Broken, loose or disconnected wiring in the starting circuit (see previous Section).
10 Distributor loose, thus changing ignition timing. Turn the distributor body as necessary to start the engine, then set ignition timing as soon as possible (Chapter 5).
11 Ignition condenser faulty (Chapter 5).
12 Broken, loose or disconnected wires at the ignition coil, or faulty coil (Chapter 5).

3 Starter motor operates without rotating engine

1   Starter pinion sticking. Remove the starter (Chapter 5) and inspect.
2   Starter pinion or engine flywheel teeth worn or broken. Remove the inspection cover at the rear of the engine and inspect.

4 Engine hard to start when cold

1   Battery discharged or low. Check as described in Section 1.
2   Choke control inoperative or out of adjustment (Chapter 4).
3   Carburetor flooded (see Section 2).
4   Fuel supply not reaching the carburetor (see Section 2).
5   Carburetor worn and in need of overhauling (Chapter 4).

5 Engine hard to start when hot

1   Choke sticking in the closed position (Chapter 1).
2   Carburetor flooded (see Section 2).
3   Air filter in need of replacement (Chapter 1).
4   Fuel not reaching the carburetor (see Section 2).

6 Starter motor noisy or excessively rough in engagement

1   Pinion or flywheel gear teeth worn or broken. Remove the inspection cover at the rear of the engine and inspect.
2   Starter motor retaining bolts loose or missing.

7 Engine starts but stops immediately

1   Loose or faulty electrical connections at distributor, coil or alternator.
2   Insufficient fuel reaching the carburetor. Disconnect the fuel line at the carburetor and remove the filter (Chapter 1). Place a container under the disconnected fuel line. Observe the flow of fuel from the line. If little or none at all, check for blockage in the lines and/or replace the fuel pump (Chapter 4).
3   Vacuum leak at the gasket surfaces or the intake manifold and/or carburetor. Check that all mounting bolts (nuts) are tightened to specifications and all vacuum hoses connected to the carburetor and manifold are positioned properly and are in good condition.

8 Engine 'lopes' while idling or idles erratically

1   Vacuum leakage. Check mounting bolts (nuts) at the carburetor and intake manifold for tightness. Check that all vacuum hoses are connected and are in good condition. Use a doctor's stethoscope or a length of fuel line hose held against your ear to listen for vacuum leaks while the engine is running. A hissing sound will be heard. A soapy water solution will also detect leaks. Check the carburetor and intake manifold gasket surfaces.
2   Leaking EGR valve or plugged PCV valve (see Chapter 6).
3   Air cleaner clogged and in need of replacement (Chapter 1).
4   Fuel pump not delivering sufficient fuel to the carburetor (see Section 7).
5   Carburetor out of adjustment (Chapter 4).
6   If a leaking head gasket is suspected, take the vehicle to a repair shop or dealer where this can be pressure checked without the need to remove the head.
7   Timing chain or gears worn and in need of replacement (Chapter 1).
8   Camshaft lobes worn, necessitating the removal of the camshaft for inspection (Chapter 1).

9 Engine misses at idle speed

1   Spark plugs faulty or not gapped properly (Chapter 1).
2   Faulty spark plug wires (Chapter 1).
3   Carburetor choke not operating properly (Chapter 4).
4   Sticking or faulty emissions systems (see Troubleshooting in Chapter 3).
5   Clogged fuel filter and/or foreign matter in fuel. Remove the fuel filter (Chapter 4) and inspect.
6   Vacuum leaks at carburetor, intake manifold or at hose connections. Check as described in Section 8.
7   Incorrect idle speed or idle mixture (Chapter 4).
8   Incorrect ignition timing (Chapter 1).
9   Uneven or low cylinder compression. Remove plugs and use compression tester as per manufacturer's instructions.

10 Engine misses throughout driving speed range

1   Carburetor fuel filter clogged and/or impurities in the fuel system (Chapter 4). Also check fuel output at the carburetor (see Section 7).
2   Faulty or incorrectly gapped spark plugs (Chapter 1).
3   Incorrectly set ignition timing (Chapter 1).
4   Check for a cracked distributor cap, disconnected distributor wires or damage to the distributor components (Chapter 1).

5   Leaking spark plug wires (Chapter 1).
6   Emission system components faulty (Chapter 6).
7   Low or uneven cylinder compression pressures. Remove spark plugs and test compression with gauge.
8   Weak or faulty EEC ignition system (see Chapter 5).
9   Vacuum leaks at carburetor, intake manifold or vacuum hoses (see Section 8).

11 Engine stalls

1   Carburetor idle speed incorrectly set (Chapter 1).
2   Carburetor fuel filter clogged and/or water and impurities in the fuel system (Chapter 4).
3   Choke improperly adjusted or sticking (Chapter 1).
4   Distributor components damp, points out of adjustment or damage to distributor cap, rotor etc. (Chapter 5).
5   Emission system components faulty (Troubleshooting section, Chapter 6).
6   Faulty or incorrectly gapped spark plugs (Chapter 5). Also check spark plug wires (Chapter 1).
7   Vacuum leak at the carburetor, intake manifold or vacuum hoses. Check as described in Section 8.
8   Valve lash incorrectly set (Chapter 2).

12 Engine lacks power

1   Incorrect ignition timing (Chapter 1).
2   Excessive play in distributor shaft. At the same time check for worn or maladjusted contact rotor, faulty distributor cap, wires, etc. (Chapter 5).
3   Faulty or incorrectly gapped spark plugs (Chapter 1).
4   Carburetor not adjusted properly or excessively worn (Chapter 4).
5   Weak coil or condensor (Chapter 5).
6   Faulty EEC system coil (Chapter 5).
7   Brakes binding (Chapter 9).
8   Automatic transmission fluid level incorrect, causing slippage (Chapter 7).
9   Manual transmission clutch slipping (Chapter 7).
10   Fuel filter clogged and/or impurities in the fuel system (Chapter 4).
11   Emission control system not functioning properly (Chapter 6).
12   Use of sub-standard fuel. Fill tank with proper octane fuel.
13   Low or uneven cylinder compression pressures. Test with compression tester, which will detect leaking valves and/or blown head gasket.

13 Engine backfire

1   Emission system not functioning properly (Chapter 6).
2   Ignition timing incorrect (Section 2).
3   Carburetor in need of adjustment or worn excessively (Chapter 4).
4   Vacuum leak at carburetor, intake manifold or vacuum hoses. Check as described in Section 8.
5   Valve lash incorrectly set, and/or valves sticking (Chapter 2).

14 Pinging or knocking engine sounds on hard acceleration or uphill

1   Incorrect grade of fuel. Fill tank with fuel of the proper octane rating.
2   Ignition timing incorrect (Chapter 5).
3   Carburetor in need of adjustment (Chapter 4).
4   Improper spark plugs. Check plug type with that specified on tune-up decal located inside engine compartment. Also check plugs and wires for damage (Chapter 1).
5   Worn or damaged distributor components (Chapter 5).
6   Faulty emission system (Chapter 6).
7   Vacuum leak. (Check as described in Section 8).

15 Engine 'diesels' (continues to run) after switching off

1   Idle speed too fast (Chapter 5).

2   Electrical solenoid at side of carburetor not functioning properly (not all models, see Chapter 4).
3   Ignition timing incorrectly adjusted (Chapter 1).
4   Air cleaner valve not operating properly (Chapter 4).
5   Excessive engine operating temperatures. Probable causes of this are: malfunctioning thermostat, clogged radiator, faulty water pump (see Chapter 3).

Engine electrical

16 Battery will not hold a charge

1   Alternator drivebelt defective or not adjusted properly (Chapter 1).
2   Electrolyte level too low or too weak (Chapter 5).
3   Battery terminals loose or corroded (Chapter 5).
4   Alternator not charging properly (Chapter 5).
5   Loose, broken or faulty wiring in the charging circuit (Chapter 5).
6   Short in vehicle circuitry causing a continual drain on battery.
7   Battery defective internally.

17 Ignition light fails to go out

1   Fault in alternator or charging circuit (Chapter 5).
2   Alternator drivebelt defective or not properly adjusted (Chapter 5).

18 Ignition light fails to come on when key is turned

1   Ignition light bulb faulty (Chapter 10).
2   Alternator faulty (Chapter 5).
3   Fault in the printed circuit, dash wiring or bulb holder (Chapter 10).

Engine fuel system

19 Excessive fuel consumption

1   Dirty or choked air filter element (Chapter 1).
2   Incorrectly set ignition timing (Chapter 1).
3   Choke sticking or improperly adjusted (Chapter 1).
4   Emission system not functioning properly (not all vehicles, see Chapter 6).
5   Carburetor idle speed and/or mixture not adjusted properly (Chapter 4).
6   Carburetor internal parts excessively worn or damaged (Chapter 4).
7   Low tire pressure or incorrect tire size (Chapter 1).

20 Fuel leakage and/or fuel odor

1   Leak in a fuel feed or vent line (Chapter 4).
2   Tank overfilled. Fill only to automatic shut-off.
3   Emission system filter in need of replacement (Chapter 6).
4   Vapor leaks from system lines (Chapter 4).
5   Carburetor internal parts excessively worn or out of adjustment (Chapter 4).

Engine cooling system

21 Overheating

1   Insufficient coolant in system (Chapter 3).
2   Fault in electric fan motor wiring (Chapter 3).
3   Radiator core blocked or radiator grille dirty and restricted (Chapter 3).
4   Thermostat faulty (Chapter 3).
5   Fan blades broken or cracked (Chapter 3).
6   Radiator cap not maintaining proper pressure. Have cap pressure tested by gas station or repair shop.
7   Ignition timing incorrect (Chapter 1).

22 Overcooling

1   Thermostat faulty (Chapter 3).
2   Inaccurate temperature gauge (Chapter 10).

23 External water leakage

1   Deteriorated or damaged hoses. Loosen clamps at hose connections (Chapter 1).
2   Water pump seals defective. If this is the case, water will drip from the water pump body (Chapter 3).
3   Leakage from radiator core or header tank. This will require the radiator to be professionally repaired (see Chapter 3 for removal procedures).
4   Engine drain plugs or water jacket freeze plugs leaking (see Chapters 2 and 3).

24 Internal water leakage

Note: *Internal coolant leaks can usually be detected by examining the oil. Check the dipstick and inside of valve cover for water deposits and an oil consistency like that of a milkshake.*
1   Faulty cylinder head gasket. Have the system pressure-tested professionally or remove the cylinder heads (Chapter 2) and inspect.
2   Cracked cylinder bore or cylinder head. Dismantle engine and inspect (Chapter 2).

25 Water loss

1   Overfilling system (Chapter 3).
2   Coolant boiling away due to overheating (see causes in Section 15).
3   Internal or external leakage (see Sections 22 and 23).
4   Faulty radiator cap. Have the cap pressure tested.

26 Poor coolant circulation

1   Inoperative water pump. A quick test is to pinch the top radiator hose closed with your hand while the engine is idling, then let it loose. You should feel a surge of water if the pump is working properly (Chapter 3).
2   Restriction in cooling system. Drain, flush and refill the system (Chapter 3). If it appears necessary, remove the radiator (Chapter 3) and have it reverse-flushed or professionally cleaned.
3   Fan drivebelt defective or not adjusted properly (Chapter 3).
4   Thermostat sticking (Chapter 3).

Clutch

27 Fails to release (pedal pressed to the floor – shift lever does not move freely in and out of reverse)

1   Improper linkage adjustment (Chapter 8).
2   Clutch linkage malfunction (Chapter 8).
3   Clutch disc warped, bent or excessively damaged (Chapter 8).

28 Clutch slips (engine speed increases with no increase in road speed)

1   Linkage in need of adjustment (Chapter 8).
2   Clutch disc oil soaked or facing worn. Remove disc (Chapter 8) and inspect.
3   Clutch disc not seated in. It may take 30 or 40 normal starts for a new disc to seat.

29 Grabbing (juddering) on take-up

1   Oil on clutch disc facings. Remove disc (Chapter 8) and inspect.

Correct any leakage source.
2   Worn or loose engine or transmission mounts. These units may move slightly when clutch is released. Inspect mounts and bolts.
3   Worn splines on clutch gear. Remove clutch components (Chapter 8) and inspect.
4   Warped pressure plate or flywheel. Remove clutch components and inspect.

30 Squeal or rumble with clutch fully engaged (pedal released)

1   Improper adjustment; no lash (Chapter 8).
2   Release bearing binding on transmission bearing retainer. Remove clutch components (Chapter 8) and check bearing. Remove any burrs or nicks, clean and relubricate before reinstallation.
3   Weak linkage return spring. Replace the spring.

31 Squeal or rumble with clutch fully disengaged (pedal depressed)

1   Worn, faulty or broken release bearing (Chapter 8).
2   Worn or broken pressure plate springs (or diaphragm fingers) (Chapter 8).

32 Clutch pedal stays on floor when disengaged

1   Bind in linkage or release bearing. Inspect linkage or remove clutch components as necessary.
2   Linkage springs being over-traveled. Adjust linkage for proper lash. Make sure proper pedal stop (bumper) is installed.

Manual transaxle
Note: *All the following Sections contained within Chapter 7 unless noted.*

33 Noisy in Neutral with engine running

1   Input shaft bearing worn.
2   Damaged main drive gear bearing.
3   Worn countergear bearings.
4   Worn or damaged countergear anti-lash plate.

34 Noisy in all gears

1   Any of the above causes, and/or:
2   Insufficient lubricant (see checking procedures in Chapter 7).

35 Noisy in one particular gear

1   Worn, damaged or chipped gear teeth for that particular gear.
2   Worn or damaged synchronizer for that particular gear.

36 Slips out of high gear

1   Damaged shift linkage.
2   Interference between the floor shift handle and console.
3   Broken or loose engine mounts.
4   Shift mechanism stabilizer bar loose.
5   Damaged or worn transaxle internal components.
6   Improperly installed shifter boot.

37 Difficulty in engaging gears

1   Clutch not releasing fully (see clutch adjustment, Chapter 8).
2   Loose, damaged or maladjusted shift linkage. Make a thorough inspection, replacing parts as necessary. Adjust as described in Chapter 7.

38 Fluid leakage

1   Excessive amount of lubricant in transmission (see Chapter 7 for correct checking procedures. Drain lubricant as required).
2   Side cover loose or gasket damaged.
3   Rear oil seal or speedometer oil seal in need of replacement (Section 6).

Automatic transaxle
Note: *Due to the complexity of the automatic transaxle, it is difficult for the home mechanic to properly diagnose and service this component. For problems other than the following, the vehicle should be taken to a reputable mechanic.*

39 Fluid leakage

1   Automatic transmission fluid is a deep red color, and fluid leaks should not be confused with engine oil which can easily be blown by air flow to the transmission.
2   To pinpoint a leak, first remove all built-up dirt and grime from around the transmission. Degreasing agents and/or steam cleaning will achieve this. With the underside clean, drive the vehicle at low speeds so that air flow will not blow the leak far from its source. Raise the vehicle and determine where the leak is coming from. Common areas of leakage are:

   a)   *Fluid pan:* tighten mounting bolts and/or replace pan gasket as necessary (see Chapter 7)
   b)   *Rear extension:* tighten bolts and/or replace oil seal as necessary (Chapter 7)
   c)   *Filler pipe:* replace the rubber oil seal where pipe enters transmission case
   d)   *Transmission oil lines:* tighten connectors where lines enter transmission case and/or replace lines
   e)   *Vent pipe:* transmission over-filled and/or water in fluid (see checking procedures, Chapter 7)
   f)   *Speedometer connector:* replace the O-ring where speedometer cable enters transmission case

40 General shift mechanism problems

1   Chapter 7 deals with checking and adjusting the shift linkage on automatic transaxles. Common problems which may be attributed to maladjustment linkage are:

   a)   Engine starting in gears other than Park or Neutral
   b)   Indicator on quadrant pointing to a gear other than the one actually being used
   c)   Vehicle will not hold firm when in Park position
   Refer to Chapter 7 to adjust the manual linkage.

41 Transaxle will not downshift with accelerator pedal pressed to the floor

1   Chapter 7 deals with adjusting the downshift cable or downshift switch to enable the transaxle to downshift properly.

42 Engine will start in gears other than Park or Neutral

1   Chapter 7 deals with adjusting the Neutral start switches used with automatic transaxles.

43 Transaxle slips, shifts rough, is noisy or has no drive in forward or reverse gears

1   There are many probable causes for the above problems, but the home mechanic should concern himself only with one possibility: fluid level.
2   Before taking the vehicle to a specialist, check the level of the fluid and condition of the fluid as described in Chapter 7. Correct fluid level

as necessary or change the fluid and filter if needed. If problem persists, have a professional diagnose the probable cause.

Drive axles

44 Clicking noise in turns

1   Worn or damaged outboard joint. Check for cut or damaged seals. Repair as necessary (Chapter 8).

45 Knock or clunk when accelerating from a coast

1   Worn or damaged inboard joint. Check for cut or damaged seals. Repair as necessary (Chapter 8).

46 Shudder or vibration during acceleration

1   Excessive joint angle. Have checked and correct as necessary (Chapter 8).
2   Worn or damaged inboard or outboard joints. Repair or replace as necessary (Chapter 8).
3   Sticking inboard joint assembly. Correct or replace as necessary (Chapter 8).

Brakes
Note: *Before assuming a brake problem exists, check that the tires are in good condition and are inflated properly (see Chapter 1): the front end alignment is correct (See Chapter 11): and that the vehicle is not loaded with weight in an unequal manner.*

47 Vehicle pulls to one side under braking

1   Defective, damaged or oil-contaminated disc pad on one side. Inspect as described in Chapter 1. Refer to Chapter 9 if replacement is required.
2   Excessive wear of brake pad material or disc on one side. Inspect and correct as necessary.
3   Loose or disconnected front suspension components. Inspect and tighten all bolts to specifications (Chapter 1).
4   Defective caliper assembly. Remove caliper and inspect for stuck piston or damage (Chapter 9).

48 Noise (high-pitched squeak without brake applied)

1   Front brake pads worn out. This noise comes from the wear sensor rubbing against the disc. Replace pads with new ones immediately (Chapter 9).

49 Excessive brake pedal travel

1   Partial brake system failure. Inspect entire system (Chapter 1) and correct as required.
2   Insufficient fluid in master cylinder. Check (Chapter 1) and add fluid and bleed system if necessary (Chapter 9).
3   Rear brakes not adjusting properly. Make a series of starts and stops while the vehicle is in Reverse. If this does not correct the situation remove drums and inspect self-adjusters (Chapter 1).

50 Brake pedal appears spongy when depressed

1   Air in hydraulic lines. Bleed the brake system (Chapter 9).
2   Faulty flexible hoses. Inspect all system hoses and lines. Replace parts as necessary.
3   Master cylinder mountings insecure. Inspect master cylinder bolts (nuts) and torque tighten to specifications.
4   Master cylinder faulty (Chapter 9).

51 Excessive effort required to stop vehicle

1 Power brake booster not operating properly (Chapter 9).
2 Excessively worn linings or pads. Inspect and replace if necessary (Chapter 1).
3 One or more caliper pistons (front wheels) or wheel cylinders (rear wheels) seized or sticking. Inspect and rebuild as required (Chapter 9).
4 Brake linings or pads contaminated with oil or grease. Inspect and replace as required (Chapter 1),
5 New pads or linings fitted and not yet "bedded in". It will take a while for the new material to seat against the drum (or rotor).

52 Pedal travels to floor with little resistance

1 Little or no fluid in the master cylinder reservoir caused by: leaking wheel cylinder(s); leaking caliper piston(s); loose, damaged or disconnected brake lines. Inspect entire system and correct as necessary.

53 Brake pedal pulsates during brake application

1 Wheel bearings not adjusted properly or in need of replacement (Chapter 1).
2 Caliper not sliding properly due to improper installation or obstructions. Remove and inspect (Chapter 9).
3 Rotor not within specifications. Remove the rotor (Chapter 9) and check for excessive lateral run-out and parellelism. Have the rotor professionally machined or replace it with a new one.
4 Out-of-round rear brake drums. Remove the drums (Chapter 9) and have them professionally machined, or replace them.

Suspension and steering

54 Vehicle pulls to one side

1 Tire pressures uneven (Chapter 1).
2 Defective tire (Chapter 1).
3 Excessive wear in suspension or steering components (Chapter 1).
4 Front end in need of alignment. (Chapter 11).
5 Front brakes dragging. Inspect braking system as described in Chapter 1.

55 Shimmy, shake or vibration

1 Tire or wheel out of balance or out of round. Have professionally balanced.
2 Loose or worn wheel bearings (Chapter 1). Replace as necessary (Chapter 11).
3 Shock absorbers and/or suspension components worn or damaged (Chapter 11).

56 Excessive pitching and/or rolling around corners or during braking

1 Defective shock absorbers. Replace as a set (Chapter 11).
2 Broken or weak coil springs and/or suspension components. Inspect as described in Chapter 11.

57 Excessively stiff steering

1 Lack of lubricant in power steering fluid reservoir (Chapter 1).
2 Incorrect tire pressures (Chapter 1).
3 Lack of lubrication at ball joints (Chapter 1).
4 Front end out of alignment.
5 Rack and pinions out of adjustment or lacking lubrication.

6 See also Section 63 'Lack of power assistance'.

58 Excessive play in steering

1 Loose wheel bearings (Chapter 1).
2 Excessive wear in suspension or steering components (Chapter 1).
3 Rack and pinion out of adjustment (Chapter 11).

59 Lack of power assistance

1 Steering pump drivebelt faulty or not adjusted properly (Chapter 1).
2 Fluid level low (Chapter 1).
3 Hoses or pipes restricting the flow. Inspect and replace parts as necessary.
4 Air in power steering system. Bleed system (Chapter 11).

60 Excessive tire wear (not specific to one area)

1 Incorrect tire pressures (Chapter 1).
2 Tires out of balance. Have professionally balanced.
3 Wheels damaged. Inspect and replace as necessary.
4 Suspension or steering components excessively worn (Chapter 1).

61 Excessive tire wear on outside edge

1 Inflation pressures not correct (Chapter 1).
2 Excessive speed on turns.
3 Front end alignment incorrect (excessive toe-in). Have professionally aligned (Chapter 11).
4 Suspension arm bent or twisted.

62 Excessive tire wear on inside edge

1 Inflation pressures incorrect (Chapter 1).
2 Front end alignment incorrect (toe-out). Have professionally aligned (Chapter 11).
3 Loose or damaged steering components (Chapter 1).

63 Tire tread worn in one place

1 Tires out of balance. Balance tires professionally.
2 Damaged or buckled wheel. Inspect and replace if necessary.
3 Defective tire.

64 General vibration at highway speeds

1 Out-of-balance front wheels or tires. Have them professionally balanced.
2 Front or rear wheel bearings worn. Check (Chapter 1) and replace as necessary (Chapter 11).
3 Defective tire or wheel. Have them checked and replaced if necessary.

65 Noise – whether coasting or in drive

1 Road noise. No corrective procedures available.
2 Tire noise. Inspect tires and tire pressures (Chapter 1).
3 Front wheel bearings loose, worn or damaged. Check (Chapter 1) and replace if necessary (Chapter 11).
4 Lack of lubrication in the balljoints or tie rod ends (Chapter 1).
5 Damaged shock absorbers or mountings. (Chapter 1).
6 Loose wheel nuts. Check and tighten as necessary (Chapter 11).

Safety first!

Regardless of how enthusiastic you may be about getting on with the job at hand, take the time to ensure that your safety is not jeopardized. A moment's lack of attention can result in an accident, as can failure to observe certain simple safety precautions. The possibility of an accident will always exist, and the following points should not be considered a comprehensive list of all dangers. Rather, they are intended to make you aware of the risks and to encourage a safety conscious approach to all work you carry out on your vehicle.

Essential DOs and DON'Ts

DON'T rely on a jack when working under the vehicle. Always use approved jackstands to support the weight of the vehicle and place them under the recommended lift or support points.

DON'T attempt to loosen extremely tight fasteners (i.e. wheel lug nuts) while the vehicle is on a jack — it may fall.

DON'T start the engine without first making sure that the transmission is in Neutral (or Park where applicable) and the parking brake is set.

DON'T remove the radiator cap from a hot cooling system — let it cool or cover it with a cloth and release the pressure gradually.

DON'T attempt to drain the engine oil until you are sure it has cooled to the point that it will not burn you.

DON'T touch any part of the engine or exhaust system until it has cooled sufficiently to avoid burns.

DON'T siphon toxic liquids such as gasoline, antifreeze and brake fluid by mouth, or allow them to remain on your skin.

DON'T inhale brake lining dust — it is potentially hazardous (see *Asbestos* below)

DON'T allow spilled oil or grease to remain on the floor — wipe it up before someone slips on it.

DON'T use loose fitting wrenches or other tools which may slip and cause injury.

DON'T push on wrenches when loosening or tightening nuts or bolts. Always try to pull the wrench toward you. If the situation calls for pushing the wrench away, push with an open hand to avoid scraped knuckles if the wrench should slip.

DON'T attempt to lift a heavy component alone — get someone to help you.

DON'T rush or take unsafe shortcuts to finish a job.

DON'T allow children or animals in or around the vehicle while you are working on it.

DO wear eye protection when using power tools such as a drill, sander, bench grinder, etc. and when working under a vehicle.

DO keep loose clothing and long hair well out of the way of moving parts.

DO make sure that any hoist used has a safe working load rating adequate for the job.

DO get someone to check on you periodically when working alone on a vehicle.

DO carry out work in a logical sequence and make sure that everything is correctly assembled and tightened.

DO keep chemicals and fluids tightly capped and out of the reach of children and pets.

DO remember that your vehicle's safety affects that of yourself and others. If in doubt on any point, get professional advice.

Asbestos

Certain friction, insulating, sealing, and other products — such as brake linings, brake bands, clutch linings, torque converters, gaskets, etc. — contain asbestos. *Extreme care must be taken to avoid inhalation of dust from such products since it is hazardous to health.* If in doubt, assume that they *do* contain asbestos.

Fire

Remember at all times that gasoline is highly flammable. Never smoke or have any kind of open flame around when working on a vehicle. But the risk does not end there. A spark caused by an electrical short circuit, by two metal surfaces contacting each other, or even by static electricity built up in your body under certain conditions, can ignite gasoline vapors, which in a confined space are highly explosive. Do not, under any circumstances, use gasoline for cleaning parts. Use an approved safety solvent.

Always disconnect the battery ground (−) cable *at the battery* before working on any part of the fuel system or electrical system. Never risk spilling fuel on a hot engine or exhaust component.

It is strongly recommended that a fire extinguisher suitable for use on fuel and electrical fires be kept handy in the garage or workshop at all times. Never try to extinguish a fuel or electrical fire with water.

Fumes

Certain fumes are highly toxic and can quickly cause unconsciousness and even death if inhaled to any extent. Gasoline vapor falls into this category, as do the vapors from some cleaning solvents. Any draining or pouring of such volatile fluids should be done in a well ventilated area.

When using cleaning fluids and solvents, read the instructions on the container carefully. Never use materials from unmarked containers.

Never run the engine in an enclosed space, such as a garage. Exhaust fumes contain carbon monoxide, which is extremely poisonous. If you need to run the engine, always do so in the open air, or at least have the rear of the vehicle outside the work area.

If you are fortunate enough to have the use of an inspection pit, never drain or pour gasoline and never run the engine while the vehicle is over the pit. The fumes, being heavier than air, will concentrate in the pit with possibly lethal results.

The battery

Never create a spark or allow a bare light bulb near the battery. The battery normally gives off a certain amount of hydrogen gas, which is highly explosive.

Always disconnect the battery ground (−) cable *at the battery* before working on the fuel or electrical systems.

If possible, loosen the filler caps or cover when charging the battery from an external source. Do not charge at an excessive rate or the battery may burst.

Take care when adding water and when carrying a battery. The electrolyte, even when diluted, is very corrosive and should not be allowed to contact clothing or skin.

Always wear eye protection when cleaning the battery to prevent the caustic deposits from entering your eyes.

Household current

When using an electric power tool, inspection light, etc., which operates on household current, always make sure that the tool is correctly connected to its plug and that, where necessary, it is properly grounded. Do not use such items in damp conditions and, again, do not create a spark or apply excessive heat in the vicinity of fuel or fuel vapor.

Secondary ignition system voltage

A severe electric shock can result from touching certain parts of the ignition system (such as the spark plug wires) when the engine is running or being cranked, particularly if components are damp or the insulation is defective. In the case of an electronic ignition system, the secondary system voltage is much higher and could prove fatal.

Chapter 1 Tune-up and maintenance

Refer to Chapter 13 for specifications and information applicable to later USA models

Contents

Specifications

Note: *Additional specifications can be found in the appropriate Chapters.*

Recommended fluids and capacities

	Capacity	Type
Engine oil	4 US qts	Class SE or SF
Engine coolant	5.8 US qts	50/50 mix of ethylene glycol-type and water
Automatic transaxle	6.0 US qts	Type F automatic transmission fluid
Manual transaxle		
1981	3.4 US qts	Consult dealer for latest recommendations
1982	3.4 US qts	80 to 90 wt. gear oil
Brake fluid	–	Dot 3 or Dot 4

Valve adjustment clearance

	in	mm
Valve side		
Intake	0.010	0.25
Exhaust	0.012	0.30
Cam side		
Intake	0.007	0.18
Exhaust	0.009	0.23

Ignition system

Spark plug type and gap	See tune-up decal
Ignition timing	8° BTDC
Battery electrolyte specific gravity (fully charged)	1.25 to 1.27

Cooling system

Thermostat rating	203°F

Drivebelt deflection

	in	mm
Alternator		
New	0.47 to 0.5	12 to 13
Used	0.5 to 0.55	13 to 14
Air pump		
New (without air conditioning)	0.63 to 0.7	16 to 18
New (with air conditioning)	0.43 to 0.5	11 to 13
Used (without air conditioning)	0.67 to 0.75	17 to 19
Used (with air conditioning)	0.5 to 0.6	13 to 15

1

	in	mm
Clutch pedal free travel	0.43 to 0.67	11 to 17

Brakes

Disc brake lining thickness

	in	mm
New	0.39	10
Replace at	0.04	1

Drum brake lining thickness

	in	mm
New	0.16	4
Replace at	0.04	1.0

Torque specifications

	Ft-lb	Nm
Alternator adjusting bolt	27 to 46	38 to 64
Automatic transaxle oil pan bolts	3.6 to 5.8	5 to 8

1 General information

Caution: *The negative battery cable should be disconnected whenever you are working in the vicinity of the fan.*

This vehicle was designed with reduced maintenance in mind and as a result, the maintenance schedule varies somewhat from usual automotive practice. For example, the suspension, steering and constant velocity joints are "lubricated for life" and have no provision for lubrication. These components should not be forgotten however, and should be inspected periodically for leaking, looseness or wear. It should also be noted that the aluminum cylinder head requires the use of proper coolant.

Consult the *General information* Section of each Chapter to determine what components may require special maintenance techniques.

2 Introduction

This Chapter was designed to help the home mechanic maintain his (or her) car for peak performance, economy, safety and longevity.

On the following pages you will find a maintenance schedule along with Sections which deal specifically with each item on the schedule. Included are visual checks, adjustments and item replacements.

Servicing your car using the time/mileage maintenance schedule and the sequenced Sections will give you a planned program of maintenance. Keep in mind that it is a full plan, and maintaining only a few items at the specified intervals will not give you the same results.

You will find as you service your car that many of the procedures can, and should, be grouped together, due to the nature of the job at hand. Examples of this are as follows:

If the car is fully raised for a chassis lubrication, for example, this is the ideal time for the following checks: exhaust system, suspension, steering and the fuel system.

If the tires and wheels are removed, as during a routine tire rotation, go ahead and check the brakes and wheel bearings at the same time.

If you must borrow or rent a torque wrench, you will do best to service the spark plugs and/or repack (or replace) the wheel bearings all in the same day to save time and money.

The first step of this or any maintenance plan is to prepare yourself before the actual work begins. Read through the appropriate Sections for all work that is to be performed before you begin. Gather together all necessary parts and tools. If it appears you could have a problem during a particular job, don't hesitate to ask advice from your local parts man or dealer service department.

Note: *The following maintenance intervals are recommended by the manufacturer. In the interest of vehicle longevity, we recommend shorter intervals on certain operations such as fluid and filter replacements.*

Weekly or every 250 miles (400 km)

Check the engine oil level, adding as necessary
Check the engine drivebelt tension
Check the engine coolant level, adding as necessary

Check the tire condition and pressures
Check the automatic transaxle fluid level
Check the brake master cylinder fluid level
Check the battery condition and electrolyte level
Check the windshield washer fluid level
Check the operation of all lights
Check horn operation

7500 miles (12 000 km) or 7.5 months

Change engine oil and filter (Chapter 1)
Check battery electrolyte level and specific gravity (Chapter 1)
Check the brake master cylinder fluid level (Chapter 1)
Check manual transaxle fluid level (Chapter 1)
Check automatic transaxle fluid level (Chapter 1)
Check steering wheel play (Chapter 11)
Check steering gear, linkage and boots (Chapter 11)
Check front disc brakes and pads (Chapter 1)
Check brake pedal, clutch pedal and parking brake mechanisms (Chapters 8 and 9)
Inspect drive axle dust boots (Chapter 1)

15 000 miles (24000 km) or 15 months

Change engine oil and filter (Chapter 1)
Replace fuel filter (Chapter 1)
Check battery electrolyte level and specific gravity (Chapter 1)
Check brake hoses (Chapter 1)
Check brake master cylinder fluid level (Chapter 1)
Check front disc brakes and pads (Chapter 1)
Check rear drum brakes (Chapter 1)
Inspect cooling system and hoses (Chapter 3)
Check manual transaxle fluid level (Chapter 1)
Check automatic transaxle fluid level (Chapter 1)
Check steering wheel play (Chapter 11)
Inspect drive axle dust boots (Chapter 1)

22 500 miles (36 000 km) or 22.5 months

Change engine oil and filter (Chapter 1)
Check brake master cylinder fluid level (Chapter 1)
Check clutch pedal, brake pedal and parking brake mechanisms (Chapters 8 and 9)
Check front disc brakes and pads (Chapter 1)
Check manual transaxle fluid level (Chapter 1)
Check automatic transaxle fluid level (Chapter 1)
Check battery electrolyte level and specific gravity (Chapter 1)
Inspect drive axle dust boots (Chapter 1)

30 000 miles (48 000 km) or 30 months

Change engine oil and filter (Chapter 1)
Check drivebelt tension (Chapter 1)
Replace air cleaner filter element (Chapter 1)
Replace spark plugs (Chapter 1)
Drain and refill cooling system (Chapter 1)
Inspect cooling system and hoses (Chapter 3)
Check battery electrolyte level and specific gravity (Chapter 1)
Inspect brake lines (Chapter 9)
Replace brake fluid (Chapter 9)
Check clutch pedal, brake pedal and parking brake mechanisms

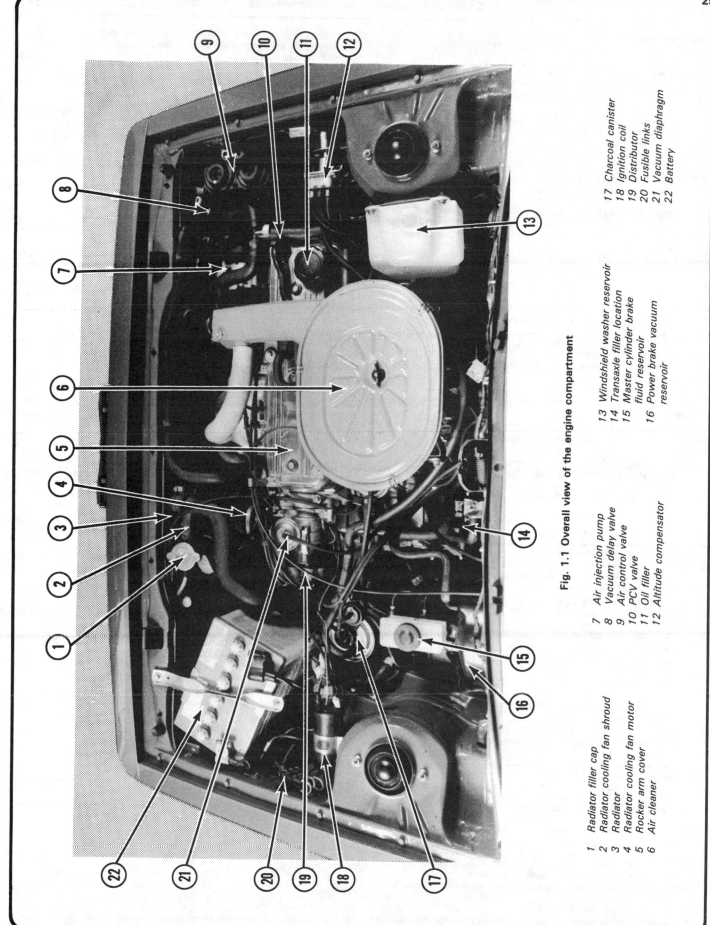

Fig. 1.1 Overall view of the engine compartment

1 Radiator filler cap
2 Radiator cooling fan shroud
3 Radiator
4 Radiator cooling fan motor
5 Rocker arm cover
6 Air cleaner

7 Air injection pump
8 Vacuum delay valve
9 Air control valve
10 PCV valve
11 Oil filler
12 Altitude compensator

13 Windshield washer reservoir
14 Transaxle filler location
15 Master cylinder brake
   fluid reservoir
16 Power brake vacuum
   reservoir

17 Charcoal canister
18 Ignition coil
19 Distributor
20 Fusible links
21 Vacuum diaphragm
22 Battery

1

(Chapters 8 and 9)
Check front disc brakes and pads (Chapter 1)
Check rear drum brakes (Chapter 1)
Inspect power brake hoses (Chapter 9)
Replace manual transaxle fluid (Chapter 1)
Check automatic transaxle fluid (Chapter 1)
Check steering gear, linkage and dust boots (Chapter 11)
Check front suspension balljoints (Chapter 11)
Check exhaust system shields (Chapter 4)
Inspect drive axle dust boots (Chapter 1)

37 500 miles (60 000 km) or 37.5 months

Change engine oil and filter (Chapter 1)
Check battery electrolyte level and specific gravity (Chapter 1)
Check brake pedal, clutch pedal and parking brake mechanisms
Check brake pedal, clutch pedal and parking brake mechanism
(Chapters 8 and 9)
Check manual transaxle fluid level (Chapter 1)
Check automatic transaxle fluid level (Chapter 1)
Inspect drive axle dust boots (Chapter 1)

45 000 miles (72 000 km) or 45 months

Change engine oil and filter (Chapter 1)
Adjust valve clearance (Chapter 1)
Check battery electrolyte level and specific gravity
Inspect brake hoses (Chapter 1)
Check brake master cylinder fluid level (Chapter 1)
Check brake pedal, clutch pedal and parking brake mechanisms
(Chapters 8 and 9)
Check front disc brakes and pads (Chapter 1)
Check rear drum brakes and shoes (Chapter 1)
Check power brake hoses (Chapter 9)
Check manual transaxle fluid level (Chapter 1)
Check automatic transaxle fluid level (Chapter 1)
Check steering gear, linkage and dust boots (Chapter 11)
Inspect drive axle dust boots (Chapter 1)

52 500 miles (84 000 km) or 52.5 months

Change engine oil and filter (Chapter 1)
Check battery electrolyte level and specific gravity (Chapter 1)
Check front disc brakes and pads (Chapter 1)
Check manual transaxle fluid level (Chapter 1)
Check automatic transaxle fluid level (Chapter 1)
Inspect drive axle dust boots (Chapter 1)

60 000 miles (96 000 km) or 60 months

Change engine oil and filter (Chapter 1)
Check battery electrolyte level and specific gravity (Chapter 1)
Adjust valve clearance (Chapter 1)
Replace air cleaner filter element (Chapter 1)
Replace spark plugs (Chapter 1)
Drain and refill engine coolant (Chapter 1)
Inspect cooling system and hoses (Chapter 1)

After 60 000 miles (96 000 km)

Return to the 7500 mile schedule and begin again
Inspect drive axle dust boots (Chapter 1)

Severe operating conditions

Severe operating conditions are defined as:
    Frequent short trips or long periods of idling
    Driving at sustained high speeds during hot weather (over 90°F,
    + 32°C)
    Driving in severe dust conditions
    Driving in temperatures below 10°F (–12°C) for 60 or more
    days

Driving 2000 miles (3200 km) or more per month
Driving in extremely humid conditions
Continuous mountain driving or where the brakes are used
extensively
If the vehicle has been operated under severe conditions, follow these
maintenance intervals:
    Change the air and fuel filters more frequently
    Change the engine oil and filter every 2000 miles (3200 km) or
    two months
    Clean and regap the spark plugs every 6000 miles (9600 km)
    Change the brake fluid annually
    Drain and refill the automatic transaxle every 22 500 miles
    (36 000 km)

3   Fluid levels check

1   There are a number of components on a vehicle which rely on the
use of fluids to perform their job. Through the normal operation of the
car, these fluids are used up and must be replenished before damage
occurs. See the *Recommended Lubricants* Section for the specific fluid
to be used when adding is required. When checking fluid levels it is
important that the car is on a level surface.

Engine oil
2   The engine oil level is checked with a dipstick which is located at
the side of the engine block. This dipstick travels through a tube and
into the oil pan at the bottom of the engine.
3   The oil level should be checked preferably before the car has been
driven, or about 15 minutes after the engine has been shut off. If the
oil is checked immediately after driving the car, some of the oil will
remain in the upper engine components, thus giving an inaccurate
reading on the dipstick.
4   Pull the dipstick from its tube and wipe all the oil from the end
with a clean rag. Insert the clean dipstick all the way back into the oil
pan and pull it out again. Observe the oil at the end of the dipstick.
At its highest point, the level should be between the 'L' and 'F' marks.
5   It takes approximately one quart of oil to raise the level from the
'L' mark to the 'F' mark on the dipstick. Do not allow the level to drop
below the 'L' mark as this may cause engine damage due to oil
starvation. On the other hand, do not overfill the engine by adding oil
above the 'F' mark as this may result in oil-fouled spark plugs, oil leaks
or oil seal failures.
6   Oil is added to the engine after removing a twist-off cap located
on the rocker cover. An oil can spout or funnel will reduce spills as the
oil is poured in.
7   Checking the oil level can also be a step towards preventative
maintenance. If you find the oil level dropping abnormally, this is an
indication of oil leakage or internal engine wear which should be
corrected. If there are water droplets in the oil, or it is milky looking,
this also indicates component failure and the engine should be
checked immediately. The condition of the oil can also be checked
along with the level. With the dipstick removed from the engine, take
your thumb and index finger and wipe the oil up the dipstick, looking
for small dirt particles or engine filings which will cling to the dipstick.
This is an indication that the oil should be drained and fresh oil added
(Section 5).

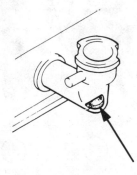

Fig. 1.2 Coolant level gauge location (Sec 3)

Engine coolant

8   The coolant level gauge in the radiator filler neck should be covered with coolant.

9   The coolant level should be checked when the engine is cold.

10   Remove the radiator cap to check the coolant level. However, **the cap should not under any circumstances be removed while the system is hot**, as escaping steam could cause serious injury. Wait until the engine has completely cooled, then wrap a thick cloth around the cap and turn it to its first stop. If any steam escapes from the cap, allow the engine to cool further. Then remove the cap and check the level in the radiator. It should be about two to three inches below the bottom of the filler neck.

11   If only a small amount of coolant is required to bring the system up to the proper level, regular water can be used. However, to maintain the proper antifreeze/water mixture in the system, both should be mixed together to replenish a low level. High-quality antifreeze offering protection to −20° should be mixed with water in the proportion specified on the container. Do not allow antifreeze to come in contact with your skin or painted surfaces of the car. Flush contacted areas immediately with plenty of water.

12   On systems with a recovery tank, coolant should be added to the reservoir after removing the cap at the top of the reservoir. Coolant should be added directly into the radiator on systems without a coolant recovery tank.

13   As the coolant level is checked, observe the condition of the coolant. It should be relatively clear. If the fluid is brown or a rust color, this is an indication that the system should be drained, flushed and refilled (Section 27).

14   If the cooling system requires repeated additions to keep the proper level, have the pressure radiator cap checked for proper sealing ability. Also check for leaks in the system (cracked hoses, loose hose connections, leaking gaskets, etc).

Windshield washer

15   The fluid for the windshield washer system is located in a plastic reservoir. The level inside the reservoir should be maintained at the 'Full' mark.

16   An approved washer solvent should be added through the plastic cap whenever replenishing is required. Do not use plain water alone in this system, especially in cold climates where the water could freeze.

Battery

Note: *There are certain precautions to be taken when working on or near the battery: a) Never expose a battery to open flame or sparks which could ignite the hydrogen gas given off by the battery; b) Wear protective clothing and eye protection to reduce the possibility of the corrosive sulfuric acid solution inside the battery harming you (if the fluid is splashed or spilled, flush the contacted area immediately with plenty of water); c) Remove all metal jewelry which could contact the positive terminal and another grounded metal source, thus causing a short circuit; d) Always keep batteries and battery acid out of the reach of children.*

17   Vehicles equipped with maintenance-free batteries require no maintenance as the battery case is sealed and has no removal caps for adding water.

18   If a maintenance-type battery is installed, the caps on the top of the battery should be removed periodically to check for a low water level. This check will be more critical during the warm summer months.

19   Remove each of the caps and add distilled water to bring the level of each cell to the split ring in the filler opening.

20   At the same time the battery water level is checked, the overall condition of the battery and its related components should be inspected. If corrosion is found on the cable ends or battery terminals, remove the cables and clean away all corrosion using a baking soda/water solution or a wire brush cleaning tool designed for this purpose. See Section 30 for complete battery care and servicing.

Brake master cylinder

21   The brake master cylinder is located on the left side of the engine compartment firewall and has a cap which must be removed to check the fluid level.

22   Before removing the cap, use a rag to clean all dirt, grease, etc. from around the cap area. If any foreign matter enters the master cylinder with the cap removed, blockage in the brake system lines can occur. Also make sure all painted surfaces around the master cylinder

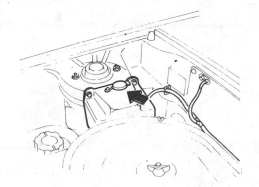

Fig. 1.3 Windshield washer reservoir location (Sec 3)

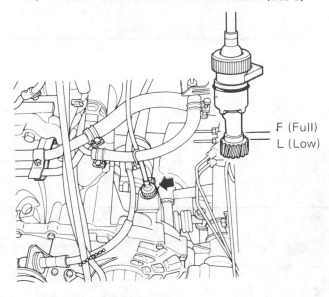

F (Full)
L (Low)

Fig. 1.4 Manual transaxle-driven gear and oil level gauge (Sec 3)

are covered, as brake fluid will ruin paintwork.

23   Unscrew the cap which threads into the top of the master cylinder reservoir.

24   Carefully lift the cap off the cylinder and observe the fluid level. It should be approximately $\frac{1}{4}$-inch below the top edge of each reservoir.

25   If additional fluid is necessary to bring the level up to the proper height, carefully pour the specified brake fluid into the master cylinder. Be careful not to spill the fluid on painted surfaces. Be sure the specified fluid is used, as mixing different types of brake fluid can cause damage to the system. See *Recommended Lubricants* or your owner's manual.

26   At this time the fluid and master cylinder can be inspected for contamination. Normally, the braking system will not need periodic draining and refilling, but if rust deposits, dirt particles or water droplets are seen in the fluid, the system should be dismantled, drained and refilled with fresh fluid.

27   Reinstall the master cylinder cap. Make sure the lid is properly seated to prevent fluid leakage and/or system pressure loss.

28   The brake fluid in the master cylinder will drop slightly as the brake shoes or pads at each wheel wear down during normal operation. If the master cylinder requires repeated replenishing to keep it at the proper level, this is an indication of leakage in the brake system which should be corrected immediately. Check all brake lines and their connections, along with the wheel cylinders and booster (see Chapter 9 for more information).

29   If upon checking the master cylinder fluid level you discover one or both reservoirs empty or nearly empty, the braking system should be bled (Chapter 9). When the fluid level gets low, air can enter the system and should be removed by bleeding the brakes.

Manual transaxles

30   Manual shift transaxles do not have a dipstick. The fluid level is

checked by removing the speedometer driven gear.

31 Remove the retaining bolt, withdraw the gear and check that the fluid covers the collar above the gear (Fig. 1.4).

32 If the transaxle needs more fluid, use a syringe to squeeze the

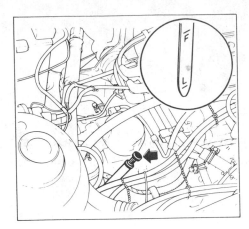

Fig. 1.5 Automatic transaxle dipstick (Sec 3)

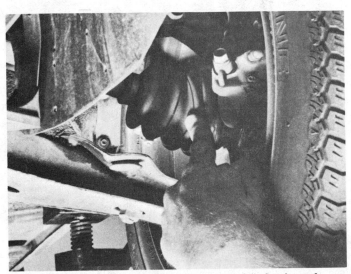

3.42 Check the constant velocity joint boots carefully for signs of cracks or leaking lubricant

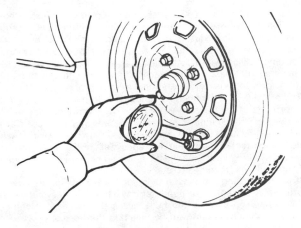

Fig. 1.6 Checking tire pressure (Sec 4)

appropriate lubricant into the speedometer gear hole to bring the fluid up to the proper level.

33 Install the gear and thread the attaching bolt into the transaxle and tighten it securely. Drive the car and check for leaks.

Automatic transaxle

34 The fluid inside the transaxle must be at normal operating temperature to get an accurate reading on the dipstick. This is done by driving the car for several miles, making frequent starts and stops to allow the transaxle to shift through all gears.

35 Park the car on a level surface, place the selector lever in Park and leave the engine running at an idle.

36 Remove the transaxle dipstick (located on the right side, near the rear of the engine) and wipe all the fluid from the end of the dipstick with a clean rag.

37 Push the dipstick back into the transaxle until the cap seats firmly on the dipstick tube. Now remove the dipstick again and observe the fluid on the end. The highest point of fluid should be between the 'Full' mark and $\frac{1}{4}$ inch below the 'Full' mark.

38 If the fluid level is at or below the 'Low' mark on the dipstick, add sufficient fluid to raise the level to the 'Full' mark. One pint of fluid will raise the level from 'Low' to 'Full'. Fluid should be added directly into the dipstick guide tube, using a funnel to prevent spills.

39 It is important that the transaxle not be overfilled. Under no circumstances should the fluid level be above the 'Full' mark on the dipstick, as this could cause internal damage to the transaxle. The best way to prevent overfilling is to add fluid a little at a time, driving the car and checking the level between additions.

40 Use only transaxle fluid specified by the manufacturer. This information can be found in the *Recommended Lubricants* Section.

41 The condition of the fluid should also be checked along with the level. If the fluid at the end of the dipstick is a dark reddish-brown color, or if the fluid has a 'burnt' smell, the transaxle fluid should be changed. If you are in doubt about the condition of the fluid, purchase some new fluid and compare the two for color and smell.

Driveshaft

42 The driveshaft constant velocity joints are lubricated for life at the time of manufacture. It is important to inspect the protective boots for cracks, tears or splits (photo).

43 With the vehicle raised securely, inspect the area around the boots for signs of grease splattering, indicating damage to the boots or retaining clamps.

44 Inspect around the inboard joint for signs of fluid leakage from the transaxle differential seal.

4	Tire and tire pressure checks

1 Periodically inspecting the tires can not only prevent you from being stranded with a flat tire, but can also give you clues as to possible problems with the steering and suspension systems before major damage occurs.

2 Proper tire inflation adds miles to the lifespan of the tires, allows the car to achieve maximum miles per gallon figures, and helps the overall riding comfort of the car.

3 When inspecting the tire, first check the wear on the tread. Irregularities in the tread pattern (cupping, flat spots, more wear on one side than the other) are indications of front end alignment and/or balance problems. If any of these conditions are found you would do best to take the car to a competent repair shop which can correct the problem.

4 Also check the tread area for cuts or punctures. Many times a nail or tack will embed itself into the tire tread and yet the tire will hold its air pressure for a short time. In most cases, a repair shop or gas station can repair the punctured tire.

5 It is also important to check the sidewalls of the tire, both inside and outside. Check for the rubber being deteriorated, cut or punctured. Also inspect the inboard side of the tire for signs of brake fluid leakage, indicating a thorough brake inspection is needed immediately (Section 25).

6 Incorrect tire pressure cannot be determined merely by looking at the tire. This is especially true for radial tires. A tire pressure gauge must be used. If you do not already have a reliable gauge, it is a good idea to purchase one and keep it in the glove box. Built-in pressure

gauges at gas stations are often unreliable. If you are in doubt as to the accuracy of your gauge, many repair shops have 'master' pressure gauges which you can use for comparison purposes.

7   Always check tire inflation when the tires are cold. Cold, in this case, means the car has not been driven more than one mile after sitting for three hours or more. It is normal for the pressure to increase 4 to 8 pounds or more when the tires are hot.

8   Unscrew the valve cap protruding from the wheel or hubcap and firmly press the gauge onto the valve stem. Observe the reading on the gauge and check this figure against the recommended tire pressure listed on the tire placard. This tire placard is usually found attached to the rear portion of the driver's door.

9   Check all tires and add air as necessary to bring all tires up to the recommended pressure levels. Do not forget the spare tire. Be sure to reinstall the valve caps which will keep dirt and moisture out of the valve stem mechanism.

5   Engine oil and filter change

1   Frequent oil changes may be the best form of preventative maintenance available for the home mechanic. When engine oil ages, it gets diluted and contaminated which ultimately leads to premature parts wear.

2   Although some sources recommend oil filter changes every other oil change, we feel that the minimal cost of an oil filter and the relative ease with which it is installed dictates that a new filter be used whenever the oil is changed.

3   The tools necessary for a normal oil and filter change are: a wrench to fit the drain plug at the bottom of the oil pan; an oil filter wrench to remove the old filter; a container with at least a five-quart capacity to drain the old oil into; and a funnel or oil can spout to help pour fresh oil into the engine.

4   In addition, you should have plenty of clean rags and newspapers handy to mop up any spills. Access to the underside of the car is greatly improved if the car can be lifted on a hoist, driven onto ramps or supported by jack stands. Do not work under a car which is supported only by a bumper, hydraulic or scissors-type jack.

5   If this is your first oil change on the car, it is a good idea to crawl underneath and familiarize yourself with the locations of the oil drain plug and the oil filter. Since the engine and exhaust components will be warm during the actual work, it is best to figure out any potential problems before the car and its accessories are hot (photo).

6   Allow the car to warm up to normal operating temperature. If the new oil or any tools are needed, use this warm-up time to gather everything necessary for the job. The correct type of oil to buy for your application can be found in *Recommended Lubricants* near the front of this Chapter.

7   With the engine oil warm (warm engine oil will drain better and more built-up sludge will be removed with the oil), raise the vehicle for access beneath. Make sure the car is firmly supported. If jack stands are used they should be placed towards the front of the frame rails which run the length of the car.

8   Move all necessary tools, rags and newspaper under the car. Position the drain pan under the drain plug. Keep in mind that the oil will initially flow from the pan with some force, so place the pan accordingly.

9   Being careful not to touch any of the hot exhaust pipe components, use the wrench to remove the drain plug near the bottom of the oil pan. Depending on how hot the oil has become, you may want to wear gloves while unscrewing the plug the final few turns.

10   Allow the old oil to drain into the pan. It may be necessary to move the pan further under the engine as the oil flow reduces to a trickle.

11   After all the oil has drained, clean the drain plug thoroughly with a clean rag. Small metal filings may cling to this plug which could immediately contaminate your new oil.

12   Clean the area around the drain plug opening and reinstall the drain plug. Tighten the plug securely with your wrench.

13   Move the drain pan in position under the oil filter.

14   Now use the filter wrench to loosen the oil filter. Chain or metal band-type filter wrenches may distort the filter canister, but don't worry too much about this as the filter will be discarded anyway.

15   Sometimes the oil filter is on so tight it cannot be loosened, or it is positioned in an area which is inaccessible with a filter wrench. As a last resort, you can punch a metal bar or long screwdriver directly through the **bottom** of the canister and use this as a T-bar to turn the

5.5 Oil filter and drain plug locations

filter. If this must be done, be prepared for oil to spurt out of the canister as it is punctured.

16   Completely unscrew the old filter. Be careful, it is full of oil. Empty the old oil inside the filter into the drain pan.

17   Compare the old filter with the new one to make sure they are of the same type.

18   Use a clean rag to remove all oil, dirt and sludge from the area where the oil filter mounts to the engine. Check the old filter to make sure the rubber gasket is not stuck to the engine mounting surface. If this gasket is stuck to the engine (use a flashlight if necessary), remove it.

19   Open one of the cans of new oil and fill the new filter with fresh oil. Also smear a light coat of this fresh oil onto the rubber gasket of the new oil filter.

20   Screw the new filter to the engine following the tightening directions printed on the filter canister or packing box. Most filter manufacturers recommend against using a filter wrench due to possible overtightening or damage to the canister.

21   Remove all tools, rags, etc. from under the car, being careful not to spill the oil in the drain pan. Lower the car off its support devices.

22   Move to the engine compartment and locate the oil filler cap on the engine.

23   If an oil can spout is used, push the spout into the top of the oil can and pour the fresh oil through the filler opening. A funnel placed into the opening may also be used.

24   Pour 4 quarts of fresh oil into the engine. Wait a few minutes to allow the oil to drain to the pan, then check the level on the oil dipstick (see Section 2 if necessary). If the oil level is at or near the lower 'Add' mark, start the engine and allow the new oil to circulate.

25   Run the engine for only about a minute and then shut it off. Immediately look under the car and check for leaks at the oil pan drain plug and around the oil filter. If either is leaking, tighten with a bit more force.

26   With the new oil circulated and the filter now completely full, recheck the level on the dipstick and add enough oil to bring the level to the 'Full' mark on the dipstick.

27   During the first few trips after an oil change, make a point to check for leaks and also the oil level.

28   The old oil drained from the engine cannot be reused in its present state and should be disposed of. Oil reclamation centers, auto repair shops and gas stations will normally accept the oil which can be refined and used again. After the oil has cooled, it can be drained into a suitable container (capped plastic jugs, topped bottles, milk cartons, etc) for transport to one of these disposal sites.

6   Chassis lubrication

1   There is no provision for lubrication of chassis or steering components on all models as they are lubed for life. Only the rear wheel bearings (Chapter 11), clutch linkage (Chapter 8) and parking

1

brake linkage (Chapter 9) require periodic lubrication.

2   The door, hood and liftgate hinges should be lubricated periodically with polyethylene grease.

3   Open the hood and smear a little grease on the hoot latch mechanism. Have an assistant pull the release knob from inside the vehicle as you lubricate the cable at the latch.

4   Lubricate the door weatherstripping with silicone spray. This will reduce chafing and retard wear.

5   The key lock cylinders should be lubricated with spray-on graphite, available at auto parts stores.

7   Cooling system check

Caution: *Disconnect the battery negative cable when working in the vicinity of the fan.*

1   Many major engine failures can be attributed to a faulty cooling system. If equipped with an automatic transaxle the cooling system also plays an integral role in transaxle longevity.

2   The cooling system should be checked with the engine cold. Do this before the car is driven for the day or after it has been shut off for one or two hours.

3   Remove the radiator cap and thoroughly clean the cap (inside and out) with clean water. Also clean the filler neck on the radiator. All traces of corrosion should be removed.

4   Carefully check the upper and lower radiator hoses along with the smaller diameter heater hoses. Inspect their entire length, replacing any hose which is cracked, swollen or shows signs of deterioration. Cracks may become more apparent if the hose is squeezed.

5   Also check that all hose connections are tight. A leak in the cooling system will usually show up as white or rust colored deposits on the areas adjoining the leak.

6   Use compressed air or a soft brush to remove bugs, leaves, etc. from the front of the radiator or air conditioning condensor. Be careful not to damage the delicate cooling fins, or cut yourself on the sharp fins.

7   Finally, have the cap and system tested for proper pressure. If you do not have a pressure tester, most gas stations and repair shops will do this for a minimal charge.

8   Exhaust system check

1   With the exhaust system cold (at least three hours after being driven), check the complete exhaust system from its starting point at the engine to the end of the tailpipe. This is best done on a hoist where full access is available.

2   Check the pipes and their connections for signs of leakage and/or corrosion indicating potential failure. Check that all brackets and hangers are in good condition and are tight.

3   At the same time, inspect the underside of the body for holes, corrosion, open seams, etc, which may allow exhaust gases to enter the trunk or passenger compartment. Seal all body openings with silicone or body putty.

4   Rattles and other driving noises can often be traced to the exhaust system, especially the mounts and hangers. Try to move the pipes, muffler and catalytic converter (if equipped). If the components can come into contact with the body or driveline parts, secure the exhaust system with new mountings.

5   This is also an ideal time to check the running condition of the engine by inspecting the very end of the tailpipe. The exhaust deposits here are an indication of engine tune. If the pipe is black and sooty or bright white deposits are found here, the engine is in need of a tune-up including a thorough carburetor inspection and adjustment.

9   Suspension and steering check

1   Whenever the front of the car is raised for service it is a good idea to visually check the suspension and steering components for wear.

2   Indications of a fault in these systems are: excessive play in the steering wheel before the front wheels react; excessive sway around corners or body movement over rough roads; binding at some point as the steering wheel is turned.

3   Before the car is raised for inspection, test the shock absorbers by

pushing downward to rock the car at each corner. If you push the car down and it does not come back to a level position within one or two bounces, the shocks are worn and need to be replaced. As this is done, check for squeaks and strange noises from the suspension components. Information on shock absorber and suspension components can be found in Chapter 11.

4   Now raise the front end of the car and support firmly by jack stands placed under the frame rails. Because of the work to be done, make sure the car cannot fall from the stands.

5   Check the front wheel hub nut for looseness and make sure that it is properly crimped in place.

6   Crawl under the car and check for loose bolts, broken or disconnected parts and deteriorated rubber bushings on all suspension and steering components. Look for grease or fluid leaking from around the steering box. Check the power steering hoses and their connections for leaks. Check the steering joints for wear.

7   Have an assistant turn the steering wheel from side to side and check the steering components for free movement, chafing or binding. If the steering does not react with the movement of the steering wheel, try to determine where the slack is located.

10   Fuel system check

1   There are certain precautions to take when inspecting or servicing the fuel system components. Work in a well ventilated area and do not allow open flames (cigarettes, appliance pilot lights, etc.) to get near the work area. Mop up spills immediately and do not store fuel-soaked rags where they could ignite.

2   The fuel system is under some amount of pressure, so if any fuel lines are disconnected for servicing, be prepared to catch the fuel as it spurts out. Plug all disconnected fuel lines immediately after disconnection to prevent the tank from emptying itself.

3   The fuel system is most easily checked with the car raised on a hoist where the components under the car are readily visible and accessible.

4   If the smell of gasoline is noticed while driving, or after the car has sat in the sun, the system should be thoroughly inspected immediately.

5   Remove the gas filler cap and check for damage, corrosion and a proper sealing imprint on the gasket. Replace the cap with a new one if necessary.

6   With the car raised, inspect the gas tank and filler neck for punctures, cracks or any damage. The connection between the filler neck and the tank is especially critical. Sometimes a rubber filler neck will leak due to loose clamps or deteriorated rubber; problems a home mechanic can usually rectify.

7   Do not under any circumstances try to repair a fuel tank yourself (except rubber components) unless you have considerable experience. A welding torch or any open flame can easily cause the fuel vapors to explode if the proper precautions are not taken.

8   Carefully check all rubber hoses and metal lines leading away from the fuel tank. Check for loose connections, deteriorated hose, crimped lines or damage of any kind. Follow these lines up to the front of the car, carefully inspecting them all the way. Repair or replace damaged sections as necessary.

9   If a fuel odor is still evident after the inspection, refer to Section 28 on the evaporative emissions system and Chapter 4 for carburetor adjustment.

11   Engine drivebelt check and adjustment

Caution: *Disconnect the battery negative cable when working in the vicinity of the fan.*

1   The drivebelts, or V-belts as they are sometimes called, at the front of the engine play an important role in the overall operation of the car and its components. Due to their function and material make-up, the belts are prone to failure after a period of time and should be inspected and adjusted periodically to prevent major engine damage.

2   The number of belts used on a particular car depends on the accessories installed. Drivebelts are used to turn: the generator (alternator); AIR smog pump; water pump; and air conditioning compressor. Depending on the pulley arrangement, a single belt may be used for more than one of these ancillary components.

3   With the engine off, open the hood and locate the various belts at the front of the engine. Using your fingers (and a flashlight if

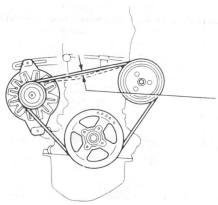

Fig. 1.7 Checking alternator/air pump belt tension (arrows) (Sec 11)

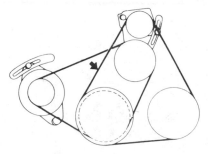

Fig. 1.8 Checking drivebelt tension on air conditioned vehicles (Sec 11)

necessary), move along the belts checking for cracks or separation. Also check for fraying and for glazing which gives the belt a shiny appearance. Both sides of the belts should be inspected, which means you will have to twist the belt to check the underside.

4   The tension of each belt is checked by pushing on the belt at a distance halfway between the pulleys. Push firmly with your thumb and see how much the belt moves downward (deflects). Refer to the Specifications Section to make sure that deflection is within limits.

5   If it is found necessary to adjust the belt tension, either to make the belt tighter or looser, this is done by moving the belt-driven accessory on its bracket.

6   For each component there will be an adjustment or strap bolt and a pivot bolt. Both bolts must be loosened slightly to enable you to move the component.

7   After the two bolts have been loosened, move the component away from the engine (to tighten the belt) or toward the engine (to loosen the belt). Hold the accessory in this position and check the belt tension. If it is correct, tighten the two bolts until snug, then recheck the tension. If it is alright, fully tighten the two bolts.

8   It will often be necessary to use some sort of pry bar to move the accessory while the belt is adjusted. If this must be done to gain the proper leverage, be very careful not to damage the component being

moved, or the part being pried against.

12 Air filter and PCV filter replacement

1   At the specified intervals, the air filter and PCV filter should be replaced with new ones. A thorough program of preventative maintenance would call for the two filters to be inspected periodically between changes.

2   The air filter is located inside the air cleaner housing on the top of the engine. To remove the filter, unscrew the wing nut at the top of the air cleaner and lift off the top plate. If there are vacuum hoses connected to this plate, note their positions and disconnect them.

3   While the top plate is off, be careful not to drop anything down into the carburetor.

4   Lift the air filter out of the housing (photo).

5   To check the filter, hold it up to strong sunlight, or place a flashlight or droplight on the inside of the ring-shaped filter. If you can see light coming through the paper element, the filter is alright. Check all the way around the filter.

6   Wipe the inside of the air cleaner clean with a rag.

7   Place the old filter (if in good condition) or the new filter (if specified interval has elapsed) back into the air cleaner housing. Make sure it seats properly in the bottom of the housing.

8   Connect any disconnected vacuum hoses to the top plate and reinstall the top plate with the wing nut.

9   On nearly all cars the PCV filter is also located inside the air cleaner housing. Remove the top plate as described previously and locate the filter on the side of the housing.

10 Insert a screwdriver into the PCV filter cavity and lift the filter out (photo).

11 Compare the new filter with the old one to make sure they are the same and insert it into the filter cavity.

12 Reinstall the air cleaner top plate.

13 For more information on these systems and the systems they are part of, see Chapters 4 and 6.

13 Positive Crankcase Ventilation (PCV) valve replacement

1   The PCV valve can usually be found pushed into one of the rocker arm covers at the side of the engine. There will be a hose connected to the valve which runs to either the carburetor or the intake manifold.

2   When purchasing a replacement PCV valve, make sure it is for your particular vehicle, model year and engine size.

3   Pull the valve (with the hose attached) from its rubber grommet in the rocker arm cover (photo).

4   Now pull the PCV valve from the end of the hose, noting its installed position and direction.

5   Compare the old valve with the new one to make sure they are the same.

6   Push the new valve into the end of the hose until it is fully seated.

7   Move the hose clamp down the hose and tighten the clamp securely around the end of the hose.

8   Inspect the rubber grommet in the cover for damage and replace it with a new one if faulty.

9   Push the PCV valve and hose securely into the rocker arm cover.

1

12.4 Removing the air filter element

12.10 Using a screwdriver to remove the PCV filter

13.3 Removing the PCV valve from the rocker cover

10 More information on the PCV system can be found in Chapter 6.

14 Clutch pedal free travel check

1   If equipped with a manual shift transaxle, it is important to have the clutch free play at the proper point. Basically, free play at the clutch pedal is the point at which time the clutch components engage and the car starts moving. When the pedal is pushed all the way to the floor, the clutch parts are disengaged and the car doesn't travel. As the pedal travels away from the floor, the parts engage and the vehicle is set into motion. It is the measured distance which the pedal moves between these two points which indicates free travel.

2   With the car on a level surface, turn on the engine and allow it to idle. Apply the parking brake to prevent the car from moving.

3   Depress the clutch pedal until it is approximately $\frac{1}{2}$ inch from the floor mat or carpeting.

4   Hold the pedal in this position and move the shift lever between first and reverse gears several times. If this can be done smoothly, the clutch is fully releasing and no adjustment is necessary. If the shift is not smooth, the clutch pedal free play should be adjusted.

5   If adjustment is necessary, refer to Chapter 8 for the step-by-step sequence to follow.

15 Tire rotation

1   The tires should be rotated at the specified intervals and whenever uneven wear is noticed. Since the car will be raised and the tires removed anyway, this is a good time to check the brakes (Section 25) and/or repack the wheel bearings (Chapter 11). Read over these Sections if this is to be done at the same time.

2   The location for each tire in the rotation sequence depends on the type of tire used on your car. Tire type can be determined by reading the raised printing on the sidewall of the tire. Do not use the temporary type spare in the tire rotation sequence.

3   See the information in *Jacking and Towing* at the front of this manual for the proper procedures to follow in raising the car and changing a tire; however, if the brakes are to be checked do not apply the parking brake as stated. Make sure the tires are blocked to prevent the car from rolling.

4   Preferably, the entire car should be raised at the same time. This can be done on a hoist or by jacking up each corner of the car and then lowering the car onto jack stands placed under the frame rails. Always use four jack stands and make sure the car is firmly supported all around.

5   After rotation, check and adjust the tire pressures as necessary and be sure to check wheel nut tightness.

16 Thermo controlled air cleaner check

1   All models are equipped with a thermostatically controlled air cleaner which draws air to the carburetor from different locations depending upon engine temperature.

2   This is a simple visual check; however, if access is tight, a small mirror may have to be used.

3   Open the hood and find the vacuum flapper door on the air cleaner assembly. It will be located inside the long 'snorkel' of the metal air cleaner. Check that the flexible air hose(s) are securely attached and are not damaged.

4   If there is a flexible air duct attached to the end of the snorkel, leading to an area behind the grille, disconnect it at the snorkel. This will enable you to look through the end of the snorkel and see the flapper door inside.

5   The testing should preferably be done when the engine and outside air are cold. Start the engine and look through the snorkel at the flapper door which should move to a closed position. With the door closed, air cannot enter through the end of the snorkel, but rather air enters the air cleaner through the flexible duct attached to the exhaust manifold.

6   As the engine warms up to operating temperature, the door should open to allow air through the snorkel end. Depending on ambient temperature, this may take 10 to 15 minutes. To speed up this check you can reconnect the snorkel air duct, drive the car and then check that the door is fully open.

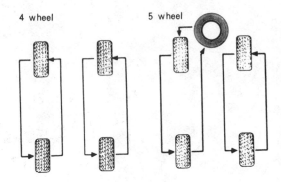

Fig. 1.9 Radial tire rotation patterns (Sec 15)

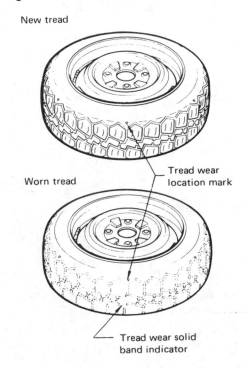

Fig. 1.10 Tread wear indicators (Sec 15)

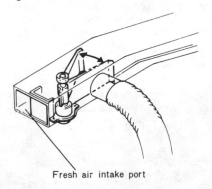

Fig. 1.11 Thermostatic air cleaner doors (Sec 16)

7   If the thermo controlled air cleaner is not operating properly, see Chapter 4 for more information.

17 Engine idle speed adjustment

1   Engine idle speed is the speed at which the engine operates when

no accelerator pedal pressure is applied. This speed is critical to the performance of the engine itself, as well as many engine sub-systems.

2   A hand-held tachometer must be used when adjusting idle speed to get an accurate reading. The exact hook-up for these meters varies with the manufacturer, so follow the particular directions included.

3   Chapter 4 contains information on each individual carburetor used. The carburetor used on your particular engine can be found in the Specifications Section of Chapter 4. However, all vehicles covered in this manual should have a tune-up decal in the engine compartment, usually placed near the top of the radiator. The printed instructions for setting idle speed can be found on this decal, and should be followed since they are for your particular engine.

4   Basically, for most applications, the idle speed is set by turning an adjustment screw located at the side of the carburetor. This screw changes the linkage, in essence, depressing or letting up on your accelerator pedal. This screw may be on the linkage itself or may be part of the idle stop solenoid. Refer to the tune-up decal or Chapter 4.

5   Once you have found the idle screw, experiment with different length screwdrivers until the adjustments can be easily made, without coming into contact with hot or moving engine components.

6   Follow the instructions on the tune-up decal or in Chapter 4, which will probably include disconnecting certain vacuum or electrical connections. To plug a vacuum hose after disconnecting it, insert a properly-sized metal rod into the opening, or thoroughly wrap the open end with tape to prevent any vacuum loss through the hose.

7   If the air cleaner is removed, the vacuum hose to the snorkel should be plugged.

8   Make sure the parking brake is firmly set and the wheels blocked to prevent the car from rolling. This is especially true if the transaxle is to be in Drive. An assistant inside the car pushing on the brake pedal is the safest method.

9   For all applications, the engine must be completely warmed-up to operating temperature, which will automatically render the choke fast idle inoperative.

18 Fuel filter replacement

1   The fuel filter is located in the engine compartment below the brake master cylinder.

2   Position newspapers and/or rags to help absorb the fuel, then disconnect the fuel lines at both ends of the filter.

3   On 1981 models, release the clips and lift the filter from the engine compartment (photo).

4   On 1982 models, loosen the retaining bolt and remove the filter.

5   To install, place the new filter in position and reinstall the clips (1981 models) or tighten the installing bolt. On 1981 models the flat metal end must face forward and on 1982 models the arrow on the top of the filter must point forward.

6   Install the fuel lines to the filter.

19 Ignition timing – adjustment

1   All vehicles are equipped with a tune-up decal inside the engine compartment. This decal gives important ignition timing settings and procedures to be followed specific to that vehicle. If information on the tune-up decal supersedes the information given in this Section, the decal should be followed.

2   At the specified intervals, the ignition timing must be checked and adjusted if necessary.

3   Before attempting to check the timing, make sure the idle speed is as specified (Chapter 4).

4   Disconnect the vacuum hose from the distributor and plug the now-open end of the hose with a rubber plug, rod or bolt of the proper size. Make sure the idle speed remains correct; adjust as necessary.

5   Connect a timing light in accordance with the manufacturer's instructions. Generally, the light will be connected to power and ground sources and to the number 1 spark plug in some fashion.

6   Locate the numbered timing tag on the front cover of the engine (Fig. 1.13). It is just behind the lower crankshaft pulley. Clean it off with solvent if necessary to read the printing and small grooves.

7   Locate the notched groove across the crankshaft pulley. It may be necessary to have an assistant temporarily turn the ignition off and on in short bursts without starting the engine to bring this groove into a position where it can easily be cleaned and marked. Stay clear of all

18.3 The fuel filter on 1981 models is held in place with clips

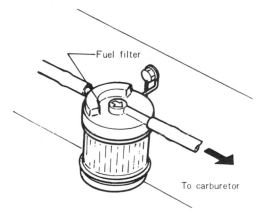

Fig. 1.12 Fuel filter installation (1982 models) (Sec 18)

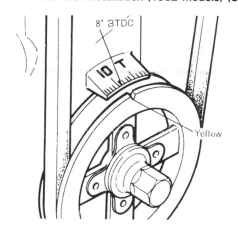

Fig. 1.13 Ignition timing marks (Sec 19)

moving engine components if the engine is turned over in this manner.

8   Use white soap-stone, chalk or paint to mark the groove on the crankshaft pulley. Also put a mark on the timing tab in accordance with the number of degrees called for in the Specifications (Chapter 5) or on the tune-up decal inside the engine compartment. Each peak or notch on the timing tab represents 2°. The word 'Before' or the letter 'A' indicates advance and the letter 'O' indicates Top Dead Center (TDC). Thus if your vehicle specifications call for 8° BTDC (Before Top

Dead Center), you will make a mark on the timing tab 4 notches before the 'O'.

9   Check that the wiring for the timing light is clear of all moving engine components, then start the engine.

10   Point the flashing timing light at the timing marks, again being careful not to come in contact with moving parts. The marks you made should appear stationary. If the marks are in alignment, the timing is correct. If the marks are not aligned, turn off the engine.

11   Loosen the locknut at the base of the distributor. Loosen the locknut only slightly, just enough to turn the distributor. (See Chapter 5 for further details, if necessary).

12   Now restart the engine and turn the distributor until the timing marks coincide.

13   Shut off the engine and tighten the distributor locknut, being careful not to move the distributor.

14   Start the engine and recheck the timing to make sure the marks are still in alignment.

15   Disconnect the timing light, unplug the distributor vacuum hose and connect the hose to the distributor.

16   Drive the car and listen for 'pinging' noises. These will be most noticeable when the engine is hot and under load (climbing a hill, accelerating from a stop). If you hear engine pinging, the ignition timing is too far advanced (Before Top Dead Center). Reconnect the timing light and turn the distributor to move the mark 1° or 2° in the retard direction. Road test the car again for proper operation.

17   To keep 'pinging' at a minimum, yet still allow you to operate the car at the specified timing setting, it is advisable to use gasoline of the same octane at all times. Switching fuel brands and octane levels can decrease performance and economy, and possibly damage the engine.

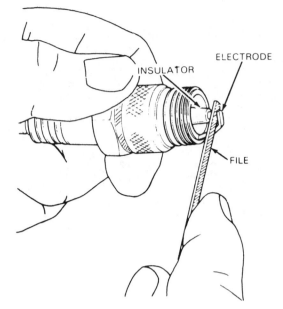

Fig. 1.14 Cleaning the spark plug electrodes with a file (Sec 21)

20 Exhaust Gas Recirculation (EGR) valve check

1   The EGR valve is located on the intake manifold, adjacent to the carburetor. The majority of the time, when a fault develops in the EGR system it is due to a stuck or corroded valve.

2   With the engine idling, remove the vacuum hose from the EGR valve and apply vacuum to the valve port.

3   The engine should either run roughly or stop. If it does not, the valve is faulty and should be replaced with a new one.

4   Further testing of the EGR system and its components can be found in Chapter 6.

21 Spark plug replacement

1   The spark plugs are located on the front (radiator) side of the engine. If the car is equipped with air conditioning, some of the plugs may be tricky to service In which case special extension or swivel tools will be necessary. Make a survey under the hood to ascertain if special tools will be needed.

2   In most cases the tools necessary for a spark plug replacement job are: a plug wrench or spark plug socket which fits onto a ratchet wrench (this special socket will be insulated inside to protect the porcelain insulator) and a feeler gauge to check and adjust the spark plug gap.

3   The best policy to follow when replacing the spark plugs is to purchase the new spark plugs beforehand, adjust them to the proper gap and then replace each plug one at a time. When buying the new spark plugs it is important that the correct plug is purchased for your specific engine. This information can be found in the Specifications Section of Chapter 5, but should be checked against the information found on the tune-up decal located under the hood of your car or in the factory owner's manual. If differences exist between these sources, purchase the spark plug type specified on the tune-up decal as this information was printed for your specific engine.

4   With the new spark plugs at hand, allow the engine to thoroughly cool before attempting the removal. During this cooling time, each of the new spark plugs can be inspected for defects and the gap can be checked.

5   The gap is checked by inserting the proper thickness gauge between the electrodes at the tip of the plug. The gap between these electrodes should be the same as that given in the Specifications or on the tune-up decal. The wire should just touch each of the electrodes. If the gap is incorrect, use the notched adjuster on the feeler gauge body to bend the curved side electrode slightly until the proper gap is

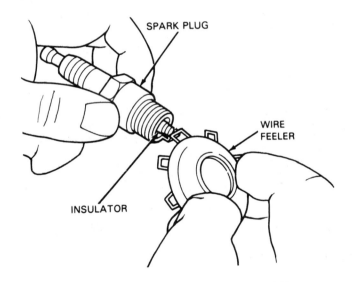

Fig. 1.15 Setting spark plug gap (Sec 21)

achieved. Also at this time check for cracks in the spark plug body, indicating the spark plug should be replaced with a new one. If the side electrode is not exactly over the center one, use the notched adjuster to align the two.

6   Cover the fenders of the car to prevent damage to exterior paint.

7   With the engine cool, remove the spark plug wire from one spark plug. Do this by grabbing the boot at the end of the wire, not the wire itself. Sometimes it is necessary to use a twisting motion while the boot and plug wire is pulled free. Using a plug wire removal tool is the easiest and safest method.

8   If compressed air is available, use this to blow any dirt or foreign material away from the spark plug area. A common bicycle pump will also work. The idea here is to eliminate the possibility of material falling into the engine cylinder as the spark plug is replaced.

9   Now place the spark plug wrench or socket over the plug and remove it from the engine by turning in a counter-clockwise motion.

10   Compare the spark plug with those shown on page 35 to get an indication of the overall running condition of the engine (photo).

11   Lubricate the first few spark plug threads with a small amount of anti-seize compound or molybdenum-type thread lubricant. Insert one of the new plugs into the engine, tightening it as much as possible by hand. The spark plug should screw easily into the engine. If it doesn't,

CARBON DEPOSITS

Symptoms: Dry sooty deposits indicate a rich mixture or weak ignition. Causes misfiring, hard starting and hesitation.

Recommendation: Check for a clogged air cleaner, high float level, sticky choke and worn ignition points. Use a spark plug with a longer core nose for greater anti-fouling protection.

OIL DEPOSITS

Symptoms: Oily coating caused by poor oil control. Oil is leaking past worn valve guides or piston rings into the combustion chamber. Causes hard starting, misfiring and hesition.

Recommendation: Correct the mechanical condition with necessary repairs and install new plugs.

TOO HOT

Symptoms: Blistered, white insulator, eroded electrode and absence of deposits. Results in shortened plug life.

Recommendation: Check for the correct plug heat range, over-advanced ignition timing, lean fuel mixture, intake manifold vacuum leaks and sticking valves. Check the coolant level and make sure the radiator is not clogged.

PREIGNITION

Symptoms: Melted electrodes. Insulators are white, but may be dirty due to misfiring or flying debris in the combustion chamber. Can lead to engine damage.

Recommendation: Check for the correct plug heat range, over-advanced ignition timing, lean fuel mixture, clogged cooling system and lack of lubrication.

HIGH SPEED GLAZING

Symptoms: Insulator has yellowish, glazed appearance. Indicates that combustion chamber temperatures have risen suddenly during hard acceleration. Normal deposits melt to form a conductive coating. Causes misfiring at high speeds.

Recommendation: Install new plugs. Consider using a colder plug if driving habits warrant.

GAP BRIDGING

Symptoms: Combustion deposits lodge between the electrodes. Heavy deposits accumulate and bridge the electrode gap. The plug ceases to fire, resulting in a dead cylinder.

Recommendation: Locate the faulty plug and remove the deposits from between the electrodes.

NORMAL

Symptoms: Brown to grayish-tan color and slight electrode wear. Correct heat range for engine and operating conditions.

Recommendation: When new spark plugs are installed, replace with plugs of the same heat range.

ASH DEPOSITS

Symptoms: Light brown deposits encrusted on the side or center electrodes or both. Derived from oil and/or fuel additives. Excessive amounts may mask the spark, causing misfiring and hesitation during acceleration.

Recommendation: If excessive deposits accumulate over a short time or low mileage, install new valve guide seals to prevent seepage of oil into the combustion chambers. Also try changing gasoline brands.

WORN

Symptoms: Rounded electrodes with a small amount of deposits on the firing end. Normal color. Causes hard starting in damp or cold weather and poor fuel economy.

Recommendation: Replace with new plugs of the same heat range.

DETONATION

Symptoms: Insulators may be cracked or chipped. Improper gap setting techniques can also result in a fractured insulator tip. Can lead to piston damage.

Recommendation: Make sure the fuel anti-knock values meet engine requirements. Use care when setting the gaps on new plugs. Avoid lugging the engine.

SPLASHED DEPOSITS

Symptoms: After long periods of misfiring, deposits can loosen when normal combustion temperature is restored by an overdue tune-up. At high speeds, deposits flake off the piston and are thrown against the hot insulator, causing misfiring.

Recommendation: Replace the plugs with new ones or clean and reinstall the originals.

MECHANICAL DAMAGE

Symptoms: May be caused by a foreign object in the combustion chamber or the piston striking an incorrect reach (too long) plug. Causes a dead cylinder and could result in piston damage.

Recommendation: Remove the foreign object from the engine and/or install the correct reach plug.

change the angle of the spark plug slightly, as chances are the threads are not matched (cross-threaded).

12 Firmly tighten the spark plug with the wrench or socket. It is best to use a torque wrench for this to ensure the plug is seated correctly. The correct torque figure is shown in Specifications.

13 Before pushing the spark plug wire onto the end of the plug, inspect it following the procedures outlined in Section 26.

14 Install the plug wire to the new spark plug, again using a twisting motion on the boot until it is firmly seated on the spark plug. Make sure wire is routed away from the hot exhaust manifold.

15 Follow the above procedures for the remaining spark plugs, replacing each one at a time to prevent mixing up the spark plug wires.

22 Wheel bearing check and repack

1   The front wheel bearings are adjusted and lubricated at the factory and normally need only be checked for looseness indicating bearing wear or improperly tightened hub nut. Refer to Chapter 11 for checking and maintenance of the front wheel bearings.

2   Adjustment, removal and installation and repacking procedures for the rear wheel bearings are also described in Chapter 11.

23 Automatic transaxle fluid change

1   The transaxle fluid should be periodically changed. Since removing the drain plug will not fully drain the transaxle, it will also be necessary to remove the oil pan.

2   Before draining, purchase the specified transaxle fluid (see *Recommended lubricants* in the Specification Section at the front of this Chapter) and a pan gasket.

3   Other tools necessary for this job include
   A wrench to remove the pan bolts
   A drain pan of at least 9-pint capacity
   Jack stands to support the vehicle
   Newspapers and clean rags

4   The fluid should be drained immediately after the vehicle has been driven. This will remove sediment better during draining than if the fluid were cold. It may be wise to wear protective gloves during this job as fluid temperature can exceed 350° in a hot transaxle.

5   After the vehicle has been driven and the fluid warmed up, raise the vehicle and support it securely.

6   Move the necessary equipment under the vehicle, being careful not to touch any of the hot exhaust components.

7   Place the drain pan under the transaxle and remove the drain plug which is accessible through the hole in the crossmember. Loosen, but do not remove, the bolts at the front of the pan.

8   Carefully pry the pan downward at the rear, allowing the remaining hot fluid to drain into the drain pan. If necessary, use a screwdriver to break the gasket seal at the rear of the pan, taking care not to damage the pan or transaxle in the process.

9   Support the pan and remove the remaining bolts at the front of the pan. Lower the pan and drain the remaining fluid into the drain receptacle. As this is done, check the fluid for signs of contamination.

10 Thoroughly clean the transaxle oil pan with solvent and inspect for metal filings or foreign matter. Dry with compressed air if possible. Remove any remaining gasket material from the oil pan mounting flange, using a gasket scraper or putty knife.

11 Apply a bead of gasket sealant around the oil pan mounting surface, with the sealant to the inside of the bolt holes. Press the new gasket into place on the pan, making sure all bolt holes line up.

12 Lift the pan up to the bottom of the transmission and install the mounting bolts. Tighten the bolts in a diagonal fashion, working around the pan. Using a torque wrench, tighten the bolts to specification.

13 Lower the vehicle.

14 Open the hood and remove the transmission fluid dipstick from its guide tube.

15 Add a little fluid at a time, continually checking the level with the dipstick, allowing time for the fluid to drain into the pan. Add fluid until the level just registers on the dipstick. In most cases, a good starting point will be 4 to 5 pints added to the transaxle through the filler tube (use a funnel to prevent spills). Fluid can also be added after removing the speedometer driven gear. Reinstall the gear before starting the engine.

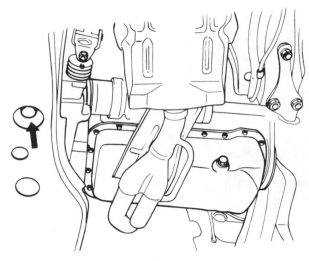

Fig. 1.16 Manual transaxle drain plug location (arrow) (Sec 24)

16 With the selector lever in Park, apply the parking brake and start the engine without depressing the accelerator pedal (if possible). *Do not race the engine at high speed*; run at slow idle only.

17 Depress the brake pedal and shift the transaxle through each gear. Place the selector back into Park and check the level on the dipstick (with the engine still idling). Look under the car for leaks around the transmission oil pan mating surface.

18 Add more fluid through the dipstick tube until the level on the dipstick is between the F and L mark. Do not allow the fluid level to go above this point, as the transaxle would be overfull, necessitating the draining of the excess fluid.

19 Push the dipstick firmly back into its tube and drive the vehicle to reach normal operating temperature (15 miles of highway driving or its equivalent in the city). Park the car on a level surface and check the fluid level on the dipstick with the engine idling and the transaxle in Park. The level should now be between the F and L mark; if not, add more fluid as necessary to bring the level to the proper point. Again, do not overfill.

24 Manual transaxle fluid change

1   Open the hood and remove the bolt retaining the speedometer driven gear. Grasp the speedometer cable and pull the gear from the transaxle (Section 2).

2   Raise the vehicle and support it securely.

3   Obtain a suitable container of at least 4 US qts to catch the fluid.

4   Remove the drain plug located in the bottom of the transaxle case (Fig. 1.16).

5   Allow the fluid several minutes to drain completely from the transaxle.

6   Replace the drain plug and lower the vehicle.

7   Add the required amount of the specified fluid through the speedometer driven gear hole, using a funnel. Check the fluid level with the gauge built into the speedometer gear (Section 2).

8   Install the speedometer gear and tighten the bolt securely.

25 Brakes check

Note: *Front-wheel drive vehicles have a tendency to wear brake components more quickly than rear drive models. Also, it is more difficult to remove the front disc should the pads wear excessively. Due to this, if at all in doubt as to the quality of the front pads or rear linings, replace them with new ones.*

1   The brakes should be inspected every time the wheels are removed or whenever a fault is suspected. Indications of a potential braking system fault are: the car pulls to one side when brake pedal is depressed; noises coming from the brakes when they are applied; excessive brake pedal travel; pulsating pedal; and leakage of fluid, usually seen on the inside of the tire or wheel.

Disc brakes

2 Disc brakes can be visually checked without the need to remove any parts except the wheels.

3 Raise the vehicle and place securely on jack stands. Remove the front wheels (see *Jacking and Towing* at the front of this manual if necessary).

4 Now visible is the disc brake caliper which contains the pads. There is an outer brake pad and an inner pad. Both should be inspected.

5 Inspect the pad thickness by looking at each end of the caliper and through the cut-out inspection hole in the caliper body. If the lining material is $\frac{1}{8}$ in or less in thickness, the pads should be replaced. Keep in mind that the lining material is riveted or bonded to a metal backing shoe and the metal portion is not included in this measuring.

6 Since it will be difficult, if not impossible, to measure the exact thickness of the remaining lining material, if you are in doubt as to the pad quality, remove the pads for further inspection or replacement. See Chapter 9 for disc brake pad replacement.

7 Before installing the wheels, check for any leakage around the brake hose connections leading to the caliper or damage (cracking, splitting, etc) to the brake hose. Replace the hose or fittings as necessary, referring to Chapter 9.

8 Also check the condition of the disc for scoring, gouging or burnt spots. If these conditions exist, the hub/rotor assembly should be removed for servicing (Chapter 8).

Drum brakes (rear)

9 Raise the vehicle and support firmly on jack stands. Block the front tires to prevent the car from rolling; however, do not apply the parking brake as this will lock the drums into place.

10 Remove the wheels, referring to *Jacking and Towing* at the front of this manual if necessary.

11 Mark the hub so it can be reinstalled in the same place. Use a scribe, chalk, etc. on drum and center hub and backing plate.

12 Pull the brake drum off the axle and brake assembly. If this proves difficult, make sure the parking brake is released, then squirt some penetrating oil around the center hub area. Allow the oil to soak in and try again to pull the drum off.

13 With the drum removed, carefully brush away any accumulations of dirt and dust. Do not blow this out with compressed air or in any similar fashion. **Note:** *Do not inhale this dust as it contains asbestos and is harmful to your health.*

14 Observe the thickness of the lining material on both the front and rear brake shoes. If the material has worn away to within $\frac{1}{8}$ in of the recessed rivets or metal backing, the shoes should be replaced. If the linings look worn, but you are unable to determine their exact thickness, compare them with a new set at the auto parts store. The shoes should also be replaced if they are cracked, glazed (shiny surface), or wet with brake fluid.

15 Check that all the brake assembly springs are connected and in good condition.

16 Check the brake components for any signs of fluid leakage. With your finger, carefully pry back the rubber cups on the wheel cylinder located at the top of the brake shoes. Any leakage is an indication that the wheel cylinders should be overhauled immediately (Chapter 9). Also check fluid hoses and connections for signs of leakage.

17 Wipe the inside of the drum with a clean rag, and denatured alcohol. Again, be careful not to breathe the dangerous asbestos dust.

18 Check the inside of the drum for cracks, scores, deep scratches or 'hard spots' which will appear as small discolorations. If these imperfections cannot be removed with fine emery cloth, the drum must be taken to a machine shop equipped to turn the drums.

19 If after the inspection process all parts are in good working condition, reinstall the brake drum. Install the wheel and lower the car to the ground.

Parking brake

20 The easiest way to check the operation of the parking brake is to park the car on a steep hill, with the parking brake set and the transmission in 'Neutral'. If the parking brake cannot prevent the car from rolling, it is in need of adjustment (see Chapter 9).

26 Spark plug wires check

1 The spark plug wires should be checked at the recommended intervals or whenever new spark plugs are installed.

2 The wires should be inspected one at a time to prevent mixing up the order which is essential for proper engine operation.

3 Disconnect the plug wire from the spark plug. A removal tool can be used for this, or you can grab the rubber boot, twist slightly and then pull the wire free. Do not pull on the wire itself, only on the rubber boot.

4 Inspect inside the boot for corrosion which will look like a white, crusty powder. Later models use a conductive white grease which should not be mistaken for corrosion.

5 Now push the wire and boot back onto the end of the spark plug. It should be a tight fit on the plug end. If not, remove the wire and use a pair of pliers to carefully crimp the metal connector inside the wire boot until the fit is secure.

6 Now using a clean rag, clean the wire its entire length. Remove all built-up dirt and grease. As this is done, inspect for burns, cracks or any other form of damage. Bend the wires in several places to ensure the conductive inside wire has not hardened.

7 Disconnect the wire at the distributor (again, pulling and twisting only on the rubber boot). Check for corrosion and a tight fit in the same manner as the spark plug end.

8 Reinstall the wire boot (or retaining ring) onto the top of the distributor.

9 Check the remaining spark plug wires in the same way, making sure they are securely fastened at the distributor and spark plug.

10 A visual check of the spark plug wires can also be made. In a darkened garage (make sure there is ventilation), start the engine and observe each plug wire. Be careful not to come into contact with any moving engine parts. If there is a break or fault in the wire, you will be able to see arcing or a small spark at the damaged area.

11 If it is decided the spark plug wires are in need of replacement, purchase a new set for your specific engine model. Wire sets can be purchased which are pre-cut to the proper size and with the rubber boots already installed. Remove and replace each wire individually to prevent mix-ups in the firing sequence.

27 Cooling system servicing (draining, flushing and refilling)

1 Periodically, the cooling system should be drained, flushed and refilled. This is to replenish the antifreeze mixture and prevent rust and corrosion which can impair the performance of the cooling system and ultimately cause engine damage.

2 At the same time the cooling system is serviced, all hoses and the fill cap should be inspected and replaced if faulty (see Section 3).

3 As antifreeze is a poisonous solution, take care not to spill any of the cooling mixture on the vehicle's paint or your own skin. If this happens, rinse immediately with plenty of clear water. Also, it is advisable to consult your local authorities about the dumping of antifreeze before draining the cooling system. In many areas reclamation centers have been set up to collect automobile oil and drained antifreeze/water mixtures rather than allowing these liquids to be added to the sewage and water facilities.

4 With the engine cold, remove the radiator pressure fill cap.

5 Move a large container under the radiator to catch the water/antifreeze mixture as it is drained.

6 Drain the radiator. The drain plug is located at the bottom of the radiator.

7 Place a cold water hose (a common garden hose is fine) in the radiator filler neck at the top of the radiator and flush the system until the water runs clean at all drain points.

8 In severe cases of contamination or clogging of the radiator, remove it (see Chapter 3) and reverse flush it. This involves simply inserting the cold pressure hose in the bottom radiator outlet to allow the clear water to run against the normal flow, draining through the top. A radiator repair shop should be consulted if further cleaning or repair is necessary.

9 Where the coolant is regularly drained and the system refilled with the correct antifreeze/inhibitor mixture there should be no need to employ chemical cleaners or descalers.

10 To refill the system, reconnect the radiator.

11 Refill the system through the radiator filler cap until the water covers the level gauge in the filler neck.

12 Run the engine until normal operating temperature is reached and with the engine idling, add coolant up to the correct level.

13 Always refill the system with a mixture of high quality antifreeze

and water in the proportion called for on the antifreeze container or in your owner's manual. Chapter 3 also contains information on anti-freeze mixtures.

14 Keep a close watch on the coolant level and the various cooling hoses during the first few miles of driving. Tighten the hose clamps and/or add more coolant mixture as necessary.

28 Evaporative emissions canister – maintenance

1 The function of the evaporative emissions system is to draw fuel vapors from the tank and carburetor, store them in a charcoal canister and then burn these fumes during normal engine operation.

2 Maintenance consists of checking the hoses for cracks and secure connections and periodic testing of the canister purge valves (Chapter 6).

3 The canister does not have a replaceable filter element but should be checked by tapping on it to hear for a rattling noise. If there is a rattle, the canister should be replaced.

29 Underhood hoses – checking and replacement

Caution: *Replacement of air conditioner hoses should be left to a dealer or a/c specialist who can de-pressurize the system and perform the work safely.*

1 The high temperatures present under the hood can cause de-terioration of the numerous rubber and plastic hoses.

2 Periodic inspection should be made for cracking, loose clamps and leaking because some of the hoses are part of the emissions system and can affect the engine's running and idling (photo).

3 Remove the air cleaner if necessary and trace the entire length of each hose. Squeeze the hose to check for cracks and look for swelling, discoloration and leaks.

4 If the vehicle has considerable mileage or one or more of the hoses is suspect, it is a good idea to replace all of the hoses at one time.

5 Measure the length and inside diameter of each hose and obtain and cut the replacement to size. As original equipment hose clamps are often good for only one or two uses, it is a good idea to replace them with screw-type clamps.

6 Replace each hose one at a time to eliminate the possibility of confusion. Hoses attached to the heater system, choke or ported vacuum switches contain radiator coolant so newspapers or rags should be kept handy to catch the spillage when they are disconnected.

7 After installation, run the engine until up to operating temperature, shut it off and check for leaks. After the engine has cooled, re-tighten all of the screw-type clamps.

30 Battery – maintenance

1 All models are equipped with maintenance-free batteries which do not require the addition of water or electrolyte.

2 The top of the battery should be kept clean and free from dirt and moisture so that the battery does not become partially discharged by leakage through dampness and dirt. Clean the top of the battery with

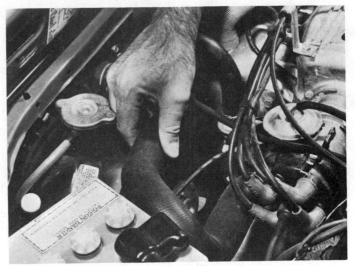

29.2 Squeezing a radiator hose to check for cracks

a baking soda and water solution, making sure that it does not enter the battery.

3 Once every three months, remove the battery and inspect the securing bolts, battery clamp bolts and leads for corrosion (white fluffy deposits which are brittle to the touch).

4 Clean the battery posts with a battery cleaning tool or wire brush.

5 Clean the battery cable terminals with a wire brush until the corrosion is removed and the metal in the terminal contact area is bright.

6 Apply grease or petroleum jelly around the base of the battery posts and install the battery cables (positive cable first) and tighten the terminal cable nuts securely.

7 If any doubt exists about the state of charge of the battery, it should be tested by a dealer or properly-equipped shop.

31 Booster battery (jump) starting

1 Certain precautions are necessary prior to using a booster battery to jump-start the vehicle.
   Before connecting the booster battery, make sure that the ignition switch is in the off position.
   The eyes should be shielded, safety goggles are a good idea.
   Make sure that the booster battery source is 12 volt and not 24 volt, which could damage the starter.
   The two vehicles must not touch each other.

2 Remove the vent caps (if equipped) from both batteries and connect the end of one jumper cable to the positive (+) terminals of each battery.

3 Connect one end of the other jumper cable to the negative (–) terminal of the good (booster) battery. The other end of this cable

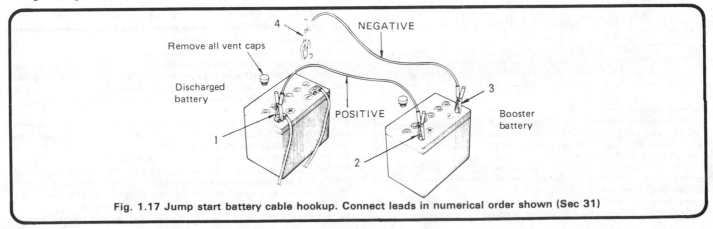

Fig. 1.17 Jump start battery cable hookup. Connect leads in numerical order shown (Sec 31)

32.5a Checking the gap on the valve side of the rocker shaft with a feeler gauge

32.5b Checking the cam side rocker gap with a feeler gauge

should be connected to a good ground on the vehicle to be started, such as a bolt on the engine block.
4   Start the engine using the jumper battery and with the engine running at idle speed, disconnect the jumper cables in the reverse sequence to connection.

32   Valve adjustment

1   The valves must be adjusted at the specified intervals with the engine at operating temperature.
2   Remove the air cleaner and any other components which interfere with the removal of the valve rocker cover. Remove the rocker cover.
3   Remove the spark plugs (Section 21) and locate Top Dead Center. To do this, place your finger over the number 1 spark plug hole and have an assistant rotate the engine in a clockwise direction with a suitable wrench on the crankshaft pulley nut until a jet of air can be felt on your finger. Continue to rotate the engine until the timing mark on the pulley is aligned with the 'T' mark on the damper.
4   Obtain a torque wrench and tighten the cylinder head bolts to specification (Chapter 2).
5   Insert a feeler gauge into the gap between the valve stem and the rocker of the number 1 intake valve on both the valve and cam side to determine if it is to specification (photos).
6   If the gap is out of specification, loosen the lock nut and turn the screw adjuster with a screwdriver to obtain the proper gap. Hold the screwdriver and tighten the lock nut (photo).
7   Repeat this procedure on the valve and cam side of the number 1 exhaust valve, number 2 intake valve, and number 3 exhaust valve.
8   Rotate the engine one complete revolution and adjust the rest of the valves, following the same procedure.
9   After all of the valves are adjusted, it is a good idea to go back and double-check the gaps to make sure that they have not been changed during the tightening of the adjustment screw.
10   Inspect the rocker cover gasket and gasket surface to make sure they are in good condition. If there is any doubt, install a new gasket after cleaning the surface. to preclude the possibility of oil leaks.

33   Compression check

1   A compression check will tell you what mechanical condition the engine is in. Specifically, it can tell you if the compression is down due to leakage caused by worn piston rings, defective valves and seats or a blown head gasket.
2   Begin by cleaning the area around the spark plugs before you remove them. This will keep dirt from falling into the cylinders while you are performing the compression test.
3   Remove the coil high-tension lead from the distributor and ground it on the engine block. Block the throttle and choke valves wide open.

32.6 Adjust the rocker gap with a screwdriver after loosening the lock nut

4   With the compression gauge in the number one cylinder's spark plug hole, crank the engine over at least four compression strokes and observe the gauge (the compression should build up quickly in a healthy engine). Low compression on the first stroke, followed by gradually increasing pressure on successive strokes, indicates worn piston rings. A low compression reading on the first stroke, which does not build up during successive strokes, indicates leaking valves or a defective head gasket. Record the highest gauge reading obtained.
5   Repeat the procedure for the remaining cylinders and compare the results to the Specifications. Compression readings approximately 10% above or below the specified amount can be considered normal.
6   Pour a couple of teaspoons of engine oil (a squirt can works great for this) into each cylinder, through the spark plug hole, and repeat the test.
7   If the compression increases after the oil is added, the piston rings are definitely worn. If the compression does not increase significantly, the leakage is occurring at the valves or head gasket.
8   If two adjacent cylinders have equally low compression, there is a strong possibility that the head gasket between them is blown. The appearance of coolant in the combustion chambers or the crankcase would verify this condition.
9   If the compression is higher than normal, the combustion chambers are probably coated with carbon deposits. If that is the case, the cylinder head should be removed and decarbonized.
10   If compression is way down, or varies greatly between cylinders, it would be a good idea to have a 'leak-down' test performed by a reputable automotive repair shop. This test will pinpoint exactly where the leakage is occurring and how severe it is.

Chapter 2 Engine

Contents

Specifications

General

Type	Inline 4-cylinder
Displacement	90.9 cu in (1.5 liter)
Bore and stroke	3.03 in X 3.15 in (77.0 mm X 89.0 mm)
Compression ratio	9.0 to 1
Compression pressure	170 psi at 300 rpm (pressures within 70 per cent of this figure are normal)

Valve timing
Intake valve:
Opens	15° BTDC
Closes	58° ABDC

Exhaust valve:
Opens	58° BBDC
Closes	15° ATDC

Engine block

Cylinder bore
Diameter	3.0315 in (77.0 mm)
Service limit	0.0035 in (0.09 mm)
Deck warpage limit	0.006 in (0.15 mm)

Pistons and rings

Piston diameter	3.0297 to 3.305 in (76.954 to 76.974 mm)

Piston-to-cylinder bore clearance
Standard	0.0010 to 0.0026 in (0.026 to 0.065 mm)
Service limit	0.0059 in (0.15 mm)

Piston ring-to-groove clearance
Top ring	0.0012 to 0.0028 in (0.03 to 0.07 mm)
Second ring	0.0012 to 0.0028 in (0.03 to 0.07 mm)
Service limit	0.006 in (0.15 mm)

Piston ring end gap
Top ring	0.008 to 0.0016 in (0.2 to 0.4 mm)
Second ring	0.008 to 0.0016 in (0.2 to 0.4 mm)
Oil ring	0.012 to 0.035 in (0.3 to 0.9 mm)
Service limit (all)	0.039 in (1.0 mm)
Piston pin diameter	0.7865 to 0.7869 in (19.976 to 19.988 mm)
Piston pin-to-piston clearance	0.0009 in (0.024 mm)

Crankshaft and flywheel

Main journal
Diameter .... 1.9661 to 1.9668 in (49.938 to 49.956 mm)
Taper limit .... 0.002 in (0.05 mm)
Out-of-round limit .... 0.0012 in (0.03 mm)
Main bearing oil clearance
Standard .... 0.0009 to 0.0017 in (0.023 to 0.042 mm)
Service limit .... 0.0031 in (0.08 mm)
Connecting rod journal
Diameter .... 1.5724 to 1.5734 in (39.940 to 39.956 mm)
Service limit .... 0.0020 in (0.05 mm)
Connecting rod side clearance .... 0.012 in (0.3 mm)
Crankshaft end play
Standard .... 0.0039 to 0.0059 in (0.10 to 0.15 mm)
Service limit .... 0.0118 in (0.030 mm)
Flywheel clutch face runout limit .... 0.008 in (0.20 mm)

Camshaft

Bearing journal diameter
Front .... 1.6515 to 1.6522 in (41.949 to 41.965 mm)
Center .... 1.6504 to 1.651 in (41.919 to 41.935 mm)
Rear .... 1.6515 to 1.6522 in (41.949 to 41.965 mm)
Service limit .... 0.0020 in (0.05 mm)
Bearing oil clearance .... 0.0059 in (0.15 mm)
Lobe height
Intake
Standard .... 1.7368 in (44.114 mm)
Service limit .... 1.7289 in (43.914 mm)
Exhaust
Standard .... 1.7368 in (44.114 mm)
Service limit .... 1.7289 in (43.914 mm)
Runout limit .... 0.0012 in (0.03 mm)
End play .... 0.001 to 0.007 in (0.02 to 0.18 mm)
Service limit .... 0.008 in (0.20 mm)

Cylinder head and valve train

Head warpage limit .... 0.006 in (0.15 mm)
Resurfacing limit .... 0.008 in (0.20 mm)
Valve seat width
Intake .... 0.055 in (1.4 mm)
Exhaust .... 0.055 in (1.4 mm)
Service limit .... 0.0079 in (0.20 mm)
Valve stem diameter
Intake
Standard .... 0.3161 to 0.3167 in (8.030 to 8.045 mm)
Service limit .... 0.3142 in (7.980 mm)
Exhaust
Standard .... 0.3159 to 0.3167 in (8.025 to 8.045 mm)
Service limit .... 0.3140 in (7.975 mm)
Valve guide inner diameter .... 0.3174 to 0.3182 in (8.063 to 8.083 mm)
Valve stem-to-guide clearance
Standard .... 0.0007 to 0.0021 in (0.018 to 0.053 mm)
Service limit .... 0.0079 in (0.020 mm)
Valve spring free length
Standard .... 1.705 in (43.3 mm)
Service limit .... 1.654 in (42.0 mm)
Valve spring pressure .... 164 in-lb (2.925 Kg/mm)
Valve spring squareness limit .... 0.059 in (1.51 mm)
Valve clearance (warm engine)
Valve side
Intake .... 0.010 in (0.25 mm)
Exhaust .... 0.012 in (0.25 mm)
Cam side
Intake .... 0.007 in (0.18 mm)
Exhaust .... 0.009 in (0.22 mm)
Rocker arm shaft diameter .... 0.7464 to 0.7473 in (18.959 to 18.980 mm)
Rocker arm bore diameter .... 0.7480 to 0.7493 in (19.0 to 19.033 mm)

Oil pump

Outer rotor-to-housing clearance
Standard .... 0.0078 to 0.0116 in (0.20 to 0.294 mm)
Service limit .... 0.0137 in (0.35 mm)
Clearance between rotor lobes
Standard .... 0.0012 to 0.0047 in (0.03 to 0.12 mm)
Service limit .... 0.0098 in (0.25 mm)

2

Rotor end clearance
    Standard .... 0.0016 to 0.0039 in (0.04 to 0.010 mm)
    Service limit .... 0.0059 in (0.15 mm)
Pump shaft-to-body clearance
    Standard .... 0.0008 to 0.0022in (0.02 to 0.056 mm)
    Service limit .... 0.0039 in (0.10 mm)
Plunger spring free length .... 1.791 in (45.5 mm)
Output pressure (at 3000 engine rpm) .. 50 to 60 psi

Torque specifications

	Ft-lb	Nm
Cylinder head bolts	56 to 59	78 to 82
Intake manifold bolts	14 to 19	19 to 26
Exhaust manifold bolts	14 to 17	19 to 23
Connecting rod cap bolts	22 to 25	30 to 35
Camshaft sprocket bolt	51 to 58	70 to 80
Clutch pressure plate	13 to 20	17 to 27
Oil pan bolt	5 to 9	7 to 12
Flywheel bolts		
Automatic	51 to 61	70 to 85
Manual	60 to 65	83 to 90
Flywheel cover endplate bolts	51 to 72	70 to 100
Spark plugs	11 to 17	15 to 23
Oil pressure switch	9 to 13	12 to 18
Timing chain cover bolts	14 to 22	19 to 31
Thermostat cover nuts	14 to 22	19 to 31
Water pump bolts	14 to 22	19 to 31
Oil pump bolts	14 to 22	19 to 31

1 General information

The removable aluminium cylinder head features an overhead mounted camshaft which is driven by the crankshaft through a timing chain. The valves are operated by the camshaft through the rocker arms.

The oil pump is located in the oil pan and is also driven by the crankshaft through a separate chain. The removable throwaway type oil filter screws into the cylinder block.

The crankshaft is supported in the cylinder block by five main bearings. The bearing shells for the crankshaft and connecting rods are removable.

The distributor is mounted horizontally and is driven directly by a tang inserted into the end of the camshaft, eliminating the need for gears or shafts.

The intake and exhaust manifolds, water pump, timing cover and transaxle housing can all be unbolted from the cylinder block.

2 Repair operations possible with the engine in the vehicle

1 Many major repair operations can be carried out without removing the engine from the vehicle.
2 It is a very good idea to clean the engine compartment and the exterior of the engine with some type of pressure washer before any work is begun. A clean engine will make the job easier and will prevent the possibility of getting dirt into the inside of the engine.
3 Remove the hood and cover the fenders to provide as much working room as possible as well as to prevent damage to the painted surfaces.
4 If oil or coolant leaks develop, indicating the need for gasket or seal replacement, the repairs can generally be made with the engine in the vehicle. The oil pan gasket, the cylinder head gasket, intake and exhaust gaskets and the front and rear crankshaft oil seals are accessible with the engine in place. In the case of the rear crankshaft oil seal, the transaxle, clutch components and the flywheel must be removed first.
5 Exterior engine components, such as the starter motor, alternator, distributor, fuel pump and carburetor, as well as the intake and exhaust manifolds, are easily removed for repair with the engine in place.
6 Since the cylinder head can be removed without pulling the engine, valve servicing can also be accomplished with the engine in the vehicle.
7 Repairs or inspection of the camshaft, timing chain assembly and the oil pump are all possible with the engine in place.
8 In extreme cases caused by lack of necessary equipment, repair or replacement of piston rings, pistons, connecting rods and rod bearings

and reconditioning of the cylinder bores is possible with the engine in the vehicle. However, this is not recommended because of the cleaning and preparation work that must be done to the components involved.

3 Engine overhaul – general note

1 It is not always easy to determine when, or if, an engine should be completely overhauled, as a number of factors must be considered.
2 High mileage is not necessarily an indication that an overhaul is needed while low mileage, on the other hand, does not preclude the need for an overhaul. Frequency of servicing is probably the single most important consideration. An engine that has regular (and frequent) oil and filter changes, as well as other required maintenance, will most likely give many thousands of miles of reliable service. Conversely, a neglected engine may require an overhaul very early in its life.
3 Excessive oil consumption is an indication that piston rings and/or valve guides are in need of attention (make sure that oil leaks are not responsible before deciding that the rings and guides are bad). Do a cylinder compression test (see Chapter 1) or have a leak-down test performed by an experienced tune-up mechanic to determine for certain the extent of the work required.
4 If the engine is making obvious 'knocking' or rumbling noises, the connecting rod and/or main bearings are probably at fault. Check the oil pressure with a gauge (installed in place of the oil pressure sending unit) and compare it to the Specifications. If it is extremely low, the bearings and/or oil pump are probably worn out.
5 Loss of power, rough running, excessive valve train noise and high fuel consumption rates may also point to the need for an overhaul (especially if they are all present at the same time). If a complete tune-up does not remedy the situation, major mechanical work is the only solution.
6 An engine overhaul generally involves restoring the internal parts to the specifications of a new engine. During an overhaul, the piston rings are replaced and the cylinder walls are reconditioned (rebored and/or honed). If a rebore is done, then new pistons are also required. The main and connecting rod bearings are replaced with new ones and, if necessary, the crankshaft may be reground to restore the journals. Generally, the valves are serviced as well, since they are usually in less-than-perfect condition at this point. While the engine is being overhauled, other components such as the carburetor, the distributor, the starter and the alternator can be rebuilt also. The end result should be a like-new engine that will give as many trouble-free miles as the original.
7 Before beginning the engine overhaul, read through the entire procedure to familiarize yourself with the scope and requirements of

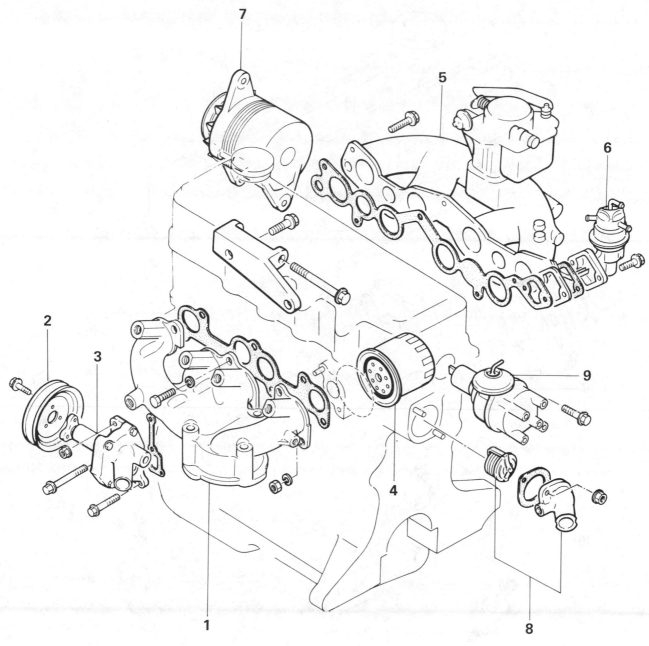

Fig. 2.1 Engine external components (Secs 2, 4, 7, 11 and 29)

1 Exhaust manifold	4 Oil filter	6 Fuel pump	8 Thermostat and cover
2 Fan pulley	5 Intake manifold	7 Alternator	9 Distributor
3 Water pump			

the job. Overhauling an engine is not that difficult, but it is time-consuming. Plan on the vehicle being tied up for a minimum of two weeks, especially if parts must be taken to an automotive machine shop for repair or reconditioning. Check on availability of parts and make sure that any necessary special tools and equipment are obtained in advance. Most work can be done with typical shop hand tools, although a number of precision measuring tools are required for inspecting parts to determine if they must be replaced. Often a reputable automotive machine shop will handle the inspection of parts and offer advice concerning reconditioning and replacement. As a general rule, time is the primary cost of an overhaul, so it doesn't pay to install worn or sub-standard parts.

8   As a final note, to ensure maximum life and minimum trouble from a rebuilt engine, everything must be assembled with care in a spotlessly clean environment.

4   Engine – removal

1   The procedure outlined here is for the removal of the engine and transaxle as a unit. A suitable means of lifting the engine is a necessity. Ideally, a small crane mounted on wheels should be rented or borrowed. These are readily available, and easy to use. An alternative would be to suspend a chain fall or cable hoist from the garage ceiling beams, or a framework fabricated from large timbers. Regardless of which type of hoist support is used, it must be strong enough to support the full weight of the engine and transaxle. Do not take chances or cut corners here, as serious injury and damage to the engine and vehicle could result.

2   The following sequence of operations does not necessarily need to be performed in the order given. It is a checklist of everything that

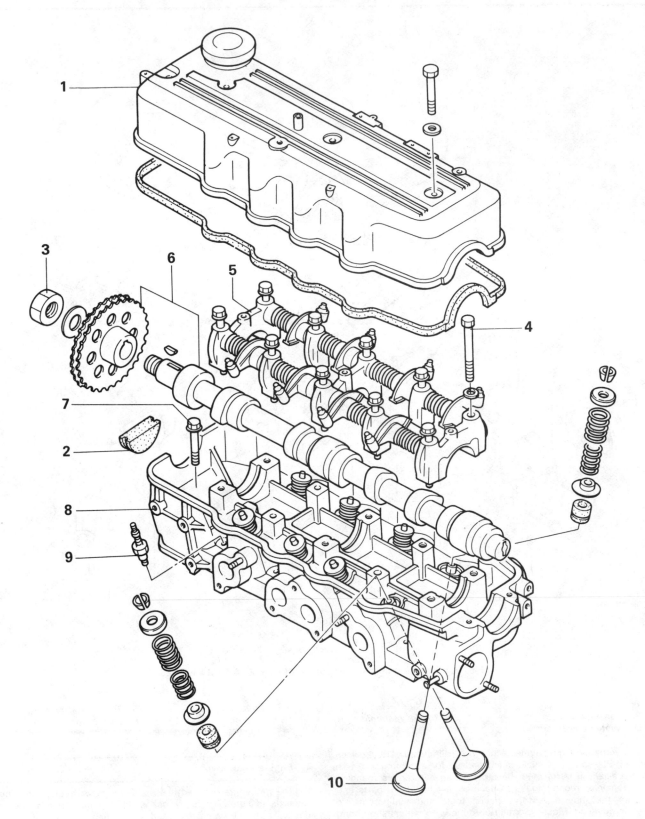

Fig. 2.2 Cylinder head components (Secs 1, 11, 21, 22, 27 and 28)

1 Valve cover	4 Cylinder head bolt	6 Camshaft and sprocket	8 Cylinder head
2 Semi-circular seal	5 Cam bearing cap	7 Cylinder head-to-timing	9 Spark plug
3 Camshaft sprocket locknut		chain cover bolt	10 Valve

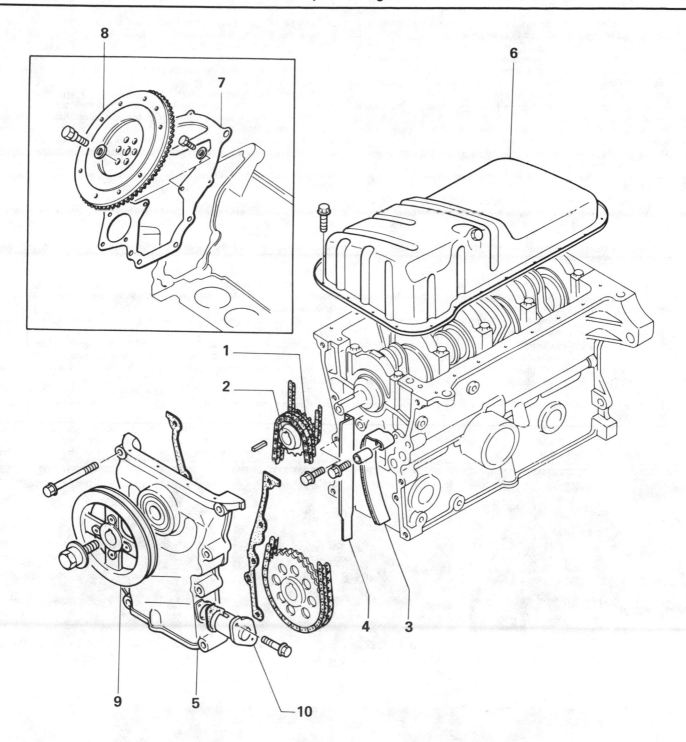

Fig. 2.3 Timing chain, oil pan and flywheel components (Secs 1, 2, 3, 6, 8, 9, 12, 26 and 28)

1	Oil pump chain and sprocket	3	Adjuster blade	6	Oil pan	9	Crankshaft pulley
2	Timing chain and sprocket	4	Chain dampener	7	End plate	10	Timing chain adjuster
		5	Timing chain cover	8	Flywheel		

must be disconnected or removed before the engine and transaxle can be lifted from the vehicle. If your vehicle is equipped with an automatic transaxle, the engine removal procedure will be slightly different. It is very important that all linkages, electrical wiring, hoses and cables are removed or disconnected before attempting to lift the engine clear of the vehicle, so double-check everything thoroughly.
3   Remove the hood (Chapter 12).
4   Disconnect the negative battery cable from the battery.

5   Raise the vehicle, support it securely and remove the front wheels.
6   Drain the engine coolant and transaxle fluid into suitable containers.
7   Remove the engine splash and side covers.
8   Remove the air cleaner.
9   Remove the manifold heat transfer and air inlet tube.
10   Disconnect the hose from the brake vacuum reservoir.
11   Disconnect the two engine harness connectors located at the rear

of the battery. Remove the positive battery cable and disconnect the wire connected to it from the fusible link (photo).

12 On manual transaxle equipped vehicles, remove the clutch cable bracket from the transaxle housing. Disconnect the cable from the lever and move the cable out of the way.

13 Disconnect the two heater hoses from the transfer tube and intake manifold located below the fuel pump.

14 Disconnect the speedometer cable from the transaxle and secure it out of the way.

15 Disconnect and plug the fuel hose attached to the left side of the fuel pump.

16 Disconnect the three vacuum hoses leading from the carburetor to the charcoal canister at the canister.

17 Disconnect the hose leading from the carburetor to the purge control valve (Chapter 6).

18 Disconnect the coil wire and the distributor lead at the coil.

19 Disconnect the No. 1 purge valve electrical connector.

20 Disconnect and plug the hose leading from the fuel tank to the charcoal canister.

21 Remove the charcoal canister.

22 Disconnect the backup light connector and release the harness strap located below the battery.

23 Disconnect the throttle cable at the bracket located on the valve cover and at the carburetor. Remove the bracket from the valve cover.

24 Remove the upper radiator hose.

25 Disconnect the vacuum hose leading from the No. 1 water thermal valve (Chapter 6).

26 Disconnect the electrical lead from the two temperature sensors located at the left front corner of the cylinder head.

27 Slide the electrical harness grommet from the retainer.

28 Disconnect the rubber hose from the air injection system check valve (photo).

29 Disconnect the hose leading from the air injection check valve located forward of the exhaust manifold.

30 Disconnect the hoses on the left side of the air pump.

31 Disconnect the air injection hose T fitting from the bracket at the front corner of the engine compartment.

32 Disconnect the large front hose from the air control valve and remove the T fitting hose assembly (photo).

33 Remove the hoses from the rear of the air control valve (Chapter 6).

34 Disconnect the three upper hoses from the altitude compensator (Chapter 6).

35 Remove the windshield washer fluid reservoir and unplug the connector. Lay the reservoir on its side and disconnect the hose.

36 Remove the reservoir mounting bracket and disconnect the vacuum hoses from the No. 1 and No. 2 solenoid valves (photo).

37 Remove the front driveaxles (Chapters 8 and 11).

38 Remove the lower radiator hose. On automatic transaxle equipped models, disconnect the fluid lines at the radiator.

39 Remove the three exhaust pipe nuts and two air intake tube bolts.

40 Remove the left-hand mounting bracket-to-engine block retaining bolt.

41 Remove the two exhaust pipe-to-rear catalytic converter nuts.

42 Remove the through-bolt for the exhaust pipe clamp and slide the clamp to the rear.

43 Pull the front of the pipe down to clear and lift it off the rear catalytic converter studs.

44 Disconnect the shifter rods and extension rods (manual transaxle) and fasten them out of the way with pieces of stiff wire.

45 Disconnect the left-hand rear catalytic converter isolation mount and the tabs of the stud on the engine mount.

46 Support the engine with a hoist and lifting chains attached to the engine hooks.

47 Remove the crossmember bolts and lower the crossmember.

48 Remove the bolt from the right-hand engine mount (photo).

49 Remove the left side mount through-bolt and then unbolt the mount from the transaxle.

50 Remove the front transaxle-to-crossmember mount.

51 Remove the battery and battery box (five bolts) and brackets (two bolts).

52 Remove the electric fan motor and shroud assembly (Chapter 3).

53 Lift the engine carefully with the lifting device.

54 When the right-hand engine mount is clear of the body mount,

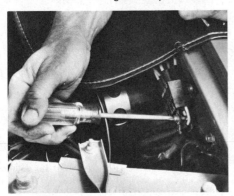
4.11 Disconnecting the battery lead from the fusible link

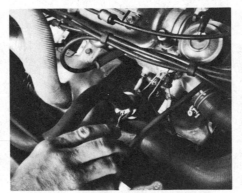
4.28 Disconnecting the air injection check valve hose

4.32 Removing the air injection T hose

4.36 Removing the solenoid vacuum hoses

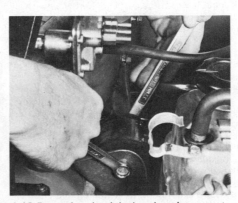
4.48 Removing the right-hand engine mount through-bolt

rotate the transaxle end cover forward for clearance.
55 Hold the engine at this angle and lift it clear of the engine compartment.
56 Lower the engine and transaxle unit to the floor or a suitable workbench.

5 Separating the engine and transaxle

1 Support the engine and transaxle in an upright position.
2 Remove the five large and three small bolts attaching the engine to the transaxle.
3 With the help of an assistant, lift the transaxle away from the engine block.

6 Clutch and flywheel – removal and installation

1 Remove the clutch disc and pressure plate assembly by referring to Chapter 8.
2 Remove the flywheel attaching bolts and separate the flywheel from the crankshaft. Remove the dust cover from the rear of the engine.
3 When installing the flywheel, be sure to install the dust cover first.
4 Hold the flywheel in position and install the attaching bolts.

7 Engine disassembly and reassembly

1 To completely disassemble the engine, remove the following items in the order given:

Engine external components	(Section 8)
Oil pan	(Section 9)
Cylinder head/valve train components	(Section 10)
Timing chain/sprockets	(Section 12)
Oil pump	(Section 13)
Piston/connecting rod assemblies	(Section 14)
Crankshaft	(Section 15)

2 Engine reassembly is basically the reverse of disassembly. Install the following components in the order given:

Crankshaft	(Section 23)
Piston/connecting rod assemblies	(Section 25)
Oil pump/timing chain and sprockets	(Section 26)
Cylinder head/valve train components	(Section 28)
Oil pan	(Section 9)
Engine external components	(Section 24)

8 External engine components – removal

Note: *When removing the external components from the engine, pay close attention to details which might be helpful or important during installation. Look for the correct positioning of gaskets, seals, spacers, pins, bolts, washers and other small items. Refer to the various accompanying illustrations and photographs as a guide during disassembly.*

1 It is much easier to dismantle and repair an engine which is mounted on an engine stand. These stands are portable and can often be rented for a reasonable fee from an equipment rental yard.
2 If a stand is not available, it is possible to dismantle the engine with it blocked up on a sturdy workbench or on the floor. When working without a stand, be very careful not to knock the engine over.
3 Remove the transaxle (Section 5), the clutch pressure plate, the clutch disc and the flywheel.
4 Remove the flywheel dust cover.
5 Disconnect the backup light switch.
6 Remove the starter.
7 Place a suitable container under the engine, remove the drain bolt in the side of the engine block and drain out any remaining coolant.
8 Remove the air injection check valve assembly from the rear of the exhaust manifold.
9 Remove the spark plugs.
10 Remove the two heat shield bolts, the check valve bolt and the heat shield.
11 Remove the catalytic converter support bracket and unbolt the converter from the exhaust manifold.
12 Unbolt and remove the exhaust manifold (five bolts and two nuts).

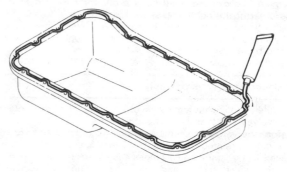

Fig. 2.4 Oil pan sealant installation (Secs 9 and 26)

13 Disconnect the water transfer tube from the water pump and the thermostat housing.
14 Loosen the alternator and air pump and remove the drivebelts.
15 Remove the alternator and air pump and their mounting brackets.
16 Remove the right-hand engine support located on the front of the engine block.
17 Disconnect the oil pressure switch connector and the throttle position sensor (adjacent to the oil filter) and remove the wiring harness.
18 Remove the PCV valve.
19 Disconnect the fuel pump hose and plug the hose and pump openings.
20 Disconnect the distributor vacuum hose from the diaphragm.
21 Remove the three nuts and two bolts retaining the intake manifold and remove the manifold. It may be necessary to grasp the manifold firmly and rock it up and down to break it loose from the gasket.
22 Remove the oil pressure sender from the cylinder block, using a suitable wrech.
23 Unbolt and remove the fuel pump.
24 Remove the spark plug wire brackets from the valve cover.
25 Remove the distributor.
26 Remove the water temperature sender and thermostat housing.

9 Oil pan – removal and installation

1 Remove the bolts securing the oil pan to the engine block.
2 Tap around the perimeter of the oil pan very carefully with a soft-faced hammer (to break the gasket seal), then separate the pan from the block.
3 Clean the oil pan with solvent and dry it thoroughly. Inspect it for cracks or distortion, particularly on the sealing surfaces.
4 Before installing the oil pan, apply a bead of silicone-type sealant to the sealing surfaces. The pan must be installed within 30 minutes after applying the compound.
5 Place the pan in position on the engine block and install the retaining bolts. Start with the bolts closest to the center of the pan and tighten them to the specified torque using a criss-cross pattern. Overtightening the bolts can cause leakage.

10 Cylinder head – removal

1 Remove the rocker arm cover.
2 Remove the rubber seal from the front of the head.
3 Remove the camshaft sprocket nut. It will be necessary to lock the crankshaft so that it will not turn during this operation. To do this, wedge a block of hardwood between the side of the engine block and the front crankshaft throw.
4 Remove the rocker arm assembly bolts by loosening them a quarter turn at a time in criss-cross pattern. Hold the rocker arm assembly together and carefully lift it from the cylinder head.
5 Disengage the camshaft from the timing chain sprocket and lift the camshaft from the engine.
6 If the engine block is to be disassembled, lower the timing chain into the block. If only the head is to be removed, tie a wire through the sprocket and chain (so that the timing will not be changed) and support the sprocket.
7 Remove the bolt in the timing chain cover.

2

8   Remove the cylinder head bolts a quarter turn at a time in the reverse order of the tightening sequence.
9   Remove the cylinder head. It may be necessary to tap the head carefully upward (with a soft-faced hammer) while using a rocking motion to break the gasket loose.

11 Cylinder head – disassembly

1   Cylinder head disassembly involves removal of the intake and exhaust valves and their related components.
2   Before the valves are removed, arrange to label and store them, along with their related components, so they can be kept separate and reinstalled in the same valve guides they were removed from. Also, inspect the valves, springs and guides as described in Section 21.
3   Compress the valve spring on the first valve with a spring compressor tool and then remove the keepers and upper spring seat. Carefully release the compressor and remove the springs, the spring seat and the valve. If the valve binds in the guide and can't be pulled through, push it back into the head and deburr the area around the keeper groove with a fine file.
4   Repeat the procedure for the remaining valves. Remember to keep all the parts for each valve in order so that they can be reinstalled in the same position.
5   Once the valves have been removed and safely stored, pull off the valve stem seals and discard them.
6   Refer to Section 21 for cylinder head cleaning and inspection procedures.

12 Timing chain/sprockets – removal and inspection

1   Detach the timing chain tensioner from the side of the timing chain cover by removing the bolts and tapping on the tensioner lightly with a soft-faced hammer to release it.
2   Remove the crankshaft bolt and pulley.
3   Remove the timing chain cover bolts and carefully tap on the cover with a soft-faced hammer to separate it from the engine block.
4   Remove the timing chain and drive gear from the crankshaft.
5   Remove the oil pump (Section 13).
6   Inspect the timing chain for stretch, wear, looseness or damaged links (replacing it with a new one if its condition is suspect).
7   Inspect the chain adjuster blade and damper for cracks, wear or distortion (replace it with a new one if necessary).
8   Check the sprocket for damaged or worn teeth. The sprocket should be replaced unless it is in very good condition, as wear here could affect cam timing.
9   Inspect the tensioner mechanism for wear or damage and check the stopper and sleeve to see how many notches are being contacted. If the sleeve is being contacted within 13 to 18 notches from the end, the chain is stretched and should be replaced with a new one.

13 Oil pump – removal and inspection

1   Remove the oil pump sprocket from the crankshaft.
2   Unbolt the oil pump and lift it from the engine.
3   Inspect the crankshaft sprocket for wear or damage to the teeth and check the chain for wear, damage, stretching and broken links. Replace either component if there is any doubt as to condition, as the engine can be severely damaged by an inadequate oil supply if the pump is not operating properly.
4   Inspect the pump sprocket teeth for wear or damage and replace the pump if any is found.
5   Remove the cotter pin and the plunger assembly and check the plunger for wear or damage and the spring for breaks or fatiguing.
6   Use a suitable press to remove the sprocket and then disassemble the oil pump.
7   Use a feeler gauge to determine the clearance between the inner and outer rotors, the body and the rotor and the rotor and cover. Check the measurements against those in the Specifications section.
8   If any components are damaged or worn beyond the service limits replace the oil pump (as a complete unit) with a new one.
9   Clean the pump components in a suitable solvent and reassemble them, making sure that the marks on the inner and outer rotors are facing the outer (cover) side.

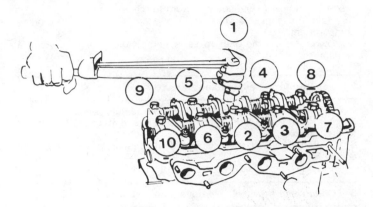

Fig. 2.5 Cylinder head bolt tightening sequence (Secs 10 and 28)

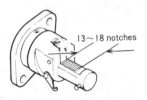

Fig. 2.6 Checking the timing chain adjuster sleeve for signs of chain stretch (Sec 12)

10 If a press is not available to check the pump's internal components for wear, it would be a good idea to replace the pump with a new unit as a matter of course, particularly if the vehicle has seen high mileage.

14 Piston/connecting rod assembly – removal

1   Prior to removing the piston/connecting rod assemblies, remove the cylinder head, oil pan, timing chain cover, timing chain and sprockets and oil pump, referring to the appropriate Sections.
2   Using a ridge reaming tool, completely remove the ridge at the top of each cylinder (follow the manufacturer's instructions provided with the tool). Failure to remove the ridge before attempting to remove the piston/connecting rod assemblies will result in piston breakage.
3   With the engine in the upside-down position, remove the oil pump (Section 13).
4   Turn the crankshaft so that the connecting rod bolts are accessible and remove the nuts. **Note:** *The rod caps should be marked with numbers (1 through 4, from front to back) and arrows (indicating the front of the engine). If they aren't, mark them with a punch or scribe now to avoid confusion during engine reassembly.*
5   Lift off the rod caps and push the piston/connecting rod assemblies through the bores and remove them. Temporarily install the rod caps and set the assemblies aside in the correct order.

15 Crankshaft – removal

1   Before removing the crankshaft, you must remove the transaxle, flywheel, flywheel dust cover (Section 8), oil pan (Section 9), cylinder head (Section 10), timing chain and cover (Section 12) and oil pump (Section 13).
2   Remove the piston assemblies from the block, as described in Section 14. Be sure to mark each connecting rod and bearing cap so that they will be properly mated during reassembly.
3   Loosen each of the main bearing cap bolts ¼ turn at a time, in sequence, starting at the center of the engine, until they can be removed by hand.
4   Gently tap the main bearing caps with a soft-faced hammer, then remove them from the engine block. If necessary, use the main bearing cap bolts as levers to remove the caps. Try not to drop the bearing shells, if they should come out with the caps. The main bearing caps are marked so you do not have to mark them.
5   Thread two oil pan bolts into the rear bearing cap so that

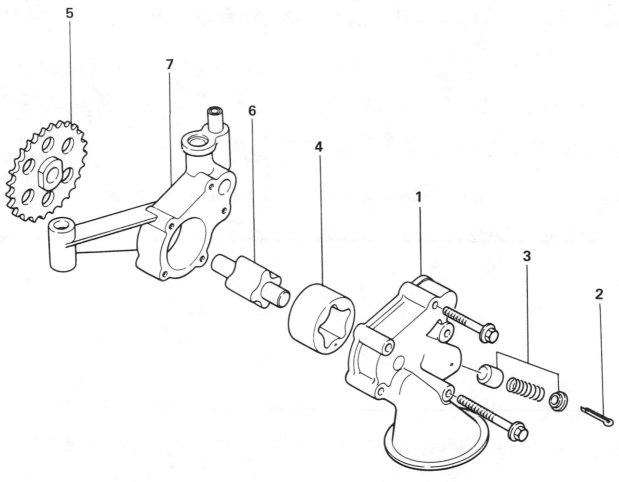

Fig. 2.7 Oil pump components (Sec 13)

| 1 | Cover | 3 | Plunger assembly | 5 | Sprocket | 7 | Pump body |
| 2 | Cotter pin | 4 | Outer rotor | 6 | Shaft and inner rotor assembly | | |

approximately $\frac{1}{2}$ inch protrudes. Use two large screwdrivers positioned under the bolt heads to lever the cap evenly out of the block. Use hardwood blocks under the screwdrivers; do not pry against the gasket surface on the block.

6   Carefully lift the crankshaft out of the engine. It is a good idea to have an assistant available as the crankshaft is rather heavy. With the bearing inserts in place in the engine block and the main bearing caps, install the caps and bolts finger tight.

16 Engine block – cleaning

1   Remove the soft plugs from the engine. To do this, knock the plugs into the block using a hammer and punch and then grasp them with pliers and pull them back through the holes.

2   Using a gasket scraper, remove all traces of gasket material from the engine block. Be very careful not to nick or gouge the gasket sealing surfaces.

3   Remove the main bearing caps and separate the bearing shells from the caps and the engine block. Tag the bearing shells according to which cylinder they were removed from (and whether they were in the cap or the block) and set them aside.

4   Remove the threaded gallery plugs from the front and back of the block.

5   If the engine is extremely dirty, it should be taken to an automotive machine shop to be steam cleaned or hot tanked. Any bearings left in the block may be damaged in the cleaning process, so plan on replacing them with new ones.

6   After the block is returned, clean all oil holes and galleries one

more time. Brushes for cleaning oil holes and galleries are available at most auto parts stores. Flush the passages with warm water until the water runs clear and then dry the block thoroughly. If you have access to compressed air, use it to speed the drying process and to blow out all the oil holes and galleries. Wipe all machined surfaces with a light rust-preventative oil.

7   If the block is not extremely dirty or sludged up, you can do an adequate job of cleaning with warm soapy water and a stiff brush. Take plenty of time and do a thorough job. Regardless of the cleaning method used, be very sure to thoroughly clean all oil holes and galleries, dry the block completely and coat all machined surfaces with light oil.

8   The threaded holes in the block must be clean to ensure proper torque readings during reassembly. Run the proper size tap into each of the holes to remove any rust, corrosion thread sealant or sludge and to restore any damaged threads. If possible, use compressed air to clear the holes of debris produced by this operation. Now is a good time to thoroughly clean the threads on the head bolts and the main bearing cap bolts as well.

9   Reinstall the main bearing caps and tighten the bolts finger tight.

10 After coating the sealing surfaces of the new soft plugs with a good quality gasket sealer, install them in the engine block. Make sure they are driven in straight and seated properly, or leakage could result. Special tools are available for this purpose, but equally good results can be obtained using a large socket (with an outside diameter slightly larger than the outside diameter of the soft plug) and a large hammer. An alternative is to have the plugs installed by a machine shop at the time of block cleaning.

11 If the engine is not going to be assembled right away, cover it with a large plastic trash bag to keep it clean.

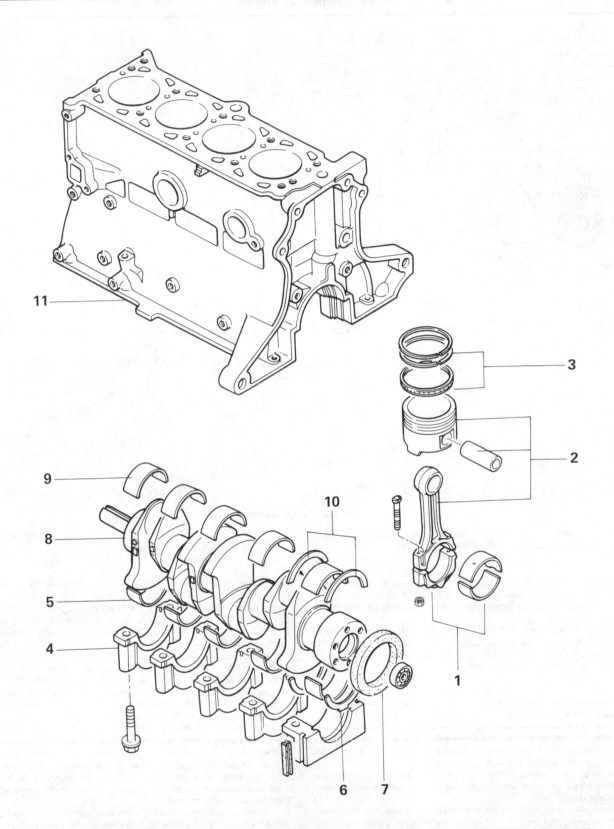

Fig. 2.8 Crankshaft, piston and engine block assembly components (Secs 14 through 20 and 23 through 25)

1 Connecting rod bearing and cap	3 Piston rings	6 Thrust bearings (lower)	9 Main bearing (upper half)
	4 Main bearing cap	7 Oil seal	10 Thrust bearings (upper)
2 Piston and connecting rod	5 Main bearing (lower half)	8 Crankshaft	11 Engine block

17 Engine block – inspection

1   Thoroughly clean the engine block as described in Section 16 and double-check to make sure that the ridge at the top of the cylinders has been completely removed.
2   Visually check the block for cracks, rust and corrosion. Look for stripped threads in the threaded holes. It is also a good idea to have the block checked for hidden cracks by an automotive machine shop that has the special equipment to do this type of work. If defects are found, have the block repaired, if possible, or replaced.
3   Check the cylinder bores for scuffing and scoring.
4   Using the appropriate precision measuring tools, measure each cylinder's diameter at the top (just under the ridge), center and bottom of the cylinder bore, parallel to the crankshaft axis. Next, measure each cylinder's diameter at the same three locations across the crankshaft axis. Compare the results to the Specifications. If the cylinder walls are badly scuffed or scored, or if they are out-of-round or tapered beyond the limits given in the Specifications, have the engine block rebored and honed at an automotive machine shop. If a rebore is done, oversized pistons and rings will be required as well (photos).
5   If the cylinders are in reasonably good condition and not worn to the outside of the limits, and if the piston-to-cylinder clearances can be maintained properly, then they do not have to be rebored; honing is all that is necessary.
6   Before honing the cylinders, install the main bearing caps (without the bearings) and tighten the bolts to the specified torque.
7   To perform the honing operation, you will need the proper size flexible hone (with fine stones), plenty of light oil or honing oil, some rags and an electric drill motor. Mount the hone in the drill motor, compress the stones and slip the hone into the first cylinder. Lubricate the cylinder thoroughly, turn on the drill and move the hone up and down in the cylinder at a pace which will produce a fine cross-hatch pattern on the cylinder walls (with the cross-hatch lines intersecting at approximately a 60° angle). Be sure to use plenty of lubricant, and do not take off any more material than is absolutely necessary to produce the desired finish. Do not withdraw the hone from the cylinder while

it is running. Instead, shut off the drill and continue moving the hone up and down in the cylinder until it comes to a complete stop, then compress the stones and withdraw the hone. Wipe the oil out of the cylinder and repeat the procedure on the remaining cylinders. Remember, do not remove too much material from the cylinder wall. If you do not have the tools or do not desire to perform the honing operation, most automotive machine shops will do it for a reasonable fee.
8   After the honing job is complete, chamfer the top edges of the cylinder bores with a small file so that the rings will not catch when the pistons are installed. Pad the tip of the file with tape to prevent scratching the cylinder walls with it.
9   Next, the entire engine block must be thoroughly washed again with warm soapy water to remove all traces of the abrasive grit produced during the honing operation. Be sure to run a brush through all oil holes and galleries and flush them with running water. After rinsing, dry the block and apply a coat of light rust preventative oil to all machined surfaces. Wrap the block in a plastic bag to keep it clean and set it aside until reassembly.

18 Crankshaft – inspection

1   Clean the crankshaft with solvent (be sure to clean the oil holes with a stiff brush and flush them with solvent) and dry it thoroughly. Check the main and connecting rod bearing journals for uneven wear, scoring, pitting and cracks. Check the remainder of the crankshaft for cracks and damage.
2   Using an appropriate size micrometer, measure the diameter of the main and connecting rod journals (photo) and compare the results to the Specifications. By measuring the diameter at a number of points around the journal's circumference, you will be able to determine whether or not the journal is worn out-of-round. Take the measurement at each end of the journal, near the crank throw, to determine whether the journal is tapered.
3   If the crankshaft journals are damaged, tapered, out-of-round or worn beyond the limits given in the Specifications, have the crankshaft reground by a reputable automotive machine shop. Be sure to use the correct undersize bearing inserts if the crankshaft is reconditioned.

19 Piston/connecting rod assembly – inspection

1   Before the inspection process can be carried out, the piston/connecting rod assemblies must be cleaned and the old piston rings removed from the pistons.
2   Using a piston ring installation tool, carefully remove the rings from the pistons. Do not nick or gouge the pistons in the process.
3   Scrape all traces of carbon from the top (or crown) of the piston. A hand-held wire brush or a piece of fine emery cloth can be used once the majority of the deposits have been scraped away. Do not, under any circumstances, use a wire brush mounted in a drill motor to remove deposits from the pistons. The piston material is soft and will be eroded away by the wire brush.
4   Use a piston ring groove cleaning tool to remove any carbon deposits from the ring grooves. If a tool is not available, a piece broken off the old ring will do the job. Be very careful to remove only the

Fig. 2.9 Cylinder bore wear check points (Sec 17)

17.4a Checking cylinder bore diameter with a telescoping gauge (gauge is measured with a micrometer to obtain diameter)

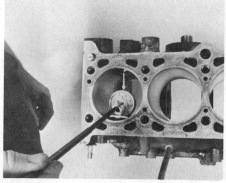

17.4b Checking the cylinder bore for taper

18.2 Measuring the crankshaft journal diameter with a micrometer carbon deposits. Do not remove any metal and do not nick or scratch the sides of the ring grooves.

5   Once the deposits have been removed, clean the piston/rod assemblies with solvent and dry them thoroughly. Make sure that the oil hole in the big end of the connecting rod and the oil return holes in the back side of the ring groove are clear.

6   If the pistons are not damaged or worn excessively, and if the engine block is not rebored, new pistons will not be necessary. Normal piston wear appears as even vertical wear on the piston thrust surfaces and slight looseness of the top ring in its groove. New piston rings, on the other hand, should always be used when an engine is rebuilt.

7   Carefully inspect each piston for cracks around the skirt, at the pin bosses and at the ring lands.

8   Look for scoring and scuffing (on the thrust faces of the skirt), holes (in the piston crown) and burned areas (at the edge of the crown). If the skirt is scored or scuffed, the engine may have been suffering from overheating and/or abnormal combustion, which caused excessively high operating temperatures. The cooling and lubrication systems should be checked thoroughly. A hole in the piston crown, an extreme to be sure, is an indication that abnormal combustion (preignition) was occurring. Burned areas at the edge of the piston crown are usually evidence of spark knock (detonation). If any of the above problems exist, the causes must be corrected or the damage will occur again.

9   Corrosion of the piston (evidenced by pitting) indicates that coolant is leaking into the combustion chamber and/or the crankcase. Again, the cause must be corrected or the problem may persist in the rebuilt engine.

10 Measure the piston ring side clearance by laying a new piston ring in the ring groove and slipping a feeler gauge in beside it (photo). Check the clearance at three or four locations around the groove. Be sure to use the correct ring for each groove; they are different. If the side clearance is greater than specified, new pistons will have to be used and the block rebored to accept them.

11 Check the piston-to-bore clearance by measuring the bore (see Section 17) and the piston diameter (photo). Make sure that the pistons and bores are correctly matched. Measure the piston across the skirt, on the thrust faces (at a 90° angle to the piston pin), about 0.100 in (2mm) up from the bottom of the skirt. Subtract the piston diameter from the bore diameter to obtain the clearance. If it is greater than specified, the block will have to be rebored and new pistons and rings installed. Check the piston pin-to-rod clearance by twisting the piston and rod in opposite directions. Any noticeable play indicates that there is excessive wear, which must be corrected. The piston/connecting rod assemblies should be taken to an automotive machine shop to have new pistons installed and the pistons and connecting rods rebored.

12 If the pistons must be removed from the connecting rods, such as when new pistons must be installed, or if the piston pins have too much play in them, they should be taken to an autmotive machine shop. While they are there, it would be convenient to have the connecting rods checked for bend and twist, as automotive machine shops have special equipment for this purpose.

13 Check the connecting rods for cracks and other damage. Temporarily remove the rod cap, lift out the old bearing inserts, wipe the rod and cap bearing surfaces clean and inspect them for nicks, gouges and scratches. After checking the rods, replace the old bearings, slip the caps in place and tighten the nuts finger-tight. *Unless new pistons or connecting rods must be installed, do not disassemble the pistons from the connecting rods.*

20 Main and connecting rod bearings – inspection

1   Even though the main and connecting rod bearings should be replaced with new ones during the engine overhaul, the old bearings should be retained for close examination, as they may reveal valuable information about the condition of the engine.

2   Bearing failure occurs mainly because of lack of lubrication, the presence of dirt or other foreign particles, overloading the engine and/or corrosion. Regardless of the cause of bearing failure, it must be corrected before the engine is reassembled to prevent it from happening again.

3   When examining the bearings, remove them from the engine block, the main bearing caps, the connecting rods and the rod caps and lay them out on a clean surface in the same general position as their location in the engine. This will enable you to match any noted bearing problems with the corrresponding crankshaft journal.

4   Dirt and other foreign particles get into the engine in a variety of ways. It may be left in the engine during assembly, or it may pass through filters or breathers. It may get into the oil, and from there into the bearings. Metal chips from machining operations and normal engine wear are often present. Abrasives are sometimes left in engine components after reconditioning, especially when parts are not thoroughly cleaned using the proper cleaning methods. Whatever the source, these foreign objects often end up embedded in the soft bearing material and are easily recognized. Large particles will not embed in the bearing and will score or gouge the bearing and shaft. The best prevention for this cause of bearing failure is to clean all parts thoroughly and keep everything spotlessly clean during engine assembly. Frequent and regular changes of engine oil, and oil filters, is also recommended.

5   Lack of lubrication (or lubrication breakdown) has a number of interrelated causes. Excessive heat (which thins the oil), overloading (which squeezes the oil from the bearing face) and oil leakage or throw-off (from excessive bearing clearances, worn oil pump or high engine speeds) all contribute to lubrication breakdown. Blocked oil passages, which usually are the result of misaligned oil holes in a bearing shell, will also oil-starve a bearing and destroy it. When lack of lubrication is the cause of bearing failure, the bearing material is wiped

19.10 Measuring piston ring side clearance with a feeler gauge

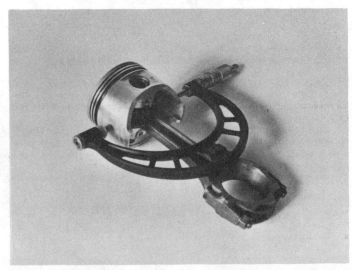

19.11 Measuring piston diameter with a micrometer

or extruded from the steel backing of the bearing. Temperatures may increase to the point where the steel backing turns blue from overheating.

6 Driving habits can have a definite effect on bearing life. Full-throttle low-speed operation (or 'lugging' the engine) puts very high loads on bearings, which tends to squeeze out the oil film. These loads cause the bearings to flex, which produces fine cracks in the bearing face (fatigue failure). Eventually the bearing material will loosen in pieces and tear away from the steel backing. Short-trip driving leads to corrosion of bearings, as insufficient engine heat is produced to drive off the condensed water and corrosive gases produced. These products collect in the engine oil, forming acid and sludge. As the oil is carried to the engine bearings the acid attacks and corrodes the bearing material.

7 Incorrect bearing installation during engine assembly will lead to bearing failure as well. Tight-fitting bearings, which leave insufficient bearing oil clearance, result in oil starvation. Dirt or foreign particles trapped behind a bearing insert result in high spots on the bearing which lead to failure.

21 Cylinder head – cleaning and inspection

1 Thorough cleaning of the cylinder head and related valve train components, followed by a detailed inspection, will enable you to decide how much valve service work must be done during the engine overhaul.

Cleaning

2 Scrape away any traces of old gasket material and sealing compound from the head gasket, the intake manifold and the exhaust manifold sealing surfaces. Work slowly and do not nick or gouge the soft aluminium of the head.

3 Carefully scrape all carbon deposits out of the combustion chamber areas. A hand-held wire brush or a piece of fine emery cloth can be used once the majority of deposits have been scraped away. Do not use a wire brush mounted in a drill motor, as the head material is soft and can be eroded away by the wire brush.

4 Remove any scale that may be built up around the coolant passages.

5 Run a stiff wire brush through the oil holes and the EGR gas ports to remove any deposits that may have formed in those areas.

6 It is a good idea to run an appropriate size tap into each of the threaded holes to remove any corrosion or thread sealant that may be present. Be very careful when cleaning aluminium threads; they can be damaged easily with a tap. If compressed air is available, use it to clear the holes of debris produced by this operation. Clean the exhaust and intake manifold stud threads in a similar manner with an appropriate size die. Clean the camshaft bearing cap bolt threads with a wire brush.

7 Next, clean the cylinder head with solvent and dry it thoroughly. Compressed air will speed the drying process and ensure that all holes and recessed areas are clean. **Note**: *Decarbonizing chemicals are available and may prove very useful when cleaning cylinder heads and valve train components. They are very caustic and should be used with caution. Be sure to follow the directions on the container.*

8 Clean the camshaft with solvent and dry it thoroughly.

9 Without dismantling the rocker arm assembly, clean it with solvent (make sure all oil holes are clear) and dry it thoroughly. Compressed air, if it is available, will speed up the drying process and make it much easier.

10 Clean all the valve springs, keepers, retainers and spring seats with solvent and dry them thoroughly. Do the parts from one valve at a time, so that no mixing of parts between valves occurs.

11 Scrape off any heavy deposits that may have formed on the valves, then use a motorized wire brush to remove deposits from the valve heads and stems. Again, make sure the valves do not get mixed up.

Inspection
Cylinder head
12 Inspect the head very carefully for cracks, evidence of coolant leakage and other damage. If cracks are found, a new head is in order.

13 Check the camshaft bearing surfaces in the head and the bearing caps. If there is evidence of excessive wear, scoring or seizure, the cylinder head will have to be replaced with a new one to restore the camshaft bearing surfaces and proper oil clearance.

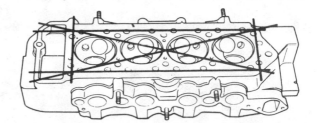

Fig. 2.10 Head warpage check (Sec 21)

14 Using a straight edge and feeler gauge, check the head gasket mating surfaces for warpage at the points shown in the accompanying illustration. If the head is warped beyond the limits given in the Specifications, it can be resurfaced at an automotive machine shop.

15 Examine the valve seats in each of the combustion chambers. If they are pitted, cracked or burned, the head will require valve service that is beyond the scope of the home mechanic.

16 Measure the inside diameters of the valve guides (at both ends and the center of the guide) with a small hole gauge and a 0 to 1 in micrometer. Record the measurements for future reference. These measurements, along with the valve stem diameter measurements, will enable you to compute the valve stem-to-guide clearance. This clearance, when compared to the Specifications, will be one factor that will determine the extent of the valve service work required. The guides are measured at the ends and at the center to determine if they are worn in a bell-mouth pattern (more wear at the ends). If they are, guide reconditioning or replacement is an absolute must.

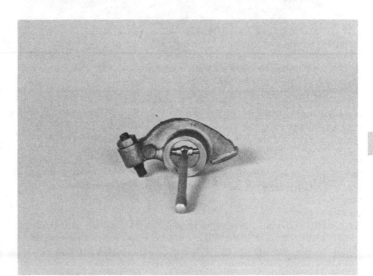

21.17 Checking the rocker arm bore diameter with a telescoping gauge (the telescoping gauge is measured with a micrometer to obtain the diameter)

Rocker arm assembly
17 Check the rocker arm faces (that contact the camshaft lobes) and the ends of the adjusting screws (that contact the valve stems) for pitting, excessive wear and roughness, measure the rocker arm bore (photo).

18 Check the adjusting screw threads for damage. Make sure they can be threaded in and out of the rocker arms.

19 Slide each rocker arm along its shaft, against the locating spring pressure, and check the rocker arm shafts for excessive wear and evidence of scoring in the areas that normally contact the rocker arms.

20 Any damaged or excessively worn parts must be replaced with new ones. Refer to the exploded view of the rocker arm assembly components, which will enable you to correctly disassemble and reassemble them.

Camshaft
21 Inspect the camshaft bearing journals for excessive wear and evidence of seizure. If the journals are damaged, the bearing surfaces in the head and bearing caps are probably damaged as well. Both the

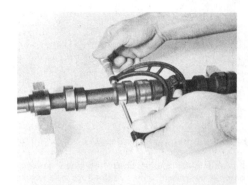

21.22 Checking the cam lobe height

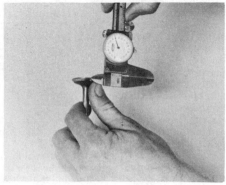

21.24 Checking the valve margin width

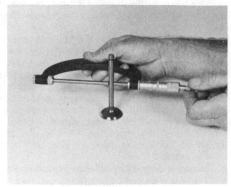

21.25 Measuring the valve stem diameter

21.26 Measuring the valve stem deflection to determine stem-to-guide clearance

21.27 Measuring the valve spring free length

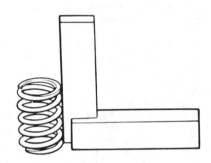

Fig. 2.11 Checking valve spring squareness (Sec 21)

camshaft and cylinder head will have to be replaced with new ones.
22 Check the cam lobes for pitting, grooves, scoring or flaking. Measure the cam lobe height and compare it to the Specifications (photo). If the lobe height is less than the minimum specified, and/or the lobes are damaged, a new camshaft must be obtained.

Valves
23 Carefully inspect each valve face for cracks, pitting and burned spots. Check the valve stem and neck for cracks. Rotate the valve and check for any obvious indication that it is bent. Check the end of the stem for pitting and excessive wear. The presence of any of the above conditions indicates a need for valve service by a professional.
24 Measure the width of the valve margin (on each valve) and compare it to the Specifications (photo). Any valve with a margin narrower than specified will have to be replaced with a new one.
25 Measure the valve stem diameter (photo). By subtracting the stem diameter from the valve guide diameter, the valve stem-to-guide clearance is obtained. Compare the results to the Specifications. If the stem-to-guide clearance is greater than specified, the guides will have to be reconditioned or replaced and new valves may have to be installed, depending on the condition of the old ones.
26 An alternative method for determining stem-to-guide clearance is to use a dial indicator to measure the valve stem deflection with the valve face about $\frac{1}{16}$ in off of the seat (photo).

Valve components
27 Check each valve spring for wear (on the ends) and pitting. Measure the free length (photo) and compare it to the Specifications. Any springs that are shorter than specified have sagged and should not be reused. Stand the spring on a flat surface and check it for squareness.
28 Check the spring retainers and keepers for obvious wear and cracks. Any questionable parts should not be reused, as extensive damage will occur in the event of failure during engine operation.

22 Valves – servicing

1 Because of the complex nature of the job and the special tools and equipment required, servicing of the valves, the valve seats and the valve guides (commonly known as a 'valve job') is best left to a professional.
2 The home mechanic can remove and disassemble the head, do the initial cleaning and inspection, then reassemble and deliver the head to a dealer service department or a reputable automotive machine shop for the actual valve servicing. It may also be possible to exchange the head for a rebuilt one, which will drastically shorten the time required to complete the service or repair procedure.
3 The dealer service department, or automotive machine shop, will remove the valves and springs, recondition or replace the valves and valve seats, recondition or replace the valve guides, check and replace the valve springs, spring retainers and keepers (as necessary), replace the valve seals with new ones, reassemble the valve components and make sure the installed spring height is correct. The cylinder head gasket surface will also be resurfaced if it is warped.
4 After the valve job has been performed by a professional, the head will be in like-new condition. When the head is returned, be sure to clean it again, very thoroughly (before installation on the engine), to remove any metal particles and abrasive grit that may still be present from the valve service or head resurfacing operations. Use compressed air, if available, to blow out all the oil holes and passages.

23 Crankshaft – installation

1 Crankshaft installation is generally one of the first steps in engine reassembly; it is assumed at this point that the engine block and crankshaft have been cleaned and inspected and repaired or reconditioned.
2 Position the engine so that the bottom is facing up.

3   Remove the main bearing caps and bolts and lay them out in the proper order to help ensure that they are installed correctly.

4   If they are still in place, remove the old bearing inserts from the block and main bearing caps. Wipe the main bearing surfaces of the block and caps with a clean, lint-free cloth (they must be kept spotlessly clean).

5   Clean the back side of the new main bearing inserts and lay one bearing half in each main bearing saddle (in the block) and the other bearing half from each bearing set in the corresponding main bearing cap. Make sure the tab on the bearing insert fits into the recess in the block or cap. Also, the oil holes in the block and cap must line up with the oil holes in the bearing insert. Do not hammer the bearing into place and do not nick or gouge the bearing faces. *No lubrication should be used at this time.*

6   Clean the faces of the bearings in the block and the crankshaft main bearing journals with a clean lint-free cloth. Check or clean the oil holes in the crankshaft, as any dirt here can only go one way – straight through the new bearings.

7   Once you are certain that the crankshaft is clean, carefully lay it in position in the main bearings with the counterweights in the horizontal position (photo).

8   Before the crankshaft can be permanently installed, the main bearing oil clearances must be checked.

9   Trim five pieces of the appropriate type of Plasti-gage (so that they are slightly shorter than the width of the main bearings) and place one piece on each crankshaft main bearing journal, parallel with the journal axis. Do not lay them across any oil holes.

10   Make sure the faces of the bearings are clean, then install the bearing caps, taking care not to disturb the Plasti-gage.

11   Install the nuts and tighten them to the specified torque. Tighten one of the bearing cap nuts $\frac{1}{2}$ turn, then the opposite nut and then return to the first one until they are both tightened to the specified torque. Start at the center main and work towards the ends. Do not rotate the crankshaft at any time during this operation.

12   Remove the bolts and carefully lift the bearing caps off.

13   Compare the width of the crushed Plasti-gage to the scale printed on the Plasti-gage container (photo).

14   Check the clearance against those given in the Specifications section.

15   If the clearance is not correct, check to make sure you have the right size bearing inserts and recheck the crankshaft main bearing journal diameters. Make sure also that no dirt or oil was trapped between the bearing inserts and the main bearing caps or the block when the clearance was measured.

16   Carefully remove all traces of the Plasti-gage from the journal and bearing surfaces with mineral spirits or equivalent and a clean lint-free cloth.

17   Carefully lift the crankshaft out of the block. Clean the bearing surfaces in the block and apply a thin, uniform layer of clean, high quality, multi-purpose grease of engine assembly lube to each bering face. Be sure to coat both sides of the thrust bearing also, as this will assist in holding it in place (photo).

18   Install the thrust bearings with the grooved surfaces facing out.

19   Carefully lower the crankshaft into position and install the bearing caps.

20   Install the bearing cap bolts and tighten them to the specified torque in a criss-cross pattern as described in Step 11.

21   Coat the rear main bearing side seal with RTV-type sealant and also apply sealant to the seal groove in the block using a screwdriver. Insert the seal carefully into the rear bearing cap. On 1981 models, the holes in the seal must face toward the sides of the block and on 1982 models toward the front and rear (photo).

22   Rotate the crankshaft a few times by hand to make sure there is no obvious binding.

23   Check the crankshaft end play by attaching a dial indicator to the block. Set the indicator at zero, lever the crankshaft forward and backward with a screwdriver and check that the total travel is within the specified limits (photo).

24   Piston rings – installation

1   Before installing the new piston rings, the ring end gaps must be checked.

23.7 Installing the crankshaft with the counterweights horizontal to the block

23.13 Measuring the Plastigage on the crankshaft journal to determine main bearing oil clearance

23.17 Lubricating the bearing surface with assembly lube

23.21 Inserting the rear main bearing cap seal

23.23 Checking the crankshaft end play

2

2   Lay out the piston/connecting rod assemblies and the new ring sets so that the rings will be matched with the same piston and cylinder during the end gap measurement and engine assembly.

3   Insert the top (number one) ring into the first cylinder and square it up with the cylinder walls by pushing it in with the top of the piston. The ring should be at least two inches below the top edge of the cylinder. To measure the end gap, slip a feeler gauge between the ends of the ring. Compare the measurement to the Specifications.

4   If the gap is larger or smaller than specified, double-check to make sure that you have the correct rings before proceeding.

5   If the gap is too small, it must be enlarged or the ring ends may come in contact with each other during engine operation, which can cause serious damage to the engine. The end gap can be increased by filing the ring ends very carefully with a fine file. Mount the ring in a vise equipped with soft jaws, holding it as close to the gap as possible. When performing this operation, file only from the outside in.

6   Excess end gap is not critical unless it is greater than 0.040 in (1 mm). Again, double-check to make sure you have the correct rings for your engine.

7   Repeat the procedure for each ring that will be installed in the first cylinder and for each ring in the remaining cylinders. Remember to keep rings, pistons and cylinders matched up.

8   Once the ring end-gaps have been checked/corrected, the rings can be installed on the pistons.

9   The oil control ring (lowest one on the piston) is installed first. It is composed of three separate components. Slip the spacer expander into the groove then install the upper side rail with the size mark and manufacturer's stamp facing up. Do not use a piston ring installation tool on the oil ring side rails, as they may be damaged. Instead, place one end of the side rail into the groove between the spacer expander and the ring land, hold it firmly in place and slide a finger around the piston while pushing the rail into the groove. Next, install the lower side rail (again, the size mark and manufacturer's stamp must face up) in the same manner.

10   After the three oil ring components have been installed, check to make sure that both the upper and lower side rails can be turned smoothly in the ring groove.

11   The number two (middle) ring is installed next. It has a stepped edge and can be readily distinguished from the top ring. Do not mix the top and middle rings up, as they have different cross sections.

12   Use a piston ring installation tool and make sure that the identification mark is facing up, then fit the ring into the middle groove on the piston. Do not expand the ring any more than is necessary to slide it over the piston.

13   Finally, install the number one (top) ring in the same manner. Make sure the identifying mark is facing up.

14   Repeat the procedure for the remaining pistons and rings. Be careful not to confuse the number one and number two rings.

25 Piston/connecting rod assembly – installation

1   Before installing the piston/connecting rod assemblies, the cylinder walls must be perfectly clean, the top edge of each cylinder must be chamfered, and the crankshaft must be in place.

2   Remove the connecting rod cap from the end of the number one connecting rod. Remove the old bearing inserts and wipe the bearing surfaces of the connecting rod and cap with a clean, lint-free cloth (they must be spotlessly clean).

3   Clean the back side of the new upper bearing half, then lay it in place in the connecting rod. Make sure that the tab on the bearing fits into the recess in the rod. Also, the oil holes in the rod and bearing insert must line up. Do not hammer the bearing insert into place, and be very careful not to nick or gouge the bearing face. *Do not lubricate the bearing at this time.*

4   Clean the back side of the other bearing insert half and install it in the rod cap. Again, make sure the tab on the bearing fits into the recess in the cap, and do not apply any lubricant. It is critically important to ensure that the mating surfaces of the bearing and connecting rod are perfectly clean and oil-free when they are assembled together.

5   Position the piston ring gaps as shown, then slip a section of plastic or rubber hose over the connecting rod cap bolts.

6   Lubricate the piston and rings with clean engine oil and install a piston ring compressor on the piston. Leave the skirt protruding about $\frac{1}{4}$ in to guide the piston into the cylinder. The rings must be

Fig. 2.12 The piston rings must be installed with the marks (arrows) facing up (Sec 24)

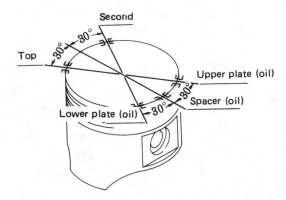

Fig. 2.13 Piston ring end gap spacing diagram (Sec 25)

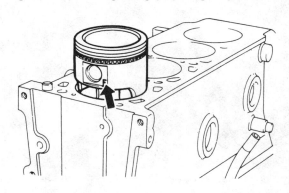

Fig. 2.14 The F on the piston must be installed facing the crankshaft pulley (front) end of the block (Sec 25)

compressed as far as possible.

7   Rotate the crankshaft so that the number one connecting rod journal is as far from the number one cylinder as possible (bottom dead center), and apply a uniform coat of engine oil to the number one cylinder walls.

8   With the F on top of the piston pointing to the front of the engine, gently place the piston/connecting rod assembly into the number one cylinder bore and rest the bottom edge of the ring compressor on the engine block. Tap the top edge of the ring compressor to make sure it is contacting the block around its entire circumference.

9   Clean the number one connecting rod journal on the crankshaft and the bearing faces in the rod.

10   Carefully tap on the top of the piston with the end of a wooden hammer handle while guiding the end of the connecting rod into place on the crankshaft journal. The piston rings may try to pop out of the ring compressor just before entering the cylinder bore, so keep some downward pressure on the ring compressor. Work slowly, and if any

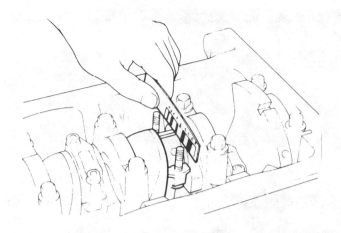

Fig. 2.15 Measuring the Plastigage on the connecting rod journal
(Sec 25)

26.2 The crankshaft key chamfer (arrow) should mate with the
chamfer in the groove next to the engine block

26.3 Install the oil pump, chain and sprocket as a unit

resistance is felt as the piston enters the cylinder, stop immediately, find out what is hanging up and fix it before proceeding. Do not, for any reason, force the piston into the cylinder, as you will break a ring and/or the piston.

11   Once the piston/connecting rod assembly is installed, the connecting rod bearing oil clearance must be checked before the rod cap is permanently bolted in place.

12   Trim a piece of the appropriate type Plasti-gage so that it is slightly shorter than the width of the connecting rod bearing and lay it in place on the number one connecting rod journal, parallel with the journal axis (it must now cross the oil hole in the journal).

13   Clean the connecting rod cap bearing face, remove the protective holes from the connecting rod bolts and gently install the rod cap in place. Make sure the mating mark on the cap is on the same side as the mark on the connecting rod. Install the nuts and tighten them to the specified torque, working up to it in three steps. Do not rotate the crankshaft at any time during this operation.

14   Remove the rod cap, being very careful not to disturb the Plasti-gage. Compare the width of the crushed Plasti-gage to the scale printed on the Plastic-gage container to obtain the oil clearance. Compare it to the Specifications to make sure the clearance is correct. If the clearance is not correct, double-check to make sure that you have the correct size bearing inserts. Also, recheck the crankshaft connecting rod journal diameter and make sure that no dirt or oil was between the bearing inserts and the connecting rod or cap when the clearance was measured.

15   Carefully scrape all traces of the Plasti-gage material off the rod journal and/or bearing face (be very careful not to scratch the bearing). Make sure the bearing faces are perfectly clean, then apply a uniform layer of clean, high quality multi-purpose grease (or engine assembly lube) to both of them. You will have to push the piston into the cylinder to expose the face of the bearing insert in the connecting rod; be sure to slip the protective hoses over the rod bolts first.

16   Slide the connecting rod back into place on the journal, remove the protective hoses from the rod cap bolts, install the rod cap and tighten the nuts to the specified torque. Again, work up to the final torque in three steps.

17   Without turning the crankshaft, repeat the entire procedure for the number four piston/connecting rod assembly. Keep the back sides of the bearing inserts and the inside of the connecting rod and cap perfectly clean when assembling them. Make sure you have the correct piston for the cylinder and that the F mark on the piston points to the front of the engine when the piston is installed. Remember, use plenty of oil to lubricate the piston before installing the ring compressor, and be sure to match up the mating marks on the connecting rod and rod cap. Also, when installing the rod caps for the final time, be sure to lubricate the bearing faces adequately.

18   After completing the procedure for piston number four, turn the crankshaft 180° and repeat the entire operation for pistons number two and three.

26   Oil pump and timing chain/sprocket assembly – installation

1   The engine should be inverted for the following operations.

2   Insert the key into the slot in the crankshaft with the chamfer down and toward the block (photo).

3   Slide the oil pump sprocket part way onto the crankshaft. Hold the oil pump above the crankshaft with the chain over the sprockets and slide the entire assembly into place (photo).

4   Install the oil pump retaining bolts and tighten them to the specified torque.

5   Slide the timing chain sprocket onto the crankshaft with the mark straight up.

6   Install the timing chain with the bright link opposite the mark on the sprocket.

7   Line up the other bright link with the mark on the camshaft sprocket (the bright links are 36 links apart) and tie the link and sprocket together with wire to hold them in position until the cylinder head is installed.

8   Install the chain dampener and guide on the block.

9   Drive out the old oil seal from the timing chain cover at the indentation, using a hammer and punch (photo).

10   Install a new oil seal by tapping it into position.

11   Coat the block lightly with RTV-type sealant and install the gaskets, using the dowels as a guide (photo).

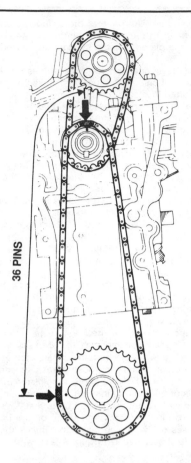

Fig. 2.16 Proper installation of the timing chain with the plated links opposite the sprocket marks (Sec 26 and 28)

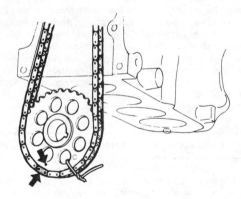

Fig. 2.17 The camshaft sprocket and timing chain wired in the proper relationship with the mark and link aligned (Secs 26 and 28)

26.9 Drive out the old oil seal at the indentation in the timing chain cover

26.11 Installing the timing chain cover gaskets

26.14 Cutting off the excess cover gasket material

12 Coat the front of the gaskets with sealant and install the timing chain cover, using the alignment dowels.
13 Install the retaining bolts and tighten them to the specified torque.
14 Cut off the excess gasket from the bottom of the cover (photo).
15 Apply RTV-type sealant to the oil pan mounting flange.
16 Lower the oil pan into position and install the retaining bolts. Tighten the bolts at the corners snugly and then work in a criss-cross pattern until all of the bolts are snug. Tighten the bolts to the specified torque, following the same pattern.
17 Apply a thin coat of lithium-base grease to the inner diameter of the crankshaft pulley and install the pulley on the crankshaft (photo).
18 Install the pulley bolt and tighten it to the specified torque, using a large screwdriver to keep the crankshaft from moving.

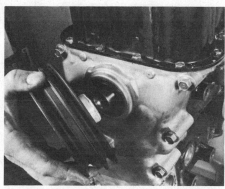

26.17 Installing the crankshaft pulley (note the white lithium grease to ease insertion into the crankshaft seal)

28.2 Installing the cylinder head over the sprocket

28.11 Tighten the sprocket nut while locking the sprocket with a screwdriver

28.12 Checking camshaft end play with a feeler gauge

28.13 Locking the chain adjuster sleeve in place with the hook (arrow)

27 Cylinder head – reassembly

1   Lay all of the spring seats in position. Install new seals on each of the valve guides, then use a hammer and an appropriate size deep socket to gently tap each seal into place until it is properly seated on its guide. Do not twist or cock the seals during installation, as they will not seal properly on the valve stems.

2   Next, install the valves (taking care not to damage the new seals), the springs, the retainers and keepers. Coat the valve stems with engine assembly lube before slipping them into the guides. When compressing the springs with the valve spring compressor, do not let the retainers contact the valve guide seals. Make certain that the keepers are securely locked in their retaining grooves.

28 Cylinder head – installation

1   With the timing chain and camshaft sprocket wired in position, rotate the engine so that it is upright.

2   Place the head gasket in position and lower the cylinder head into place (photo).

3   Check the camshaft oil clearance, using Plasti-gage (refer to Section 23 for the procedure to follow when using Plasti-gage).

4   Apply a thin coat of assembly lube to the camshaft journals.

5   Align the camshaft key with the slot in the sprocket and then slide the sprocket onto the camshaft.

6   Lower the rocker shaft assembly onto the cylinder head, making sure that the cast-in arrows are pointing forward.

7   Install the head bolts so that they are finger tight and check that all components are positioned properly and not binding.

8   Starting at the center, tighten the head bolts in a criss-cross pattern, one quarter turn at a time until they are snug. Tighten the bolts to the specified torque, following the sequence shown in Fig. 2.5.

9   Tighten the bolt inside the timing chain cover to the same torque as the head bolts.

10 Invert the engine and cut any wires holding the timing chain and remove them.

11 Turn the engine upright and install the washer and nut retaining the sprocket to the camshaft and tighten it to the specified torque (photo).

12 Check the camshaft endplay, using a feeler gauge (photo).

13 Push the chain adjuster sleeve fully into the body and retain it with the hook (photo).

14 Using a new gasket, install the adjuster. When the engine is started, the chain will contact the adjuster blade and release the sleeve.

15 Lightly lubricate the distributor O-ring with engine oil and install the distributor, making sure that the end of the shaft fits securely into the end of the camshaft.

16 Adjust the valve clearances (Chapter 1).

17 Install the valve cover.

29 External engine components – installation

1   Install the oil filter (applying a light coat of engine oil to the rubber gasket) and the dipstick.

2   Install the oil pressure switch.

3   Install the engine support at the front of the engine block.

4   Make sure that the mating surfaces of the block and intake manifold are clean and free of nicks or damage and install the manifold and gasket.

5   Install the fuel pump.

6   Install the engine lifting hook.

7   Coat the thermostat gasket surface with RTV-type sealant, then install the thermostat and gasket, followed by the housing (Chapter 3).

8   Install the coolant temperature pickup.

9   Apply a coat of RTV-type sealant to the block and install the water pump and gasket.

10 Install the lifting hook/air injection pump mount to the rear of the cylinder head.

11 Install the block drain plug.

2

12 Apply lithium based grease to the end of the water transfer tube and insert the tube into the water pump.
13 Install the exhaust manifold and gasket.
14 Hook the water transfer tube to the exhaust manifold stud and install the manifold bolts.
15 Install the transfer pipe-to-water pump hose.
16 Attach the catalytic converter to the exhaust manifold.
17 Attach the exhaust pipe bracket to the block. Tighten the two bolts which go into the block snugly, followed by fully tightening those which go into the manifold. Fully tighten the bracket-to-block bolts.
18 Install the air injection pump.
19 Install the heat shield on the exhaust manifold (four bolts). It may be necessary to remove the center two spark plugs for access.
20 Install the air injection pump adjustment brace.
21 Install the alternator mounting bracket on the block.
22 Place the alternator into position, insert the through-bolt and install the nut. Install the bolt through the adjusting brace.
23 Install and adjust the drivebelts (Chapter 1).
24 Install the carburetor (Chapter 4).
25 Engage the diaphragm link with the throttle linkage.
26 Hook the throttle return springs in place.
27 Tighten the diaphragm bracket.
28 Attach the fuel pump hose to the carburetor and engage the clamps.
29 Connect all of the vacuum hoses to their previously marked locations.

30 Engine – installation

1 Attach the lifting chain to the engine lifting hooks.
2 Remove the engine from the stand.
3 Lubricate the inner diameter of the crankshaft seal and install the seal to the rear of the crankshaft by tapping it in place with a hammer and the blunt end of a drift punch until it bottoms in the block cavity (photos).
4 Install the alignment dowels in the rear of the block.
5 Install the dust shield.
6 Install the flywheel and bolts. The holes in the flywheel are staggered so that it will only go on the crankshaft in the proper position. Apply thread locking compound to the bolt threads and tighten them to the specified torque in a criss-cross pattern, using a suitable punch to keep the flywheel from turning.
7 Center the clutch plate, place the clutch housing in position and install the retaining bolts finger tight.
8 Center the clutch plate carefully (photo) so that the transaxle shaft will be properly aligned, using a suitable socket and extension or equivalent, and then tighten the clutch pressure plate housing bolts to the specified torque.
9 Apply a small amount of molybdenum disulphide grease to the contact surfaces of the clutch fingers, the transaxle shaft splines and the release bearing.
10 With the help of an assistant, attach the transaxle to the engine and install the retaining bolts finger tight.
11 Draw the transaxle up to the engine by gradually tightening the bolts.
12 Once the engine and transaxle are properly aligned, tighten the retaining and dust cover bolts.
13 Install the starter and plug in the electrical connectors.
14 Connect the electrical wiring harness to the alternator, oil pressure switch and the starter. Route the harness around the rear of the engine and over the transaxle, securing it with the clips.
15 Raise the vehicle and support it securely.
16 Use a lifting device to raise the engine and suspend it over the engine compartment. Protect the front fenders with suitable covers.
17 Lower the engine slowly and carefully into the engine compartment with the assembly crossways so that the rear of the transaxle just clears the radiator filler spout (photo).
18 Lower the engine into place and return it to the proper position in line with the axles. Install the right-hand engine support in its mount.
19 Insert the right-hand axleshaft into the transaxle.
20 Install the through-bolt into the right-hand engine mount with the nut finger tight.
21 Lift up slightly on the transaxle to seat the axle snap-ring.
22 Install the left-hand engine mount and insulator and leave the through bolt and nut finger tight.

30.3a Installing the crankshaft seal with the inside lubricated with white lithium grease

30.3b Tapping the seal into place using the blunt end of a punch

30.8 Centering the clutch disc using a socket and extension

30.17 Lower the engine into the engine compartment with the transaxle toward the left-front corner

23 Place the crossmember in position under the vehicle and attach the rubber insulators to the bar attached to the rear of the secondary catalytic converter.

24 Attach the rear crossmember mount bracket to the transaxle.

25 Attach the front crossmember mount to the transaxle.

26 Attach the rear angled mount to the transaxle bracket wth the nut finger tight.

27 Lift the rear of the crossmember up and loosely install the bolt and washer and nut and washer on the chassis.

28 Carefully lift the front of the crossmember while aligning the rear rubber mount stud into the hole in the crossmember. Install the nut finger tight.

29 Place the front rubber mount in position on the transaxle bracket and install the nut finger tight.

30 Lift the front of the crossmember up to the chassis and align the stud on the forward mount and the two radiator mounts with the holes in the crossmember.

31 Loosely attach the forward crossmember to the chassis with the nuts and washers. The nuts on the front mount should be installed loosely at this time.

32 Tighten the nuts and bolts attaching the crossmember to the chassis to the specified torque.

33 Tighten the two bolts attaching the rear rubber mount to the transaxle.

34 Carefully lower the engine onto the mounts, making sure the tabs are properly aligned.

35 Remove the lifting chain and tighten the right and left-hand engine mount through-bolts and nuts to the specified torque.

36 Tighten the rubber mount attaching nuts.

37 Check all of the engine mount fasteners to make sure they are properly installed and tightened.

38 Install the battery tray.

39 Install the fan motor and shroud on the radiator.

40 Reconnect all vacuum hoses and electrical connectors detached during engine removal (Section 4).

41 Install the left-hand axle and reconnect the steering knuckle.

42 Reconnect the shifter and shift extension rods (Chapter 7).

43 Install the upper and lower radiator hoses and tighten the clamps. On automatic transaxle equipped vehicles, connect the cooler lines to the radiator.

44 Install the windshield washer reservoir and connect the hoses.

45 Install the exhaust pipe, clamps and brackets.

46 Connect the vacuum hoses to the No 1 and No 2 solenoid valves.

47 Connect the hoses to the altitude compensator.

48 Connect the hoses to the air control valve.

49 Reconnect the air injection system hoses.

50 Connect the hoses to the No. 1 water thermal valve.

51 Connect the throttle cable.

52 Connect the backup light wire.

53 Install the charcoal canister and connect the hoses.

54 Connect the coil wire and distributor lead to the coil.

55 Connect the fuel hose to the fuel pump.

56 Fill the transaxle with the specified lubricant and install the speedometer driven gear.

57 Connect the heater hoses to the transfer tube.

58 On manual transaxle equipped models, connect the clutch cable and bracket.

59 Install the battery. Hook up the positive cable first, followed by the negative cable.

60 Connect the hose to the brake vacuum reservoir.

61 Fill the radiator with the specified coolant (Chapter 1). After the engine is started you will have to add more coolant, so keep an eye on the level.

62 Fill the crankcase with the specified grade of oil.

63 Install the hood.

64 Double-check all of the nuts and bolts for tightness and make sure all hoses, electrical wiring and other connectors are properly installed.

65 Install the wheels and lower the vehicle.

31 Initial start-up and break-in after overhaul

1 Once the engine has been properly installed in the vehicle, double-check the engine oil and coolant levels.

2 With the spark plugs out of the engine and the coil high-tension lead grounded to the engine block, crank the engine over until oil pressure registers on the gauge (or the light goes out).

3 Install the spark plugs, hook up the plug wires and the coil high-tension lead.

4 Make sure the carburetor choke plate is closed, then start the engine. It may take a few moments for gasoline to reach the carburetor, but the engine should start without a great deal of effort.

5 As soon as the engine starts, it should be set at a fast idle (to ensure proper oil circulation) and allowed to warm up to normal operating temperature. While the engine is warming up, make a thorough check for oil and coolant leaks.

6 After the engine reaches normal operating temperature, shut it off, remove the valve cover, retorque the head bolts and recheck the valve clearances (using the hot engine specifications).

7 Install the the valve cover and recheck the engine oil and coolant levels. Also, check the ignition timing and the engine idle speed (refer to Chapter 1) and make any necessary adjustment.

8 Drive the vehicle to an area with minimum traffic, accelerate at full throttle from 30 to 50 mph, then allow the vehicle to slow to 30 mph with the throttle closed. Repeat the procedure 10 or 12 times. This will load the piston rings and cause them to seat properly against the cylinder walls. Check again for oil and coolant leaks.

9 Drive the vehicle gently for the first 500 miles (no sustained high speeds) and keep a constant check on the oil level. It is not unusual for an engine to use oil during the break-in period.

10 At approximately 500 to 600 miles, change the oil and filter, retorque the cylinder head bolts and recheck the valve clearances.

11 For the next few hundred miles, drive the vehicle normally. Do not pamper it or abuse it.

12 After 2000 miles, change the oil and filter again and consider the engine fully broken in.

2

Chapter 3 Cooling, heating and air conditioning

Refer to Chapter 13 for specifications and information applicable to later USA models

Contents

Specifications

Cooling system

Thermostat	
Type	Wax pellet
Initial opening temperature	180°F (82°C)
Fully open temperature	203°F (95°C)
Lift	0.315 in (8 mm)
Radiator pressure cap rating	13 psi (0.9 kg/cm^2)
Coolant type	50/50 mix of ethylene glycol base anti-freeze and water
Coolant capacity	5.8 US qts (5.5 liters)
Fan motor current	6.5 amps
Fan operating temperatures	
Turns on	196°F (91°C)
Turns off	188°F (84°C)
Fan belt deflection	
New	0.47 in to 0.5 in (12 mm to 14 mm)
Used	0.5 in to 0.55 in (13 mm to 14 mm)

Torque specifications

	Ft-lb	Nm
Water thermo-switch	22 to 29	30 to 40
Temperature gauge unit	4 to 7	5 to 10
Thermostat cover	14 to 22	19 to 31
Water pump	14 to 22	19 to 31

1 General information

Caution: *Whenever working in the vicinity of the fan, always make sure the ignition is turned off or the battery negative cable is disconnected.*

The cooling system on all models consists of a radiator, an electrically-driven fan mounted in the radiator shroud, a thermostat and a water pump.

Coolant is circulated through the radiator tubes and is cooled by air passing through the cooling fins. The coolant is circulated by a pump mounted on the front side of the engine and driven by a belt.

A thermostat allows the engine to warm up by remaining closed until the coolant in the radiator, heater and cylinder head is at operating temperature. The thermostat then opens, allowing full circulation of coolant throughout the cooling system.

A thermal switch actuates the electric fan when a certain temperature is reached so that it will aid in drawing air through the radiator.

The heating system operates by directing air through the heater core mounted in the dash to the interior of the vehicle by a system of ducts. Temperature is controlled by mixing heated air with fresh air by a system of flapper doors in the ducts and a heater motor.

2 Antifreeze

1 It is recommended that the cooling system is filled with a water/ethylene glycol based antifreeze solution which will give protection down to at least −20°F at all times. This provides protection against corrosion and increases the coolant boiling point. When handling antifreeze, take care that it is not spilled on the vehicle paint, since it will invariably cause damage if not removed immediately.

2 The cooling system should be drained, flushed and refilled every alternate Fall. The use of antifreeze solutions for periods of longer than two years is likely to cause damage and encourage the formation of rust and scale due to the corrosion inhibitors gradually losing their efficiency.

3 Before adding antifreeze to the system, check all hose connections and check the tightness of the cylinder head bolts as such solutions are searching.

4 The exact mixture of antifreeze to water which you should use depends upon the relative weather conditions. The mixture should contain at least 50 percent antifreeze, offering protection to −34°F.

Under no circumstances should the mixture contain more than 70 percent antifreeze.

3 Thermostat – removal and installation

1 A fault in the thermostat is indicated by a failure of the engine to reach operating temperature or to take a longer than normal time to do so.
2 Disconnect the battery negative cable.
3 Drain the radiator coolant into a suitable container (Chapter 1).
4 Remove the radiator hose from the thermostat cover.
5 Disconnect the fan switch at the thermostat cover.
6 Remove the thermostat cover nuts and lift the cover away. Note the position of the thermostat and then lift it away.
7 Clean all traces of gasket material from the mating surfaces with a scraper.
8 Install the new thermostat, with the "jiggle" pin facing outwards.
9 Coat both sides of the new gasket with sealant and place it in position on the thermostat cover.
10 Install the thermostat cover and nuts, tightening the nuts to specification.
11 Install the radiator hose, plug in the cooling fan connector and fill the radiator with the specified coolant.
12 Connect the battery negative cable and run the engine to check for proper thermostat operation and leaks.

4 Water pump – removal and installation

1 Water pump failure is indicated by a grinding noise issuing from the pump or coolant leaking from the "weep" hole.
2 Raise the vehicle and support it securely.
3 Drain the cooling system by removing the lower radiator hose.
4 Remove the radiator hose from the water pump.
5 Loosen the water pump pulley bolts while holding tension on the drivebelt (photo).
6 Relax the tension on the alternator drivebelt by loosening the pivot bolt.
7 Remove the water pump bolts and the pulley (photo).
8 Remove the nut and bolts retaining the water pump, grasp it firmly and pull it free of the mounting stud. With a twisting motion, work the water pump free of the water tube and remove it.
9 Clean the mounting surfaces of the block and remove any traces of gasket material.
10 Prior to installation, apply sealant to both sides of the new gasket and lubricate the new O-ring and water pipe with lithium-based grease.
11 Place the sealant-coated gasket on the water pump and install them. Install the mounting nut and bolts and tighten to specification.

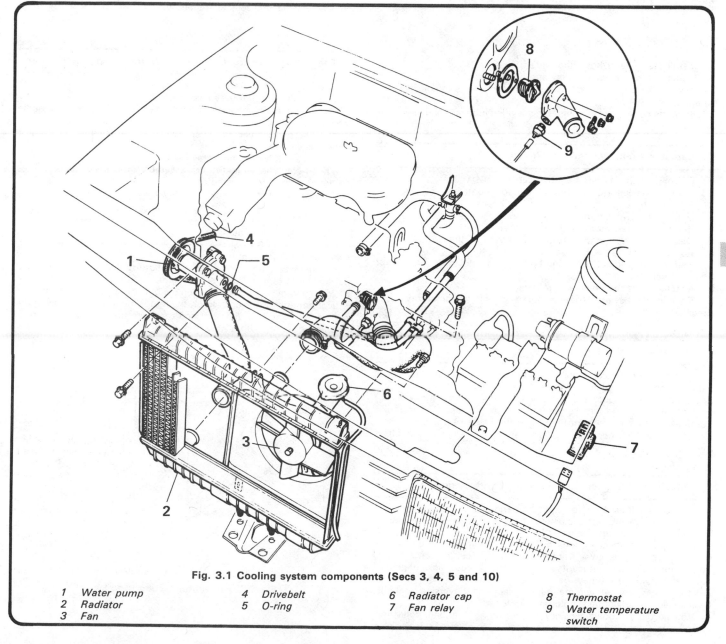

Fig. 3.1 Cooling system components (Secs 3, 4, 5 and 10)

1	Water pump	4	Drivebelt	6	Radiator cap
2	Radiator	5	O-ring	7	Fan relay
3	Fan				

8	Thermostat	
9	Water temperature switch	

3

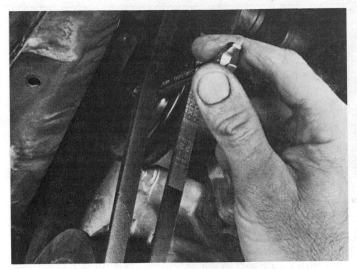

4.5 Hold the water pump drivebelt and loosen the pulley bolts

4.7 Remove the water pump bolts. Note the coolant leakage from the weep hole, indicating seal failure (arrow)

12 Install the radiator hose and water pipe.
13 Install the water pump pulley and drivebelts.
14 Tighten the alternator and water pump drivebelts to specification (Chapter 1).
15 Refill the cooling system with the specified lubricant and lower the vehicle.

5 Radiator – removal and installation

1   Disconnect the battery negative cable.
2   Drain the radiator coolant into a suitable container.
3   Remove the upper and lower radiator hoses.
4   Unplug the two fan motor connectors.
5   Remove the fan motor and shroud assembly (Section 8).
6   Disconnect the water thermo valve hoses at the bottom of the radiator.
7   Remove the radiator retaining bolts and carefully lift the radiator from the vehicle.
8   Installation is the reverse of removal.
9   Connect the battery negative cable and refill the radiator with the specified coolant.

6 Radiator – inspection

1   The radiator should be kept free of obstructions such as leaves, paper, insects, etc which could affect the cooling efficiency.
2   Periodically, inspect the radiator for bent cooling fins, signs of coolant leakage and cracks around the upper and lower tanks. Carefully straighten any bent fins, using the blade of a screwdriver.
3   Check the filler neck sealing surface for dents which could affect the radiator cap effectiveness.

7 Drivebelts – inspection, replacement and tensioning

1   The drivebelts should be inspected periodically for wear, cuts and contamination by oil, gasoline or coolant as well as for signs of glazing, indicating improper tensioning.
2   To replace a drivebelt, loosen the adjustment bolts and push the pivoting components away from the belt until it can be removed. Do not pry on the pulley surface itself as this could cause nicks or gouges which will damage the new belt.
3   Install the new belt and maintain pressure on it by using a suitable lever while the adjustment bolts are tightened,
4   Check the drivebelt tension by measuring the belt deflection, referring to Chapter 1 and the Specifications Section of this Chapter.

8 Fan motor and shroud assembly – removal and installation

1   Disconnect the battery negative cable.
2   Unplug the two fan motor connectors.
3   Remove the wiring harness from the fan shroud and loosen the tie strap.
4   Release the two vacuum hoses which are retained to the left side of the fan shroud.
5   Remove the fan shroud retaining bolts.
6   Lift the fan shroud and motor assembly from the radiator.
7   Installation is the reverse of removal.
8   Connect the battery negative cable.

9 Fan motor – testing

1   Unplug the fan motor connector.
2   Connect an ammeter between the battery negative terminal and the horizontal terminal of the connector.
3   With a wire connected between the battery negative cable and the vertical terminal of the connector, the motor must run smoothly at the specified current. If it does not and there are no faults in the wiring, replace the motor with a new one.

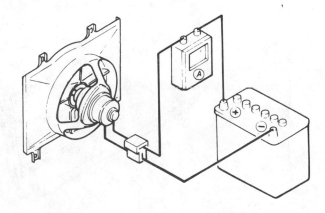

Fig. 3.2 Fan motor testing (Sec 9)

10 Fan relay – testing

1   Unplug the water temperature connector (located adjacent to the thermostat housing).
2   With the ignition switch in the On position, the fan should turn.
3   If it does not, check the fan relay and motor connectors and the fuse for faults.
4   If the motor still does not run, replace the relay.

11 Heater control – removal and installation

1   Disconnect the battery negative cable.
2   Remove the fan control knob.
3   Remove the control face plate screws.
4   In the engine compartment, disconnect the clip at the heater bracket and slide the control wire off the pin (photo).
5   Insert the wire back through the firewall.
6   Snap the wire loose from the clip on the white plastic case and slide it off the pin.
7   Disconnect the light socket from the control and withdraw the control from the dash panel.
8   Installation is a reversal of removal.

12 Heater blower motor – removal and installation

1   Disconnect the battery negative cable.
2   Remove the left dash undercover.
3   Remove the left defroster duct by removing the snap lock and pulling straight down.
4   Unplug the motor electrical connector.
5   Remove the three blower motor-to-heater screws.
6   Withdraw the blower motor from the heater housing.
7   Installation is the reverse of removal.
8   Connect the battery negative cable and check the blower motor for proper operation.

11.4 Disconnect the clip and slide the control wire off the pin

13 Air conditioning system – general information

Caution: *The air conditioning system is pressurised at the factory and requires special equipment to repair. Any work should be left to a properly equipped shop. Do not, under any circumstances, disconnect an air conditioning hose while the system is under pressure.*

The air conditioning system consists of a condenser mounted in front of the radiator, an evaporator, a suction accumulator, an evaporator mounted in the dash panel, a compressor to transfer the refrigerant through the system and associated hoses.

The temperature in the passenger compartment is lowered by transferring the heat to the refrigerant in the evaporator, passing the refrigerant through a suction accumulator and then to the condenser.

Maintenance is confined to keeping the system properly charged with refrigerant, the compressor drivebelt tensioned properly and making sure the condenser is free of leaves or accumulations of dirt or debris.

3

Chapter 4 Fuel and exhaust systems

Refer to Chapter 13 for specifications and information applicable to later USA models

Contents

Specifications

General

Fuel tank capacity	11.1 US gals (42.0 liters)
Fuel filter type	Paper cartridge element

Fuel pump

Output pressure	2.84 psi to 3.84 psi
Output volume	0.8 US qts (800cc) per minute

Carburetor

Curb idle speed		
Manual transaxle (Neutral)	850 rpm	
Automatic transaxle (Drive)	750 rpm	
	in	**mm**
Fast idle cam primary throttle valve clearance		
1981	0.033 ± 0.002	0.85 ± 0.05
1982	0.026 ± 0.002	0.67 ± 0.05
Choke valve clearance		
1981	0.039 ± 0.008	0.99 ± 0.2
1982	0.043 ± 0.008	1.08 ± 0.2
Choke unloader valve clearance		
1981	0.088 ± 0.011	2.23 ± 0.28
1982	0.130 ± 0.011	3.30 ± 0.28
Primary throttle-to-bore wall clearance		
1981	0.311 ± 0.024	7.9 ± 0.6
1982	0.236	6.0
Choke diaphragm lever clearance (at 15.7 in-hg [400 mm-hg] vacuum)		
1981 (at 46°F [8°C])	0.076 ± 0.020	1.78 ± 0.020
1981 (at 91°F [33°C])	0.1000 ± 0.020	2.54 ± 0.25
Float level height	0.435	11
Float seat lip-to-needle valve clearance	0.051 to 0.067	1.3 to 1.7
Secondary fuel cut system lever-to-plunger clearance	1.38 ± 0.008	3.5 ± 0.2

1 General information

The fuel system consists of a rear-mounted fuel tank, a fuel pump which draws the fuel to the carburetor and associated lines and filters.

The exhaust system is composed of pipes, heat shields, muffler and catalytic converters for carrying the exhaust gases from the engine to the rear of the vehicle. Catalytic converters require unleaded fuel.

2 Fuel system check

The fuel system should be inspected periodically for leaks, malfunctions and faulty components. This check is described in Chapter 1.

3   Air filter element replacement

Replace the air cleaner filter element periodically in accordance with the maintenance schedule in Chapter 1 or when it is dirty or clogged. The replacement procedure is also found in Chapter 1.

4   Thermostatically controlled air cleaner check

A malfunction of the thermostatically controlled air cleaner can affect the engine's running during warmup. Check the operation of the air cleaner flapper door and mechanism periodically as described in Chapter 1.

5   Fuel filter replacement

The fuel filter should be replaced periodically according to the maintenance schedule and procedures in Chapter 1.

6   Throttle opener (air conditioning-equipped models) – adjustment

1   Air conditioned vehicles are equipped with a throttle opener system to maintain proper engine speed during air conditioner operation.
2   To check the throttle opener operation, start the engine, disconnect the intake manifold-to-No. 3 three-way solenoid valve hose.

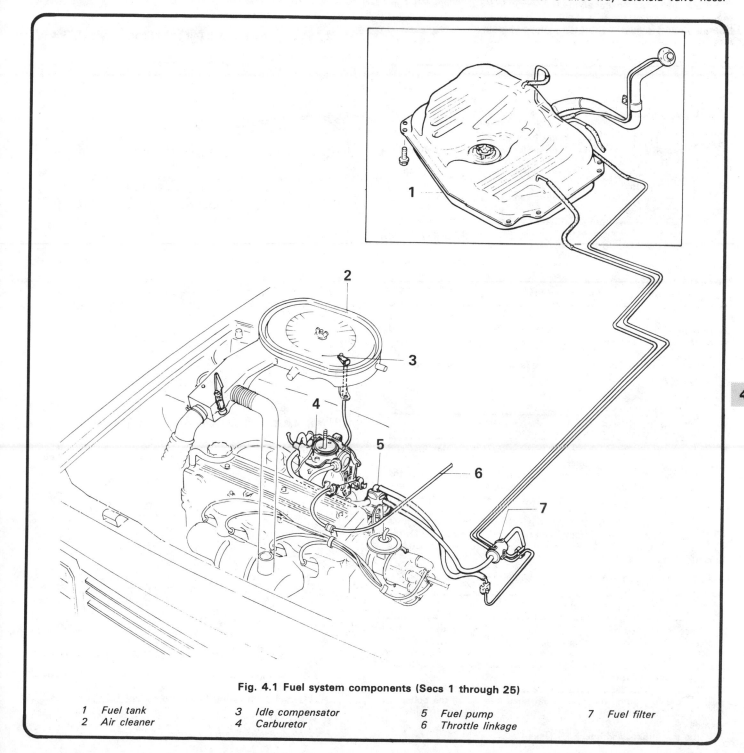

Fig. 4.1 Fuel system components (Secs 1 through 25)

1 Fuel tank	3 Idle compensator	5 Fuel pump	7 Fuel filter
2 Air cleaner	4 Carburetor	6 Throttle linkage	

Connect the hose to the throttle opener servo diaphragm.
3   The engine speed should increase approximately 1200 rpm. If it does not, turn the adjustment screw on the servo diaphragm until the increase is within specification.
4   Reconnect the vacuum hose to the No. 3 three-way solenoid valve.

7   Throttle linkage – adjustment

1   Check the throttle linkage free play at the carburetor. If the free play is not within specification, loosen the nut, adjust as necessary and retighten.
2   Push the throttle pedal all the way down to the floor and have an assistant check that the throttle valves in the carburetor are open fully. If they are not, adjust the throttle pedal stop bolt.

8   Idle compensator – testing

1   The idle compensator is located in the floor of the air cleaner assembly and is connected to the carburetor by a hose. A fault in the idle compensator is indicated by uneven idling or hard starting.
2   Remove the lid and filter element from the air cleaner.
3   Disconnect the hose from the carburetor and determine that no air flows through it or the compensator.
4   Heat the idle compensator to operating temperature (153°F [67°C]) with a suitable lamp or hair drier.
5   With the compensator at operating temperature, air should now flow through the hose.
6   If the idle compensator fails either test, replace it with a new unit.
7   Reinstall the filter element and air cleaner lid and reconnect the idle compensator hose to the carburetor.

9   Fuel pump – general information

The fuel pump is bolted to the cylinder head, adjacent to the carburetor. A lobe on the camshaft moves the pump lever up and down, actuating the diaphragm so that the fuel is drawn from the tank, through the pump to the carburetor.
The fuel pump is a sealed unit and a faulty pump must be replaced with a new one.

10   Fuel pump – testing

1   A simple test of the fuel pump is to disconnect the outlet hose and route it into a suitable container.
2   Disconnect the ignition coil wire and turn the engine over with the starter while observing the fuel pump outlet hose. The pump should exhibit definite spurts of fuel. If it does not or very little fuel is seen, replace the pump with a new one.
3   The pump can be tested for output volume by routing the hose into a suitable graduated container and turning the engine over for the specified time to determine if the proper amount of fuel is pumped (see Specifications for data).

11   Fuel pump – removal and installation

1   Place clean rags or newspaper under the fuel pump to catch any gasoline which is spilled during removal.
2   Release the clips and remove the fuel hoses from the pump. Plug the hose ends to prevent leakage.
3   Unbolt and remove the fuel pump.
4   To install, use gasket sealer to retain the new gasket in place, position the fuel pump on the cylinder head and install the bolts.
5   Install the fuel hoses to the pump and secure them with the clamps.
6   Run the engine and check for leaks.

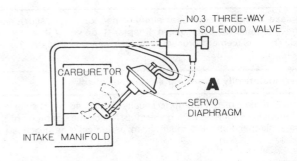

Fig. 4.2 Throttle opener check (air conditioned models) (Sec 6)

A   Adjustment screw

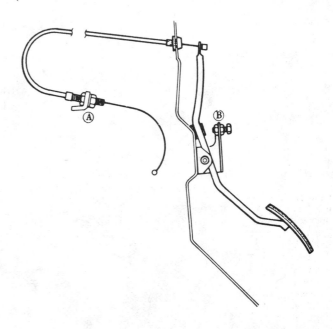

Fig. 4.3 Throttle linkage adjustment (Sec 7)

A   Cable adjustment nut   B   Throttle pedal stop bolt

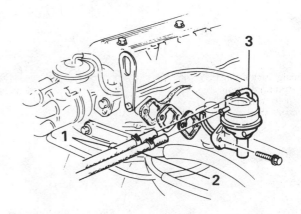

Fig. 4.4 Fuel pump installation (Sec 11)

1   Fuel inlet hose   3   Fuel pump
2   Fuel outlet and return hose

12 Carburetor – removal and installation

1   Remove the air cleaner.
2   Remove all vacuum tubes and hoses from the carburetor, tagging them for ease of installation.
3   Tag and remove all wiring connectors from the carburetor.
4   Disconnect the throttle cable.
5   Remove the retaining nuts and lift the carburetor from the intake manifold.
6   To install, place the carburetor and gasket in position and install the retaining nuts.
7   Reconnect the vacuum hoses and tubes and electrical connectors to their previously tagged positions.
8   Reconnect the throttle cable.
9   Start the engine and check for fuel leaks. The fuel level must be visible in the sight glass on the caburetor and bisect the mark on the glass.
10   Check the idle speed to make sure that it is within specifications.

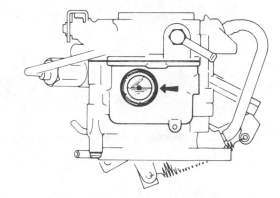

Fig. 4.5 Proper fuel level (Sec 12)

13 Carburetor – disassembly

1   With the carburetor removed from the vehicle (Section 12) and a rebuild kit in hand, disassembly can begin. Carburetor disassembly is illustrated in a step-by-step fashion with photos. Follow the photos in the proper sequence.
2   Have a large and clean work area on which to lay out the parts as they are removed from the carburetor. Many of the parts are very small and can be easily lost if the area is cluttered.
3   Take your time during reassembly. Sketch the relationship of the various components of any assembly which appears complicated or tag the various parts for ease of reassembly. Also, refer to the accompanying exploded view of the carburetor (Fig. 4.7). Care taken during disassembly will pay off with an easier job at the time of carburetor assembly. Begin disassembly by following the photo sequence starting with photo 13.3/1.

14 Carburetor – inspection

1   Clean all components in a suitable solvent or carburetor cleaner.
2   Inspect the air horn, main and throttle body housings for cracks. Check the choke and throttle shafts for wear as this could allow air leakage. Inspect the float, needle and seat for wear, rust or damage. Carefully examine the jets and air bleeds for clogging, using compressed air rather than a wire or rod to clean out any blockage. Inspect the accelerating pump plunger cup for wear, replacing any suspect unit with a new one. Check the diaphragm assembly for wear and proper operation. Inspect the length of the mixture screw for burrs, nicks or damage.
3   Test the solenoid by connecting the horizontal terminal of the connector to the battery positive (+) terminal and the vertical to the negative (–) terminal The plunger should retract; if it does not, replace the solenoid with a new one.
4   Test the choke heater for continuity by connecting an ohmmeter

13.3/1 Remove the snap-ring and lift the accelerator pump lever

13.3/2 Disengage the fast idle link

13.3/3 Remove choke cover rivets. Remove set screw, pull retaining bracket outward, rotate it ¼ turn and remove assembly

13.3/4 Remove the choke diaphragm hose

13.3/5 Remove the five retaining screws and lift the carburetor air horn from the body

13.3/6 Disconnect idle linkage at choke lever, invert air horn and remove gasket. Remove float retaining pin (arrow) and remove float

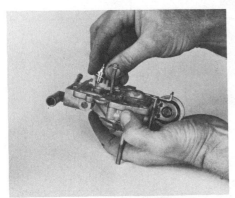
13.3/7 Remove the float needle valve

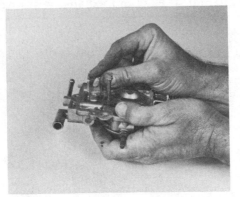
13.3/8 Remove the needle valve screen

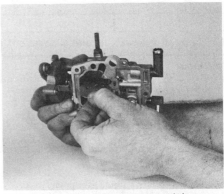
13.3/9 Remove the choke plate retaining screws. The ends are staked and will require filing. Remove the choke plates

13.3/10 Remove the choke diaphragm linkage snap-ring and choke housing retaining screw

13.3/11 Lift off the choke housing

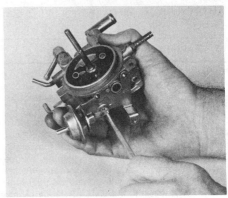
13.3/12 Remove the choke diaphragm assembly

13.3/13 Remove the accelerator pump spring

13.3/14 Remove the accelerator pump discharge weight

13.3/15 Remove the accelerator pump inlet ball

13.3/16 Remove the secondary cut system snap-ring

13.3/17 Remove the secondary cut system shaft, boot and sleeve

13.3/18 Remove the screw, spring, washer and check ball

13.3/19 Remove the slow cut solenoid valve. Be prepared to catch the plunger and spring when withdrawing the solenoid

13.3/20 Remove the inner and outer primary slow jets

13.3/21 Remove the inner and outer primary main air bleeds

13.3/22 Remove the secondary main air bleed

13.3/23 Remove the secondary inner and outer slow jets

13.3/24 Remove the power jet (arrow). Do not depress the plunger during removal as this will cause it to bend

13.3/25 Remove the idle switch assembly

13.3/26 Remove the secondary diaphragm unit

13.3/27 Remove the upper carburetor-to-base retaining screws

13.3/28 Remove the bottom retaining screw carefully as it is drilled and easily damaged. Remove the body from the base

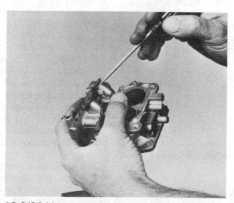
13.3/29 Use a screwdriver to remove the main jet retainers

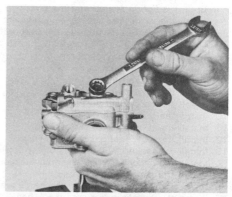
13.3/30 Remove the main jet plugs

13.3/31 Remove the main jets with a screwdriver

13.3/32 Remove the idle mixture adjusting screw by turning clockwise and unscrewing it

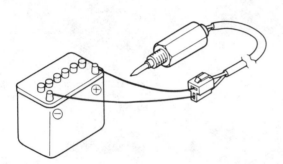

Fig. 4.6 Testing the slow cut solenoid (Sec 14)

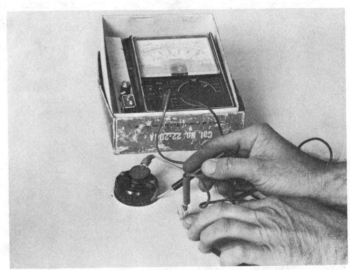

14.4 Checking the choke heater for continuity

between the heater ground and the connector (photo).
5   Replace the heater with a new one if there is no continuity.
6   If compressed air is available, blow all components dry.

15 Carburetor – reassembly

Note: *Refer to the carburetor disassembly photo sequence and to Figure 4.7.*
1   Install the idle mixture screw and spring into the shell by screwing it in until it is *lightly* seated and then backing it off four turns.
2   Install the main jets, covers, seal washers and retainers.
3   Install the carburetor body to the base with new gaskets.
4   Align the idle mixture screw with the tab on the body.
5   Install the secondary diaphragm, using a new gasket.
6   Install the idle switch.
7   Install the power jet.
8   Install the secondary slow jet.
9   Install the secondary air bleed
10   Install the primary air bleed.
11   Install the primary slow jet assembly.
12   Install the slow fuel cut solenoid valve.
13   Install the secondary cut check ball spring, seal washer and screw.
14   Install the secondary cut assembly sleeve.
15   Install the secondary cut assembly.
16   Install the accelerator pump discharge weight.
17   Install the accelerator pump check ball.
18   Install the accelerator pump spring, with the ball retaining tab turned downward.

19   Install the needle jet filter, aligning it with the protrusion on the air horn body.
20   Install the needle valve and seal.
21   Install the choke diaphragm assembly.
22   Install the choke shaft into the air horn far enough to allow the linkage to be connected.
23   After the linkage is installed, retain it with the snap-ring.
24   Install the choke housing screws.
25   Install the choke plate and screws.
26   Measure and adjust the float level clearance (Section 16).
27   Install the accelerator pump boot.
28   Lubricate the accelerator pump cup lightly with engine oil and insert it into the boot.
29   Using a new gasket, install the air horn to the carburetor body.
30   Install and tighten the air horn-to-body screws.
31   Install the choke diaphragm vacuum tube.
32   Hook the fast idle linkage to the lever and install the washer and cotter pin.
33   Install the accelerator pump lever and retaining clips.
34   Install the choke housing by sliding the choke lever and bracket into position until it is locked with the alignment lug. Secure with either suitable screws or rivets.
35   Secure the choke heater electrical harness into position with the clip which is installed on the air horn screw.

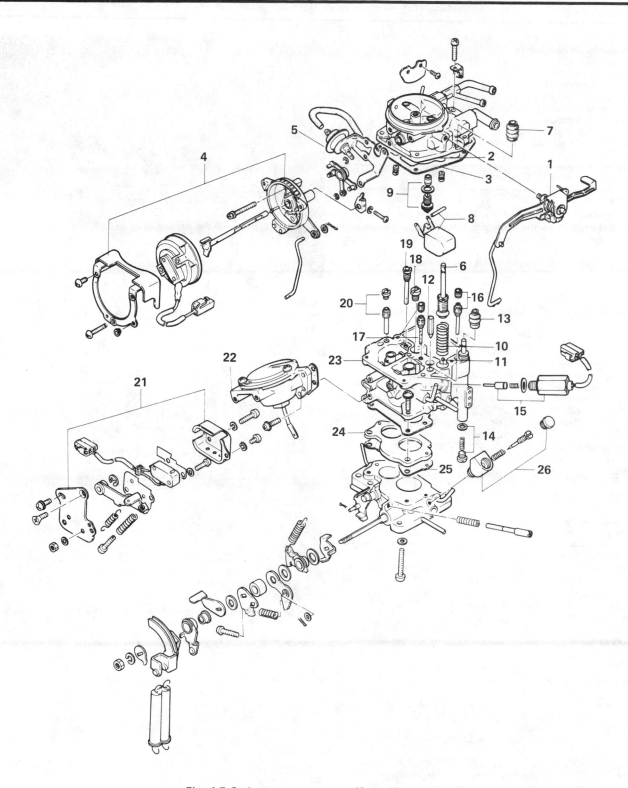

Fig. 4.7 Carburetor components (Secs 13 through 23)

1	Lever and rod	9	Needle valve	14	Secondary cut system	20	Secondary slow jet
2	Air horn	10	Spring	15	Slow fuel cut solenoid	21	Idle switch
3	Gasket	11	Accelerator pump inlet		valve	22	Diaphragm
4	Automatic choke		ball	16	Primary slow jet	23	Main body
5	Vacuum diaphragm	12	Accelerator pump	17	Primary main air bleed	24	Insulator
6	Accelerator pump		discharge weight	18	Power jet	25	Gasket
7	Boot	13	Boot	19	Secondary main air bleed	26	Idle mixture screw
8	Float						

4

36 Assembly is now complete. Install the carburetor. Check and adjust the following as necessary:

    Choke diaphragm (Section 17)
    Fast idle cam (Section 18)
    Choke valve (Section 19)
    Choke unloader (Section 20)
    Secondary throttle valve (Section 21)
    Fast idle speed (Section 22)
    Idle speed (Section 23)
    Secondary fuel cut system (Section 24)

16 Float level – checking and adjustment

Float height

1   With the gasket removed from the air horn, lift the float fully upward and then lower it so the seat lip just touches the needle.
2   Measure the distance between the bottom of the float and the top of the air horn to determine float height (photo).
3   If the float level is out of specification, bend the float tang to adjust it.

Float seat lip-to-needle valve clearance

4   Raise the float fully and measure the clearance between the seat lip and needle valve (photo).
5   Bend the float stop to adjust as necessary.

16.2 Measuring float height

17 Choke diaphragm clearance – checking and adjustment

1   Before beginning, make sure the fast idle cam lever is on the first step of the fast idle cam.
2   Apply the specified vacuum (see Specifications) to the choke diaphragm.
3   Press the choke valve lightly closed and check the clearance between the choke lever and the valve.
4   If the clearance is out of specification, adjust by bending the choke lever.
5   After adjustment, install the bi-metal cover.

18 Fast idle cam – checking and adjustment

1   Hold the choke valve closed with your finger.
2   Check the fast idle cam to make sure that it is on the proper step of the cam. On 1981 models it must be on the first step and on 1982 models, the second step.
3   Check the primary throttle valve clearance ('G' in Figs. 4.10 and 4.11) against specification.
4   If the clearance is out of specification, adjust by turning the adjusting screw. Turning the screw clockwise increases the clearance.

16.4 Measuring float seat lip-to-needle valve clearance

19 Choke valve – checking and adjustment

1   Check and adjust as necessary, the fast idle cam (Section 18).
2   With the fast idle cam lever on the second step of the cam, close the choke valve with your finger.
3   Measure the clearance between the choke valve and the choke bore wall.
4   Minor adjustments to bring the clearance within specification can be made by bending the fast idle cam. If a larger adjustment is necessary, bend the choke rod.

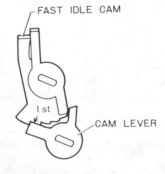

20 Choke unloader – checking

1   With the choke valve closed, open the primary throttle valve.
2   Measure the clearance between the choke valve and bore wall and check this against specification.

Fig. 4.8 The fast idle cam should be on the first step when checking the choke diaphragm (Sec 17)

21 Secondary throttle valve – checking and adjustment

1   The secondary throttle valve begins to open after the primary valve

has opened 49 degrees. Both throttles reach the completely open position at the same time.
2   Open the primary throttle until the secondary throttle begins to move and then check the primary throttle-to-bore wall clearance.
3   Bend the connecting rod, if necessary, to adjust the clearance to bring it within specification.

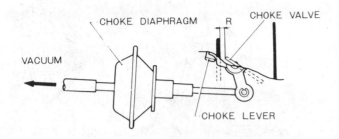

Fig. 4.9 Measuring the choke diaphragm clearance (R) (Sec 17)

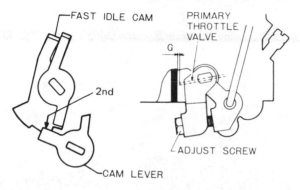

Fig. 4.11 On 1982 models, the cam lever must be on the second step of the cam when checking primary throttle valve clearance (G) (Sec 18)

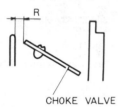

Fig. 4.13 Measuring the choke unloader valve clearance (R) (Sec 20)

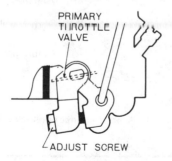

Fig. 4.15 Fast idle adjustment screw (Sec 22)

22 Fast idle speed – checking and adjustment

1 Check the idle speed, adjusting as necessary (Section 23).
2 Depress the throttle pedal.
3 Start the engine and warm it up to operating temperature.
4 Turn off the engine and remove the air cleaner.
5 Hold the throttle valve slightly open, then push the choke valve closed. Release the choke valve, followed by the throttle valve.
6 Without touching the throttle pedal, start the engine. Engine speed should increase to between 3000 and 4000 rpm.

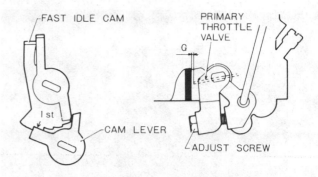

Fig. 4.10 The primary throttle valve clearance (G) is measured with the cam lever on the first step (1981 models) (Sec 18)

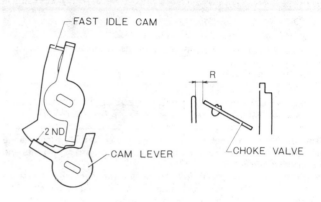

Fig. 4.12 Checking the choke valve clearance (R) (Sec 19)

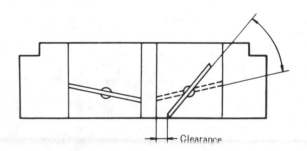

Fig. 4.14 Checking the primary throttle opening clearance (Sec 21)

7 Adjust the engine speed as necessary by turning the fast idle screw.
8 Install the air cleaner.

23 Idle speed – checking and adjustment

1 Prior to checking the idle speed, make sure that the ignition system, spark plugs and carburetor are operating properly.
2 Turn off all lights and accessories which could drain the electrical system.
3 The electrical cooling fan must not be operating while the idle speed is being checked. If the fan is running, wait until it shuts off before proceeding.
4 Connect a suitable tachometer to the engine.
5 With the engine at normal operating temperature, check the idle speed against Specifications.
6 Turn the throttle adjustment screw to adjust the idle speed (photo).

23.6 Idle speed (throttle) adjustment screw location (arrow)

Fig. 4.17 Siphoning fuel from the tank using a pump (Sec 25)

24 Secondary fuel cut system – checking and adjustment

1   The secondary fuel cut system cuts off the secondary fuel passage under certain conditions such as panic stops and hard right turns and maintains the proper idle.
2   With the throttle pedal fully released, measure the clearance between the throttle lever and the secondary fuel cut plunger.
3   Check this measurement against Specifications, bending the lever as necessary to adjust.

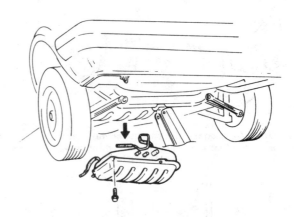

Fig. 4.18 Fuel tank removal (Sec 25)

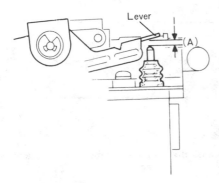

Fig. 4.16 Measuring the secondary fuel cut system lever clearance (A) (Sec 24)

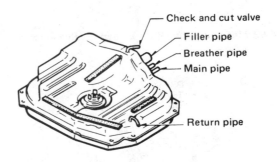

Fig. 4.19 Fuel tank hose connections (Sec 25)

25 Fuel tank – removal and installation

Caution: *This operation is potentially hazardous. Follow all precautions listed in 'Safety First' near the front of this manual.*
1   Remove the rear seat and fuel tank gauge and siphon or pump fuel from the tank.
Caution: *Do not use your mouth to start the siphoning action.*
2   Raise the vehicle and support it securely.
3   Disconnect all fuel tank hoses, identifying them well for re-installation. Unbolt the tank and lower it from the vehicle.
4   Installation is the reverse of removal. Make sure that all of the hoses are securely reconnected to their proper pipes.
5   Lower the vehicle, reinstall the tank gauge and rear seat.
6   Check for leaks.

26 Exhaust system – removal and installation

1   The exhaust system should be inspected periodically for leaks, cracks and damaged or worn components (Chapter 1).
2   Allow the exhaust system to cool for at least one hour prior to inspecting or beginning work on it.
3   Raise the vehicle and support it securely.
4   Exhaust system components can be removed by removing the heat shields, unbolting and/or disengaging them from the hangers and removing from the vehicle. If parts are rusted together, apply a rust dissolving fluid (available in automotive supply stores) and allow it to work prior to attempting removal.
5   After replacing any part of the exhaust system, check carefully for leaks before driving the vehicle.

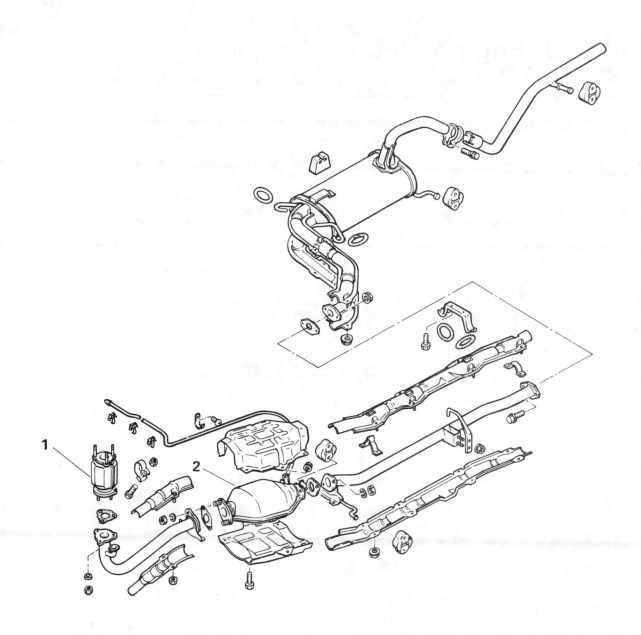

Fig. 4.20 Exhaust system layout and components (Sec 26)

1   *Front catalytic converter*   2   *Rear catalytic converter*

4

Chapter 5 Engine electrical system

Refer to Chapter 13 for specifications and information applicable to later USA models

Contents

Specifications

Spark plugs
Type .... NGK BPR-5ES or BPR-6ES
Gap .... 0.031 in (0.080 mm)
Spark plug (high tension) wire resistance .... 16 000 ohms per 3.28 ft

Ignition timing (initial)
Manual transaxle .... 8° BTDC at 850 rpm
Automatic transaxle .... 8° BTDC at 750 rpm
Timing mark location .... Crankshaft pulley

Firing order 1-3-4-2

Ignition coil
Primary resistance .... 1.15 ohms
Secondary resistance .... 10 to 30 ohms
Insulation resistance .... Over 10 000 ohms

Alternator
Brush length
    Standard .... 0.71 in   18 mm
    Service limit .... 0.31 in   8 mm
Drivebelt tension
    New .... 0.47 in to 0.5 in   12 mm to 13 mm
    Used .... 0.5 in to 0.55 in   13 mm to 14 mm

Starter motor
Brush length
    Standard .... 0.69 in   17 mm
    Service limit .... 0.45 in   11.5 mm
Shaft endplay .... 0.008 in to 0.020 in   0.2 mm to 0.5 mm
Pinion-to-stopper clearance .... 0.02 in to 0.08 in   0.5 mm to 2.0 mm

Torque specifications

	Ft-lb	Nm
Spark plug	11 to 17	15 to 23
Starter motor	27 to 46	38 to 64
Alternator	27 to 46	38 to 64

1 General information

The engine electrical system is made up of a battery, a charging system, starter and ignition system

The charging system consists of the alternator, integral voltage regulator and battery. The starting system is operated by the battery's electrical power through the starter relay which activates the starter motor. The ignition system includes the distributor, ignition wires and spark plugs.

The electrical system is of the 12-volt, negative ground type and whenever the system is to be worked on the negative battery cable should be disconnected.

Information on the maintenance of the ignition, starter and charging sytems and battery can be found in Chapter 1.

2   Battery – removal and installation

Caution: *Hydrogen gas is produced by the battery and open flames or lighted cigarettes should be kept away from the battery at all times. Also, battery acid is very corrosive. Avoid contact with skin or eyes.*
1   The battery is located at the left front corner of the engine compartment and is held in place by a metal strap across its top.
2   Always disconnect the negative (–) battery cable first, followed by the positive (+) cable.
3   After the cables are disconnected, remove the two nuts retaining the metal strap and remove the strap.
4   Remove the battery. **Note:** *When lifting the battery from the engine compartment, be careful not to twist the case as this could cause acid to spurt out of the filler openings.*
5   Installation is the reverse of removal. Be careful not to overtighten the securing nuts as this may damage the battery case.

3   Alternator – general information

The alternator is operated by a drivebelt turned by the crankshaft pulley. The rotor turns inside the stator to produce an alternating current, which is then converted to direct current by diodes. The current is adjusted to battery charging needs by an electronic voltage regulator which is incorporated into the alternator.

4   Alternator – maintenance

The alternator requires very little maintenance because the only components subject to wear are the brushes and bearings. The bearings are sealed for life. The brushes should be inspected for wear after about 75 000 miles (120 000 km) and checked for wear against Specifications.

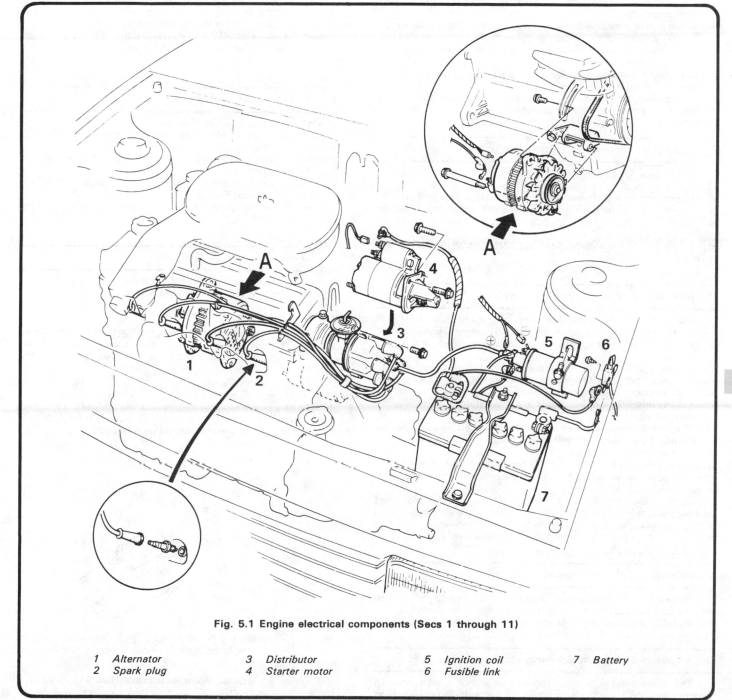

Fig. 5.1 Engine electrical components (Secs 1 through 11)

1   Alternator   3   Distributor   5   Ignition coil   7   Battery
2   Spark plug   4   Starter motor   6   Fusible link

Regular maintenance consists of cleaning the alternator of grease and dirt, checking the electrical connections for tightness and adjusting the drivebelt for proper tension.

5 Alternator – special precautions

Whenever the electrical system is being worked on or booster or external means of starting the engine are used, certain precautions must be observed to avoid damaging the alternator. They are as follows:

Make sure that the battery terminals are never reversed as this will damage the alternator diodes. The negative (–) cable must always be grounded.

The output (B) terminal must never be grounded; it should always be connected to the positive battery terminal.

Never use a high voltage tester on the alternator.

Do not operate the engine with the voltage regulator plug disconnected.

When the alternator is to be removed or its wiring disconnected, always disconnect the battery negative cable first.

The alternator must never be operated with the battery-to-alternator cable disconnected.

Disconnect the battery cables before charging the battery with an external charger.

If a booster charger or battery is to be used, always doublecheck that the battery cables are not reversed.

6 Alternator – removal and installation

1   Disconnect the battery negative cable.
2   Remove the alternator adjusting bolt.
3   Unplug the wiring connectors from the rear of the alternator.
4   Rotate the alternator toward the engine and remove the drivebelt.
5   Remove the bracket through-bolt and lift the alternator from the engine compartment.
6   Installation is the reverse of removal. After installation, check the drivebelt tension (Chapter 1).

7 Alternator – fault diagnosis and repair

1   Due to the special training and equipment necessary to test or service the alternator, it is recommended that the vehicle be taken to a dealer or other repair shop with the proper equipment if a fault is suspected.
2   The most obvious sign of a fault is the alternator warning lamp on the instrument panel lighting, particularly at low speeds. This indicates that the alternator is not charging. Other symptoms are a low battery charge, evidenced by dim headlights and the starter motor turning the engine over slowly.
3   The first check should always be of the drivebelt tension (Chapter 1) followed by making sure that all electrical connections are secure and free of dirt and corrosion.
4   If the drivebelt tension, electrical connections and battery condition are good, an internal fault in the alternator or internal voltage regulator is indicated.
5   Due to the complexity of this model and special tools and techniques required to work on the alternator, repair should be left to a properly-equipped shop. If the alternator has considerable miles on it, a good alternative is to replace it with a rebuilt unit.

8 Alternator voltage regulator – general information

Alternator voltage output is controlled by a regulator which is an integral part of the alternator. Special equipment is necessary to check for faults. This should be left to your dealer or a qualified shop.

9 Starter motor system – general information

The starter motor system consists of a motor with solenoid engagement, the battery, starter switch, a starter inhibitor switch (on some models), the starter relay and the necessary wiring.

When the ignition switch is turned to the Start position the starter relay is energized through the starter control circuit. The relay then connects the battery to the starter motor.

10 Starter motor – testing on engine

1   If the starter motor fails to operate, then check the condition of the battery by turning on the headlights. If they glow brightly for several seconds, and then gradually dim, the battery is in a discharged condition.
2   If the headlights continue to glow brightly and it is obvious that the battery is in good condition, check the tightness of the battery leads and all cables relative to the starting system. If possible, check the wiring with a voltmeter or test light for breaks or short circuits.
3   Check that there is current at the relay when the ignition switch is operated. If there is, then the relay should be suspect.
4   If there is no current at the relay, then suspect the ignition switch. On models with automatic transaxle check the inhibitor switch.
5   Should the above checks prove negative then the starter motor brushes probably need replacement or at the worst there is an internal fault in the motor.

11 Starter motor – removal and installation

1   Disconnect the battery negative cable.
2   Identify each starter wire with numbered tape, etc., and then disconnect the wiring connectors from the starter motor.
3   Remove the starter motor retaining bolts and lift the motor from the engine compartment.
4   To install, place the starter motor in position, install the retaining bolts and tighten to specification.
5   Connect the wiring connectors to the starter motor and install the battery negative cable.

12 Starter motor solenoid – testing

1   Remove the starter motor from the vehicle (Section 11).
2   Disconnect the M terminal from the solenoid.

Pull-in test (Fig. 5.3)
3   Connect the battery power between the S and M terminal for *no more than 10 seconds*. The starter pinion should move outward indicating that the pull-in coil is operating. If it does not, replace the solenoid with a new one.

Hold-in test (Fig. 5.4)
4   With battery power to the S terminal and the body of the solenoid, the pinion should not retract. If the pinion does move inward, there is an open circuit and the solenoid should be replaced.

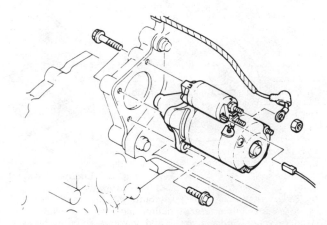

Fig. 5.2 Starter motor installation (Sec 11)

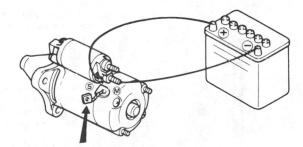

Fig. 5.3 Starter solenoid pull-in test (Sec 12)

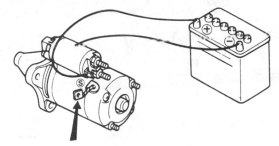

Fig. 5.4 Starter solenoid hold-in test (Sec 12)

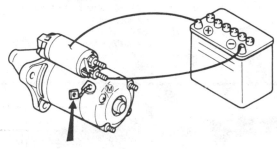

Fig. 5.5 Starter solenoid return test (Sec 12)

Return test (Fig. 5.5)
5   Connect battery power between the solenoid body and the M terminal and pull the pinion outward. When released, the pinion should return to its original position. If it does not, replace the solenoid.

13 Ignition system – general information

The ignition system consists of a pointless-type distributor, ignition coil, spark plug wires and spark plugs.

The distributor is mounted horizontally and driven directly by the camshaft. The distributor shaft turns the rotor which sends the high voltage through the high tension wires to the spark plugs. Centrifugal and vacuum advance mechanisms in the distributor vary the spark timing to conform to engine speed.

14 Distributor – removal and installation

1   Disconnect the negative battery cable and then the vacuum hose from the distributor.
2   Remove the distributor cap (photo).
3   Disconnect the electrical lead from the coil to the distributor.
4   Disconnect the two small wires which lead from the coil to the distributor.
5   Disconnect the ground lead from the distributor housing.
6   Mark the relationship of the distributor housing to the engine.
7   Mark the positions of the distributor and rotor.
8   Remove the hold-down bolts and washers and withdraw the distributor from the engine. Do not rotate the engine while the distributor is removed.

14.2 Release the distributor cap clip by pushing upward on the end

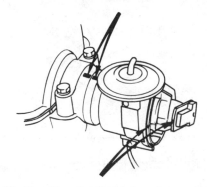

Fig. 5.6 Marking the distributor housing and rotor relationship (Sec 14)

9   To install, place the distributor in position with housing-to-engine and rotor-to-housing marks aligned.
10 Install the hold-down bolts and washers and tighten securely.
11 Install the electrical leads and vacuum hose and check the timing (Chapter 1).

15 Distributor – dismantling, inspection and reassembly

1   Remove the distributor (Section 14) and place it securely in a vise, using blocks of wood to protect the housing.
2   Lift off the rotor.
3   Remove the distributor cap seal.
4   Remove the rubber plug from the shaft.
5   Remove the retaining screw from the top of the shaft.
6   Use two screwdrivers to pry the retractor and locating pin off (photo).
7   Disengage the wiring from the distributor housing and unplug it from the coil pickup (photo).
8   Remove the two pickup coil retaining screws and lift the coil away.
9   Remove the pickup coil spacers.
10 Remove the vacuum advance diaphragm retaining screws.
11 Disengage diaphragm from the lug in the distributor housing and lift the assembly away (photo).
12 Remove the retractor breaker plate.
13 Mark on the distributor housing the position of the notch in the distributor plate prior to removal for ease of reassembly. Remove the plate.
14 Remove the pin retaining the drive tang to the distributor shaft (photo).
15 Remove the snap-ring retaining the shaft and lift the shaft from the housing.
16 Remove the clip and shims from the shaft (photo).

5

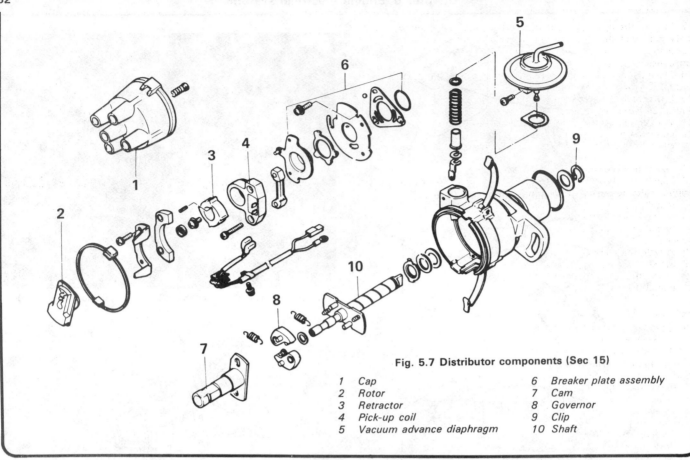

Fig. 5.7 Distributor components (Sec 15)

1	Cap	6	Breaker plate assembly
2	Rotor	7	Cam
3	Retractor	8	Governor
4	Pick-up coil	9	Clip
5	Vacuum advance diaphragm	10	Shaft

15.6 Lift the retractor off the shaft using two screwdrivers

15.7 Use needle-nose pliers to disconnect the wiring

15.11 Disengage the vacuum advance diaphragm from the housing and withdraw it from the housing

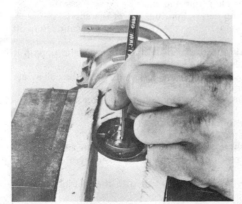

15.14 Use a punch and hammer to remove the drive tang retaining pin

15.16 Slide the shims off the distributor shaft

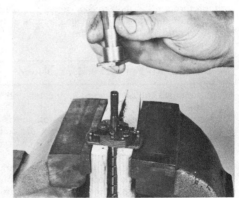

15.19 With the shaft securely in a vise protected by wood blocks, remove the retaining screw and lift the cam off

17 Inspect the distributor shaft for galling and check the weights to make sure that they are securely attached and move freely.
18 Inspect the inner and outer springs for breaks, stretching or looseness.
19 Place the shaft in the vise with the wood blocks, remove the screw and lift the cam off (photo).
20 Inspect the O-ring on the distributor housing for signs of deterioration or oil leaks.
21 With the drive tang upward, assemble the shaft components.
22 Lubricate the shaft with lithium-based grease prior to installation.
23 Hold the shaft in the inverted position and lower the housing over it.
24 Install the spacers, washers and snap-ring.
25 Install the drive tang and then tap the retaining pin into place using a suitable punch and hammer.
26 Install the distributor plate, using the mark made during disassembly and then install the vacuum diaphragm.
27 Install the retractor breaker plate followed by the pickup coil and spacers.
28 Plug in the pickup coil leads.
29 Install the retractor, retaining screw and rubber plug.
30 Install the rotor and distributor cap seal.
31 Install the distributor according to the instructions in Section 14.

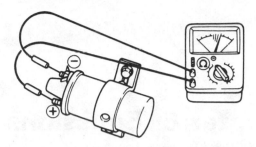

Fig. 5.8 Checking the ignition coil primary resistance (Sec 16)

16 Ignition coil and high tension wire – testing

1 Because of the high voltage involved, the ignition coil and high tension wire should be checked regularly to make sure they are in good condition to eliminate the possibility of weak spark.
2 Check the high tension wire with an ohmmeter to make sure that the value of resistance is within specification. Insert the ohmmeter probes at opposite ends of the wire and read the value of resistance on the dial.
3 The coil must be at operating temperature when being checked.
4 With the ohmmeter set on the XI scale, contact the positive (+) and negative (–) terminals on the coil with the probes. The dial should indicate continuity.
5 Set the ohmmeter on the X1000 scale and contact the high tension wire terminal with one probe and the positive (+) terminal with the other to check the secondary coil resistance. The resistance should be within specification.
6 Check the coil insulation resistance by contacting the negative (–) terminal with one ohmmeter probe and the casing with the other. Using a 500 megohm resistance range the reading should be within specification.

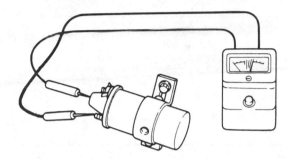

Fig. 5.9 Ignition coil secondary resistance check (Sec 16)

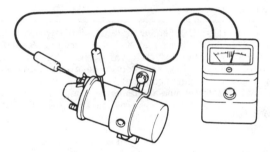

Fig. 5.10 Insulation resistance test (Sec 16)

5

Chapter 6 Emissions control systems

Refer to Chapter 13 for specifications and information applicable to later USA models

Contents

Specifications

Air injection vacuum delay valve pressure drop .... 11.8 in-Hg (300 mm-Hg) in 7.5 seconds

1 General information

In order to meet US Federal anti-pollution laws, vehicles are equipped with a variety of emissions control systems, depending on the model and the State in which it was intended for sale.

Since the emissions systems control so many of the engine's functions, driveability and fuel consumption as well as conformance to the law can be affected should any faults develop. Therefore, it is very important that the emissions systems be kept operating at peak efficiency.

This Chapter will describe all of the systems which may be installed in order to cover all models. An emissions label located under the hood contains information on the systems installed on your particular vehicle.

The catalytic converter is an integral feature of the emissions system and because it operates at high temperatures, certain precautions must be taken when operating a converter-equiped vehicle. After driving, do not park the vehicle over combustible materials such as dry grass as a fire could result. If it is necessary to push-start the vehicle, do so only when the converter is cold. A push-start will result in a certain amount of raw gasoline being pumped into the exhaust system which could ignite and cause abnormally high temperatures in the converter if it is already hot.

2 Air injection system – description and testing

1   This system injects fresh air into the exhaust stream so that carbon monoxide and hydrocarbon levels are reduced. The system consists of a belt-driven air pump and various solenoid, temperature and vacuum-actuated valves which control the air flow according to vehicle and engine speed. Replace any components which are suspect with new units.

Air pump

2   The air pump is obviously the most important part of the system and the first check should be of the drivebelt to make sure that it is not cracked or frayed and is properly tensioned (Chapter 1).
3   Inspect all hoses going to and from the pump for crimps, cracks and loose connections.
4   With the engine at operating temperature and the drivebelt properly tensioned, check for noise from the air pump itself.
5   Disconnect the pump outlet hose. Run the engine at approximately 1500 rpm and hold your hand at the disconnected hose. Air should be felt coming from the air pump.

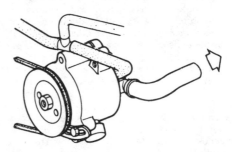

Fig. 6.1 Air injection pump test (Sec 2)

Check valve

6   Remove the check valve and blow air through the valve to make sure that the flow is only toward the large end.

Air control valve

7   The air control valve is located in the right front corner of the engine compartment. Disconnect the vacuum sensing tube from the valve (1 and 2 in Figure 6.2) and the air hose (A). With the engine running, air should flow from the port (a in the Figure). Reconnect the sensing tubes (1 and 2) and check that air blows from the ports (b and c). Disconnect the manifold vacuum (2) and with vacuum only going to the sensing tube (1) air should flow from the port (c).

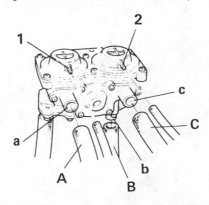

Fig. 6.2 Air control valve test (see text) (Sec 2)

8 Reconnect all hoses and tubes and check that at approximately 4000 rpm air flows from the port (a).
9 Remove the vacuum delay valve, connect a suitable vacuum gauge and with the engine at idle, apply vacuum to the valve (Fig. 6.3).
10 Remove the vacuum and check the gauge to make sure that the pressure drop is within specification. Reinstall the valve.

No. 1 water thermo valve

11 This valve is located on the bottom corner of the radiator. With the

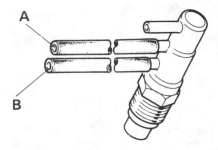

APPLY VACUUM HERE

Fig. 6.3 Vacuum delay valve test (Sec 2)

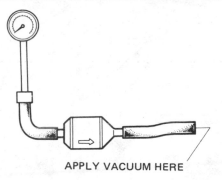

Fig. 6.4 No. 1 water thermo valve test (see text) (Sec 2)

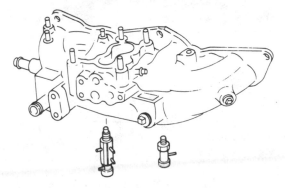

Fig. 6.5 No. 3 (left) and No. 2 thermo valve locations (Sec 2)

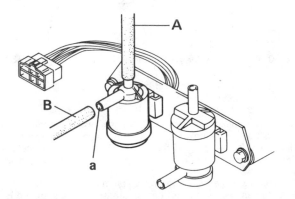

Fig. 6.6 No. 2 three-way solenoid valve test (see text) (Sec 2)

engine coolant temperature below 68°F (19°C), disconnect the sensing tubes from the vacuum delay valve and No. 2 three-way solenoid valve (A and B in Fig. 6.4).
12 With the engine at idle, connect the manifold vacuum to the sensing tube (B). Place your finger over the disconnected tube end and make sure that no vacuum can be felt.
13 With the engine at operating temperature 132°F (55°C), repeat the test. Vacuum should now be felt at the hose end (A in Fig. 6.4).

No. 2 thermo control valve

14 No. 2 thermo control valve is located in the intake manifold (Fig. 6.5). Disconnect the vacuum sensing tube leading from the valve to the air control valve at the air control valve (photo). With the engine at idle, place your finger over the end of the tube. No vacuum should be felt. After warming up the engine to operating temperature, repeat the test. Vacuum should now be felt at the tube.

No. 2 three-way solenoid valve

15 The No. 2 three-way solenoid valve is located on the firewall directly behind the carburetor and is adjacent to the deceleration control throttle positioner.
16 Disconnect the electrical connector and vacuum sensing tubes (A and B in Fig. 6.6).
17 Connect a tube to the top port of the valve.

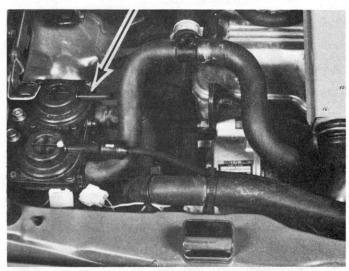

2.13 No. 2 thermo valve hose connection at the air control valve (arrow)

2.17 Air blown into the upper tube should exit through the lower port

6

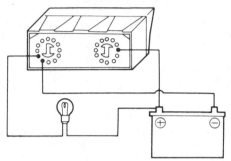

Fig. 6.7 Connector to No. 1 and No. 2 solenoid valves
(Secs 2 and 3)

Fig. 6.8 Vehicle speed switch test (Sec 2)

18 Air blown into the top port of the valve should be felt coming from
the side port (photo).
19 Apply battery power to the electrical connector terminal YB while
grounding terminal LgY with a wire (Fig. 6.7).
20 Air blown into the side port (B in the Figure) should now be
diverted out through the valve's bottom at the air filter. Replace the
valve if it fails any of the tests.

Vehicle speed switch
21 The vehicle speed switch is part of the speedometer assembly and
is accessible after the speedometer is removed (Chapter 12).
22 Connect a test lamp as shown in Figure 6.8.
23 The switch is good if the speedometer is registering less than 63
mph (100 kph) and the test light does not light.

---

3 Deceleration control system – description and testing

1 During deceleration, this system reduces increased emissions
caused by the tendency of the engine to draw in excessive fuel
because of the high manifold vacuum present.

Anti-afterburn valve
2 With the engine at idle, close the valve's intake port. The engine
speed should not change.
3 Place your hand near the bottom of the valve and increase and
then rapidly decrease engine speed. You should feel air being sucked
into the valve intake port for a period of 1 to 2 seconds (Fig. 6.9).

Throttle positioner servo diaphragm
4 Warm the engine to normal operating temperature, check that it
idles properly and turn it off.
5 Disconnect the vacuum tube from the top of the positioner and
connect a vacuum source from the engine (photo).
6 Install a tachometer, start the engine and run it at approximately
2000 rpm and then release the throttle. The engine speed should be
between 1100 and 1300 rpm. If it is not, turn the adjusting screw until
the engine speed is within specifications.
7 Reconnect the vacuum hose and remove the tachometer.

No. 1 three-way solenoid valve
8 This valve is located adjacent to the No. 2 three-way solenoid
valve of the air injection system (Section 2).
9 Disconnect the vacuum tubes from the valve (a and c in Fig. 6.10).
10 Unplug the electrical connector.
11 Blow air through the valve at the top port (c). The air should be felt
coming out at the bottom port (b).
12 Apply power from the battery to connector terminal YB while
grounding terminal LgR (Fig. 6.7).
13 Air blown through the top port (c) should now exit through the air
filter at the bottom.

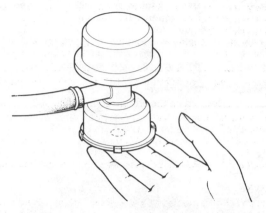

Fig. 6.9 Checking the anti-afterburn valve (Sec 3)

3.5 Throttle positioner servo diaphragm vacuum sensing tube

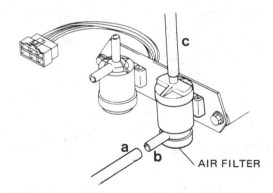

Fig. 6.10 No. 1 three-way solenoid valve test (see text) (Sec 3)

14 Reconnect the connector and hoses.

Engine speed unit
15 The engine speed unit controls idle speed in conjunction with the
throttle positioner. Failure of this unit will cause erratic idling.
16 The unit is located behind the kick panel to the left of the driver's
feet. It will be necessary to remove the panel and the attaching screws
to gain access.
17 Connect a voltmeter to the unit connector.
18 Start the engine, run it up to approximately 3000 rpm and record
the speed at which current no longer flows. This should be around
2100 rpm.

19 Slowly decrease the engine speed from 2000 rpm and record the speed at which the current begins flowing again. This should be approximately 1500 rpm.
20 Replace the switch with a new unit if it fails either test.

4 Exhaust gas recirculation (EGR) system – description and testing

1 This system reduces oxides of nitrogen (Nox) in the exhaust by recirculating a small amount of exhaust gas back through the combustion cycle. Common problems associated with malfunctioning of the EGR system are: rough idling or stalling at idle, rough engine performance during light acceleration and stalling on deceleration.

EGR valve
2 With the engine running at idle, disconnect the vacuum tube from the EGR valve. Use either a vacuum pump or manifold vacuum to apply suction to the EGR valve port (Fig. 6.11).

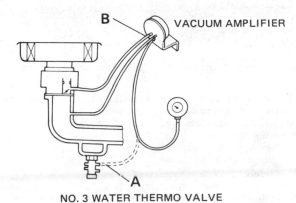

Fig. 6.11 EGR valve test (Sec 4)

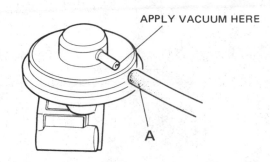

Fig. 6.12 EGR system vacuum amplifier test (see text) (Sec 4)

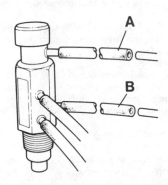

Fig. 6.13 EGR No. 3 water thermo valve test (see text) (Sec 4)

3 The engine should run roughly or stop. If it does not, replace the valve with a new one.

Vacuum amplifier
4 Disconnect the vacuum tube from the No. 3 water thermo valve and connect a vacuum gauge (Fig. 6.12).
5 With the engine idling, disconnect the vacuum tube (B in Fig. 6.12). The vacuum gauge should read 2.0 ± 0.2 in-Hg (50 ± 5 mm-Hg).
6 Reconnect the vacuum (B) and increase engine speed to 3500 rpm. The gauge should now read approximately 3.54 in-hg (90 mm-hg).

No. 3 water thermo valve
7 This valve is threaded into the underside of the intake manifold and can be located by tracing one of the vacuum tubes from the evaporative emissions canister.
8 Disconnect vacuum tubes leading from the emissions canister and vacuum amplifier at the No. 3 water thermo valve (A and B in Fig. 6.13).
9 Run the engine at 2000 rpm and check that no vacuum is present by placing your finger over the ends of the tubes.
10 Warm the engine up to operating temperature. Vacuum should now be felt at the ends of the disconnected tubes of the thermo valve.

5 Slow cut fuel system – description and testing

1 This system controls fuel supply over the entire range of driving conditions so that the exhaust emissions are within limits and the catalytic converters are not overheated and damaged.

Neutral switch
2 The Neutral switch is located in the transaxle case and is accessible from underneath by raising the vehicle and supporting it securely. Trace the wire from the Neutral switch to the connector.
3 Disconnect the Neutral switch connector.
4 On manual transaxle equipped vehicles, use an ohmmeter to test the switch for continuity by inserting the probes into the connector terminals. **Caution:** *Before attempting the following, make sure the parking brake is firmly set and the wheels sufficiently chocked to prevent movement of the car. Beware of hot exhaust components.*
5 On automatic transaxle models, start the engine and run it at idle until it is at operating temperature. With the brakes securely applied, test the switch for continuity with an ohmmeter with the engine idling and the shift lever in Neutral.

Accelerator switch
6 Unplug the accelerator switch connector and check for continuity with an ohmmeter (Fig. 6.15).
7 With the engine at operating temperature, check that the idle speed is correct (Chapter 4).
8 Back the accelerator switch adjusting screw off.
9 Tighten the screw gradually until you hear a clicking sound, indicating that the switch is turned on. Further tighten the screw $1\frac{1}{4}$ to $1\frac{1}{2}$ turns.

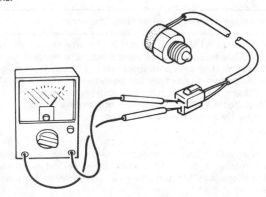

Fig. 6.14 Testing the Neutral switch for continuity (Sec 5)

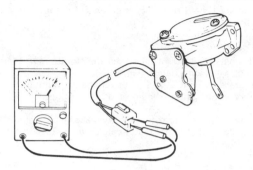

Fig. 6.15 Checking the accelerator switch connector for continuity (Sec 5)

Clutch switch

10 The clutch switch is located at the top of the clutch arm and sends a signal to the slow cut system which controls primary fuel flow under certain conditions.
11 Remove the ventilator duct to gain access to the switch.
12 Unplug the switch and connect the terminals to the contacts of a volt/ohmmeter which is set at R x 100.
13 With the clutch pedal depressed, the meter should indicate that the switch has continuity.

Altitude compensator

14 The compensator is operated by atmospheric pressure to adjust for altitude changes.
15 Mark and disconnect all of the hoses from the compensator and install a hose to the bottom port.
16 Air blown into the hose should not exit from the compensator ports at low altitude (below 1700 feet) but should exit at high altitude (above 1700 feet).

6 Positive crankcase ventilation (PCV) – description and testing

1 The PCV system reduces hydrocarbon emissions by recirculating fresh air through the crankcase to pick up blow-by gases which are then re-routed through the carburetor to be returned by the engine. The PCV system should be checked regularly as carbon and residue deposited by blow-by gases will eventually clog the PCV valve and/or system hoses. When the flow of the PCV system is reduced or stopped, common symptoms are rough idling or reduced engine speed at idle.

PCV valve

2 Remove the valve (Chapter 1).
3 To test the valve, blow air through it from the larger diameter end and verify that the air exits at the opposite end (A to B in Fig. 6.16).
4 Air blown in the opposite direction should now flow through the valve.

7 Evaporative emissions system – description and testing

1 This complicated looking system is actually one of the simplest and most trouble-free portions of the emissions network. Basically this is a closed fuel system which reroutes wasted fuel back to the gas tank and stores fuel vapors until they can be drawn into the engine instead of venting them to the atmosphere. Symptoms of malfunctions in the emissions systems are the strong odor of gasoline fumes and starving of the engine for fuel during acceleration.

Canister

2 The charcoal canister is located in the engine compartment below the brake master cylinder. It should be inspected periodically for charcoal leakage and for loose internal components by tapping the canister.

Air vent solenoid valve

3 Disconnect the vent hose at the carburetor.

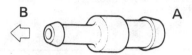

Fig. 6.16 PCV valve air flow (Sec 6)

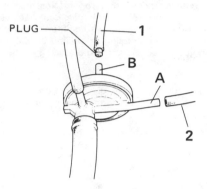

Fig. 6.17 Evaporative system No. 1 purge control valve test (1981 models) (Sec 7)

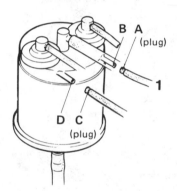

Fig. 6.18 No. 1 and No. 2 purge control valve test (see text) (Sec 7)

4 The valve can be tested by slowly blowing air through the vent hose. The air should pass through the valve.
5 With the ignition switch on, air blown through the hose should not pass through the valve.

No. 1 purge control valve
1981 models
6 Disconnect the vacuum sensing tube and evaporative hose at the purge control valve (1 and 2 in Fig. 6.17).
7 Plug the sensing tube (1).
8 Connect a rubber tube to the evaporative port (A), start the engine and run it up to 2000 rpm. Blow air at low pressure into the rubber tube and check to make sure that the air does not pass through the valve.
9 Remove the plug from the sensing tube (1) and reconnect it to the valve. Air blown into the tube should pass through the purge control valve if it is operating properly.
1982 models (refer to Fig. 6.18)
10 Disconnect and plug hose A and blow air into port B. If the valve is operating properly, the air will not flow through the valve.
11 With the engine running at 1500 rpm, blow air into port B. The air should flow through the valve.

No. 2 purge control valve
1981 models
12 Disconnect the hose at the No. 2 purge control valve and the hose leading from the No. 1 purge control valve at the No. 1 valve (1 and 2 in Fig. 6.19).
13 Blow low pressure air into the No. 2 valve through the hose leading from the No. 1 valve (2 in the Figure).

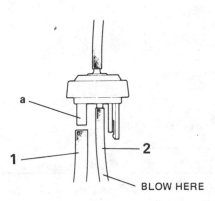

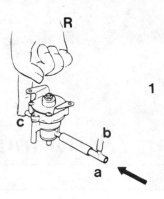

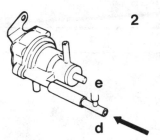

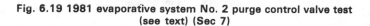

Fig. 6.19 1981 evaporative system No. 2 purge control valve test
(see text) (Sec 7)

14 If the valve is operating properly, no air will be felt at the port (a
in the Figure).
15 Run the engine at 1500 rpm and blow air into the hose leading
from the No. 1 valve to the No. 2 valve. Air should now be felt exiting
at the port (a).
1982 models (refer to Fig. 6.18)
16 Disconnect and plug hose C. Air blown into port D should not flow
through the valve.
17 Start the engine, run it up to 1500 rpm and then blow air into port
D. The air should now flow through the valve.

Check and cut valve

18 The check and cut valve is located adjacent to the fuel tank and
regulates the flow of fumes between the tank and the charcoal
canister.
19 Mark the location of the valve and remove it by disconnecting the
hoses, removing the retaining bolt and disengaging it from the
alignment tang.
20 Hold the valve in the vertical position, place your finger over port
c and blow into port a. Air should be felt at port b. See Fig. 6.20.
21 With the valve in the horizontal position, blow into port d and feel
for air escaping at port e.
22 If the valve fails any of the tests, replace it with a new one.

Fig. 6.20 Check and cut valve test (Sec 7)

1   *Vertical test*   2   *Horizontal test*

8 Catalytic converter – general information

These models use two catalytic converters, one directly adjacent
to the exhaust manifold and one behind the transaxle. The converter
consists of a ceramic honeycomb-like core housed in a stainless steel
pipe. The core is coated with a platinum and paladium catalyst which
converts unburned carbon monoxide and hydrocarbons into carbon
dioxide and water by chemical reaction.
No special maintenance of the converter is required, but it can be
damaged by the use of leaded fuels, engine misfire, excessive richness
of the carburetor mixture, incorrect operation of the air injection
system or running out of gasoline.

6

Chapter 7A Manual transaxle

Contents

Specifications

Transaxle type	4- or 5-speed with Reverse, synchromesh in all forward gears	
Transaxle oil capacity	3.4 US qts (3.2 liters)	
Transaxle oil type		
1981	Consult dealer for latest recommendations	
1982	80 to 90 wt SAE oil	

	in	mm
Lever-to-reverse idler clearance	0.004 to 0.013	0.1 to 0.32
Service limit	0.020	0.5
Shift fork-to-clutch sleeve clearance	0.008 to 0.018	0.2 to 0.46
Service limit	0.020	0.5
Gear synchronizer ring-to-gear clearance	0.059	1.5
Service limit	0.021	0.8
Thrust clearances		
First gear	0.006 to 0.015	0.14 to 0.37
Second gear	0.010 to 0.016	0.245 to 0.405
Third gear	0.004 to 0.015	0.095 to 0.38
Fourth gear	0.004 to 0.016	0.095 to 0.4
Fifth gear	0.006 to 0.011	0.15 to 0.287
Service limit (all)	0.020	0.5
Primary shaft gear bearing preload	3.5 to 6.1 in-lb	4.0 to 7.0 cm-kg
Differential side bearing preload	4 to 7 in-lb	0.5 to 0.76 Nm
Side gear and pinion gear backlash	0.004	0.1

Torque specifications	Ft-lb	Nm
Gate lock bolt	9 to 12	12 to 16
Transaxle case bolts	13 to 19	18 to 26
Rear cover	6 to 8	8 to 11
Gear shaft lock nuts	94 to 152	130 to 210
Guide bolt	7 to 10	9 to 14
Reverse idle shaft lock bolt	23 to 16	21 to 31
Ring gear bolts	51 to 61	70 to 85
Front crossmember-to-chassis nuts	44 to 63	61 to 87
Front and rear crossmember-to-engine mount nuts	23 to 34	43 to 47
Rear crossmember-to-chassis bolt	47 to 66	85 to 91

1 General information

All manual transmission models are equipped with a 4- or 5-speed transaxle which incorporates the differential assembly and is mounted in-line with the engine. Drive from the engine passes through the transaxle gears and then to the differential gears which drive the axles. All forward gears are synchromesh and the floor-mounted shift mechanism operates the transaxle internal shift assembly through a shift control rod.

2 Shift lever assembly – removal and installation

1   Raise the vehicle, support it securely and remove the shift control lever-to-rod bolt and nut.
2   Inside the passenger compartment, remove the shift lever knob and console cover (if equipped).
3   Use a screwdriver to disengage and remove the spring retaining the shift lever in the socket.
4   Lift the shift lever away and remove it from the vehicle.
5   To install, insert the shift lever into the socket and install the retaining spring.
6   Install the shift knob and boot or console cover.
7   From underneath the vehicle, install the shift control rod to the lever, making sure the lever is facing in the proper direction. Install the retaining nut and bolt.
8   Lower the vehicle and check the shifting mechanism for proper operation.

3 Manual transaxle – removal and installation

1   Raise the vehicle, support it securely and remove the splash shields and front wheels.
2   Remove the speedometer drive gear and drain the transaxle lubricant (Chapter 1).
3   Remove the lower balljoints (Chapter 11).
4   Remove the drive axles.
5   Unbolt the clutch cable bracket and remove it.
6   Disconnect the clutch cable at the lever.
7   Remove the heater water pipe bracket from the transaxle.
8   Bend the wiring harness clips back and move the harness out of the way.
9   Unplug the electrical connectors adjacent to the carbon canister and cable harness and disconnect the backup lamp.
10 Remove the starter (Chapter 5).
11 Loosen the two upper mounting bolts on the bellhousing.
12 Unbolt the shift rods and move them out of the way.
13 Remove the three clutch cover bolts located at 2:30, 5 and 7 O'clock (when viewed from the right side).
14 Loosen the two upper and lower bellhousing bolts on the transaxle side.
15 Remove the nuts from the front and rear engine mount insulators.
16 Remove the bolt and three nuts from the crossmember, taking care not to let the insulator fall. Disengage the rear of the crossmember from the catalytic converter support.
17 Support the engine with a sturdy jack, wood blocks, etc. The engine must remain supported while the transaxle is out of place.
18 Unbolt and remove the transaxle-to-chassis mount.
19 With the help of an assistant (it's quite heavy), lower the transaxle and remove it from the vehicle.
20 To install, place the transaxle in position and install the mounting bolts, tightening to specification.
21 Install the crossmember and front and rear engine mount insulators.
22 Install the shift rods.
23 Install the starter.
24 Reinstall any electrical connectors which were disconnected during removal.
25 Install the heater water pipe bracket to the transaxle.
26 Install the clutch cable and bracket.
27 Install the drive axles and lower balljoints (Chapters 8 and 11).
28 Refill the transaxle with the specified lubricant and install the speedometer drive gear.
29 Install the splash shield and the front wheels.
30 Check the gearshift for proper operation.
31 Lower the vehicle.

4 Manual transaxle – dismantling

1   Unbolt and remove the rear cover (5-speed).
2   Use a suitable punch to drive the lock nut collar back from the groove on each of the lock nuts (5-speed).
3   Carefully lock the gear teeth with a screwdriver or similar tool and remove the lock nuts (5-speed) (photos).

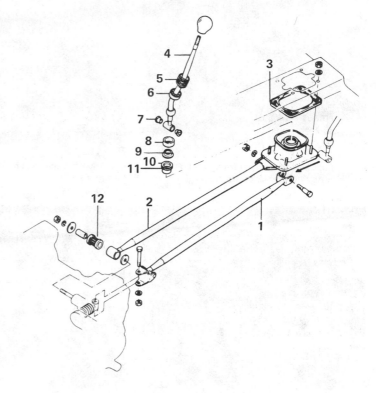

Fig. 7.1 Manual shift lever components (Secs 2 and 3)

1	Shift control rod	7 Bushing
2	Extension bar and bracket assembly	8 Lower ball sheet
3	Insulator	9 Plate
4	Gear shift lever	10 Holder
5	Spring	11 Boot
6	Upper ball sheet	12 Bushing

4.3a Insert a screwdriver into the gear teeth to lock the shafts

7A

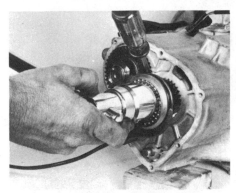

4.3b Make sure the screwdriver doesn't slip while removing the lock nuts

4.4 Drive out the shift fork retaining pin with a hammer and punch

4.6 Remove the lock bolt

4.7 Remove the guide bolt from the case

4.10a Use two screwdrivers to carefully separate the transaxle case halves

4.10b Carefully lift the case half off the shafts

4.11 Use a scraper to remove the 5th-gear oil passage

4.13 Lift out the reverse idle shaft and remove the gear

4.14 Removing the 5th gear and reverse lock plate bolt

4   Remove the 5th-gear shift fork retaining pin (5-speed) (photo).
5   Remove the 5th-gear stop plate, synchro ring, gear sleeve and gear (5-speed).
6   Remove the lock bolt from the transaxle case (photo).
7   Remove the guide bolt from the case (photo).
8   Unscrew the backup light connector from the case.
9   Mark the location of the wiring clamp on the case and remove the transaxle case bolts.
10   Carefully separate the two halves of the case (photos).
11   Remove the 5th-gear oil passage (5-speed) (photo).
12   Remove the magnet from the case.
13   Remove the reverse idle shaft and gear (photo).
14   Remove the lock bolt from the 5th gear and reverse lock plate (photo).
15   On 4-speed models, remove the shift gate and reverse lever as a unit, with the shift in Neutral.
16   Remove the 5th gear and reverse rod (5-speed) (photos).
17   Remove the 5th- and reverse gear shift gate (5-speed).

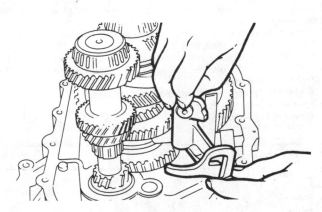

Fig. 7.2 4-speed shift gate and lever removal (Sec 4)

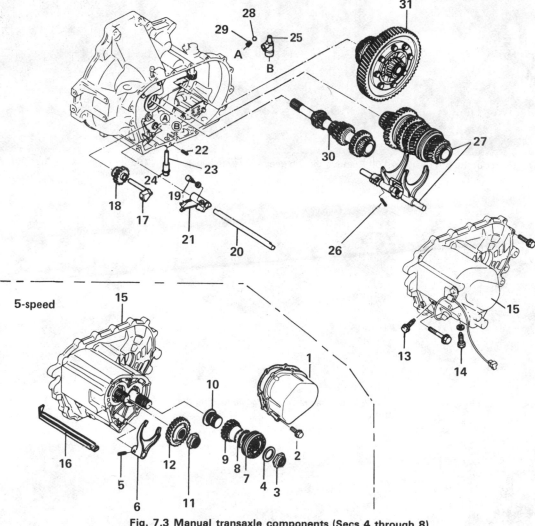

Fig. 7.3 Manual transaxle components (Secs 4 through 8)

1	Rear cover (5-speed)	8	Synchronizer ring (5-speed)
2	Rear cover bolt (5-speed)	9	5th gear (5-speed)
3	Lock nut (5-speed)	10	Gear sleeve (5-speed)
4	Stop plate (5-speed)	11	Lock nut (5-speed)
5	Spring pin (5-speed)	12	Primary gear (5-speed)
6	Shift fork (5-speed)	13	Lock bolt (5-speed)
7	Clutch hub assembly (5-speed)	14	Guide bolt (5-speed)
		15	Transaxle case

16	Oil passage (5-speed)	24	O-ring
17	Reverse idle shaft	25	Crank lever assembly
18	Reverse idle gear	26	Spring pin
19	Lock bolt	27	Secondary gearshaft and shift fork assembly
20	5th and reverse shift rod (5-speed)	28	Steel ball
21	Gate	29	Spring
22	Spring pin	30	Primary gearshaft assembly
23	Crank lever shaft	31	Differential assembly

7A

18 Drive out the crank lever retaining pin and remove the pin (5-speed) (photos).

19 Remove the crank lever assembly while moving the shift rod to assist in releasing it (5-speed) (photo).

20 Make sure the interlock sleeve end surface is flush with the control lever end surface. Turn the control rod counterclockwise as far as it will go (photo).

21 Pull up on the control rod. It may be necessary to pry upward on the interlock ball.

22 Drive out the retaining pin from the control rod (photo).

23 Place the transaxle in 4th gear by pulling upward on the upper shift fork (photo).

24 Gently pull the shift rod out of the housing. When the rod is free of the housing, the steel ball will fall from the reverse lever shaft.

25 Lift the secondary gearshaft and shift fork assembly from the transaxle case (photo).

26 Remove the primary gear assembly.

27 Remove the differential assembly (photo).

28 Remove the Neutral switch.

29 Remove the input shaft oil seals and bearing races.

30 Remove the funnel from the transaxle case.

31 Unbolt and remove the shifter guide plate and arm.

32 Drive out the shift arm retaining pin, making sure the selector lever is centered.

33 Remove the shift shaft boot from the transaxle housing and withdraw the shaft (photo).

34 Remove the reverse gate spring, bushing and selector.

35 Carefully drive out the bearing races (photo).

36 Remove the shift shaft seal.

37 Remove the axle seals by tapping them out with a hammer and suitable punch, working around their circumference.

38 Remove the differential bearing race.

39 Remove the air bleed baffle (two bolts).

40 Remove the pin retaining the lever shaft.

41 Remove the axle oil seal.

42 Lift the shift fork away from the secondary gear shaft with the control lever lug aligned with the notch in the shifter fork and remove the shaft assembly.

43 Remove the primary shaft assembly.

4.16a Use a screwdriver to lift out the 5th gear and reverse rod

4.16b Remove the 5th gear and reverse lock plate

4.18a Use a punch to drive out the crank lever retaining pin

4.18b Withdraw the crank lever pin

4.19 Lift out the crank lever while moving the shifter

4.20 Rotate the control rod counterclockwise

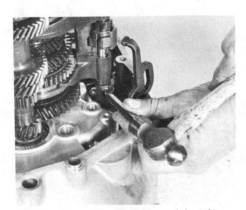
4.22 Use a punch to drive the retaining pin from the control end of the rod

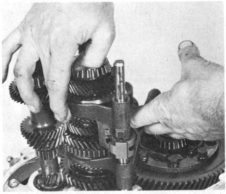
4.23 Shift into 4th gear by pulling the shift fork upward

4.25 Lift the secondary gearshaft assembly carefully upward to remove

4.27 Lift the differential assembly from the transaxle case

4.33 Withdrawing the boot and shift shaft

4.35 Driving the bearing race out by tapping around the circumference with a punch and hammer

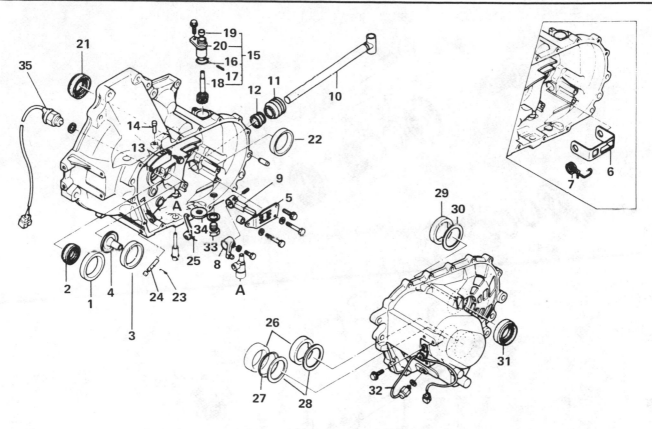

Fig. 7.4 Manual transaxle case and shift components (Secs 4 and 8)

1 Bearing outer race	10 Shift rod	18 Speedometer driven gear	27 Diaphragm spring
2 Oil seal	11 Boot	19 Oil seal	28 Adjusting shim
3 Bearing outer race	12 Oil seal	20 Speedometer gear case	29 Bearing outer race
4 Funnel	13 Breather cover	21 Oil seal	30 Adjusting shim
5 Guide plate	14 Breather	22 Bearing outer race	31 Oil seal
6 Reverse gate	15 Speedometer gear	23 Spring pin	32 Backup light switch
7 Spring	assembly	24 Reverse lever shaft	33 Drain plug
8 Shift arm	16 O-ring	25 Reverse lever	34 Magnet
9 Selector	17 Spring pin	26 Bearing outer race	35 Neutral switch

5 Secondary gearshaft assembly – inspection and overhaul

1 Remove the secondary gearshaft from the transaxle (Section 4).
2 Place the shaft in a vise, using two blocks of wood to protect it from damage. Check the gear thrust clearances with a feeler gauge and check them against specifications (photo).
3 Use a suitable puller to remove the roller bearing from the end of the shaft and lift off 4th gear.
4 Remove the synchronizer ring.
5 Remove the 3rd and 4th gear clutch hub assembly retaining rings.
6 Carefully pry the 3rd and 4th gear clutch hub assembly off the shaft.
7 Remove the 3rd gear synchronizer ring.
8 Remove the 3rd gear assembly.
9 Remove the thrust washer retaining ring, followed by the thrust washers.
10 Remove the 2nd gear.
11 Remove the synchronizer ring.
12 Remove the 1st gear retaining ring.
13 Special tools are required to press off the 1st gear and the 1st and 2nd gear synchronizer assembly. This operation will have to be performed by your dealer or a properly-equipped shop.
14 Remove the bearing with a suitable puller.
15 Inspect the gears for worn or damaged synchro cones, hub sleeve wear, worn or damaged teeth or worn sliding surfaces.

5.2 Checking gear thrust clearances

7A

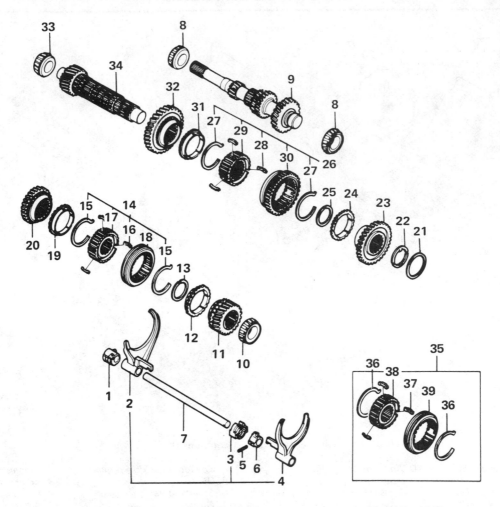

Fig. 7.5 Primary and secondary gearshaft components (Secs 5 and 6)

1	Shift fork control end	11	4th gear
2	1st and second gear shift fork	12	Synchronizer ring
		13	Retaining ring
3	Interlock sleeve	14	3rd and 4th gear clutch hub assembly
4	3rd and 4th gear shift fork		
5	Spring pin	15	Synchronizer spring
6	Control lever	16	Synchronizer key
7	Control rod	17	Clutch hub
8	Bearing inner race	18	Clutch hub sleeve
9	Primary gearshaft	19	Synchronizer ring
10	Bearing inner race	20	3rd gear

21	Ring	30	Reverse gear clutch hub sleeve
22	Thrust washer		
23	2nd gear	31	Synchronizer ring
24	Synchronizer ring	33	Inner bearing race
25	Retaining ring	34	Secondary shaft gear
26	1st and 2nd gear clutch hub assembly	35	Clutch hub assembly
		36	5th-gear synchronizer spring
27	Synchronizer spring		
28	Synchronizer key	37	Synchronizer key
29	Clutch hub	38	Clutch hub
		39	Clutch hub sleeve

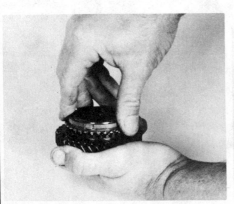

5.17 Checking the synchro ring for free movement

5.21 Checking the clutch hub and shifter clearance

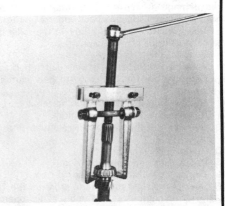

6.2 Removing the primary shaft bearing

16 Check the secondary shaft for worn or damaged sliding surfaces, splines or teeth and clogged oil passages.
17 Check the synchro rings by pressing them into position and then rotating them to make sure they slide smoothly. Measure the clearance with a feeler gauge and compare to the specifications (photo).
18 Inspect the clutch hub assembly and shifter for grooves, galling or wear.
19 Disassemble the synchronizer hub and inspect the splines and surfaces for wear and the springs to make sure they are not bent or losing tension.
20 Reassemble the hub with the raised portion of the key facing the outer edge of the hub. When installing the spring, make sure that it is in the center indentation of the keys.
21 Check the clutch hub-to-shifter clearance with a feeler gauge (photo).
22 Replace any worn or damaged components with new ones.
23 Install the bearing on the gear end of the shaft.
24 Invert the shaft and install 1st gear and the 1st gear synchro ring. This synchro ring differs from the others in that it is missing three teeth.
25 Install the 1st- and 2nd-gear clutch hub assembly with the shift fork groove downward.
26 Install the 1st- and 2nd-gear assembly snap-rings.
27 Install the synchro ring into the hub, aligning the groove with the keys in the hub.
28 Install 2nd gear.
29 Install the two halves of the thrust washer, aligning the tang with the hole in the shaft.
30 Install the thrust washer retaining rings.
31 Install 3rd gear and the 3rd-gear synchro ring.
32 Install the 3rd/4th-gear synchro hub with the grooved surfaces downward and the keys aligned. It may be necessary to have these installed using a press.
33 Install the 3rd/4th-gear retaining ring.
34 Install the 4th-gear synchro ring, followed by 4th gear.
35 To install the bearing it will be necessary to have it pressed onto the shaft.

6 Primary gearshaft assembly – inspection and overhaul

1 Remove the assembly and place it securely in a vise with wood blocks to protect the shaft.
2 Use a suitable puller to remove the bearings from both ends of the shaft (photo).
3 Inspect the shaft and gears for worn or damaged splines, sliding surfaces or damaged teeth.
4 Inspect the bearings for wear, looseness, galling or pitting of the rollers.
5 Replace any worn components with new ones.
6 Press the bearings onto the shaft and reinstall the assembly in the transaxle.

7 Differential – inspection and overhaul

1 Remove the differential from the transaxle (Section 4) and place it in a vise, protected by blocks of wood.
2 Unbolt the ring gear from the gear case and remove the gear.
3 Remove the pinion shaft lock pin by driving it out from the opposite side of the gear case.
4 Remove the pinion shaft, gears and thrust washers.
5 Remove the gear case bearing inner race using a suitable press and bearing removal tool.
6 Remove the remaining bearing with a suitable puller.
7 Remove the speedometer drive gear.
8 Inspect the gears and sliding surfaces for wear, cracks and galling.
9 Check the side and pinion gear assembly. This is done with the drive axles inserted in the differential assembly. With the axles supported on V-blocks, measure the backlash of both of the pinion gears by manually moving them the full distance of free travel. If backlash exceeds specification, obtain a suitable thrust washer of the proper thickness from your dealer and install it between the differential case and side gears. The thrust washers should be of similar thickness.
10 Prior to assembly, wash each part thoroughly in a suitable solvent.

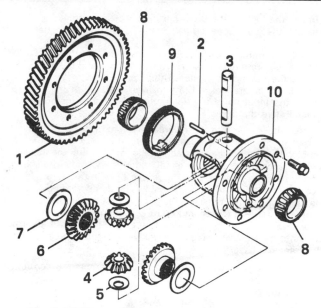

Fig. 7.6 Differential components (Secs 4, 7 and 8)

1	Ring gear	6	Side gear
2	Retaining pin	7	Thrustwasher
3	Pinion shaft	8	Side bearing inner race
4	Pinion gear	9	Speedometer drive gear
5	Thrustwasher	10	Differential gear case

11 During reassembly, apply clean transmission fluid to all sliding surfaces and replace any removed spring-pins with new ones.
12 Install the speedometer drive gear.
13 Install the side bearings using the approved special tool and hydraulic press or take the assembly to your dealer or a suitably equipped shop to have this done.
14 Install the pinion and side gears using the appropriate thrust washers.
15 Install the pinion pin, making sure the lock pin hole is aligned with the hole in the gear case.
16 Install the pinion shaft lock.
17 Stake the lock pin in place with a hammer and suitable drift or chisel, working from the ring gear side.
18 Install the ring gear and tighten the bolts to specification.
19 Install the differential to the transaxle.

8 Manual transaxle – reassembly

1 Install the drain plug.
2 Install the secondary shaft outer bearing race by placing it in position with its shim. Tap lightly around the circumference with a suitable drift punch and a hammer until the race is seated.
3 Install the differential bearing race and shims, matching the numbers on the shims with those on the removed items.
4 Install the primary shaft shim spring with the raised portion upward and the shim.
5 Install the reverse lever shaft and spring.
6 Install the oil deflector.
7 Install the shift rod oil seal and partially insert the shift rod.
8 Insert the shift rod and install the shifter, making sure the spring-pin is in the proper position.
9 Place the selector rod tip thru the right hole of the reverse gate and lower the assembly into position so that the shift rod can be inserted.
10 Place the reverse gate spring in position and insert the reverse shift rod through the spring on the end of the gate.
11 Position the shift arm onto the end of the shift rod.
12 Secure the selector to the shift rod with the spring pin.
13 Install the selector guide plate with the three bolts. The bolts are all dissimilar and the one without a washer goes on the upper right corner. The reverse gate spring must be installed around the rear bolt spacer.

7A

14 Install the lock bolt and washer onto the shift arm.

15 Install the gear lube funnel, followed by the secondary shaft bearing race.

16 Install the primary shaft seal with the open end upward.

17 Install the primary shaft bearing into the case and tap it into place.

18 Place the magnet in its slot in the case.

19 Install the differential to the transaxle case.

20 Lube the inner lip of the differential seal with transmission fluid and install it to the case.

21 Install the spring into the reverse lever shaft.

22 Position the shift fork assembly onto the secondary shaft gear assembly. Use care when installing and make sure the gears are properly meshed with the differential and primary shaft. The shift fork assembly must be inserted into the proper boss in the transaxle case.

23 Carefully pull the shift fork assembly slightly upward and outward of its boss by tilting the secondary gearshaft assembly. Slide the control up as far as it will go and rotate it 90 degrees from the Neutral position. Place the ball in the end of the reverse lever shaft and rotate the rod into the Neutral position. Carefully reinsert the rod into its boss in the transaxle case.

24 Install the spring pin into the shift fork assembly rod control end and tap it into place.

25 Install the crank lever assembly which connects the shift arm to the shift fork assembly rod control end.

26 Install a new o-ring on the crank lever shaft. Lubricate and install the crank lever and secure it with the spring retaining pin.

27 Place the reverse gate into position and slide the 5th gear and reverse rod into position with the dimple on the rod facing out. The hole in the shift rod must be aligned with the reverse gate.

28 Install the reverse idler gear and shaft. Place the gear into position, insert the shaft with the hole in the shaft in alignment with the rib on the transaxle case.

29 Place the oil passage in position on the transaxle case, using sealant to hold it in place (5-speed only).

30 Install the transaxle case to the differential half, carefully inserting it over the primary and secondary gearshafts. It may be necessary to align the magnet with the slot in the upper case half.

31 Install the transaxle case retaining bolts and tighten them to specification in a criss-cross pattern (5-speed).

32 Install the primary shift rod lock bolt and seal washer. It may be necessary to lift up on the secondary shift shaft for proper alignment of the lock bolt. Tighten the bolt (5-speed).

33 Install and tighten to specification the reverse idler shaft lock bolt (5-speed).

34 Install the primary gear and lock nut, with the nut finger-tight (5-speed).

35 Pre-lube and slide the primary shaft gear sleeve into place (5-speed).

36 Pre-lube and install 5th gear (5-speed).

37 Install the synchronizer ring (5-speed).

38 Install the clutch hub assembly and shift fork, aligning the keys with the slots in the synchronizer ring and securing the fork with the roll pin (5-speed).

39 Install the synchronizer stopper plate (5-speed).

40 Install the secondary shaft lock nut finger-tight (5-speed).

41 Tighten both lock nuts to specification and peen the collars into the shaft groove to retain them, using a suitable punch and hammer (5-speed).

42 Apply sealant to the transaxle 5th-speed cover and install the cover and bolts, tightening to specification. (5-speed).

43 Install the axle seals.

44 Install the backup light switch to the case.

45 Lightly lubricate and then install the 0-ring on the speedometer gear assembly and install the speedometer gear.

46 Install the transaxle.

Chapter 7B Automatic transaxle

Refer to Chapter 13 for specifications and information applicable to later USA models

Contents

Specifications

Transaxle type .... 3-speed, fully automatic floor-mounted shifter

Fluid
Capacity .... 5.7 US qts (6.0 liters)
Type .... Type F automatic transmission fluid

Torque specifications

	Ft-lb	Nm
Drive plate-to-crankshaft	60 to 69	83 to 95
Drive plate-to-torque converter	25 to 36	35 to 50
Converter housing-to-engine		
12 mm bolt	47 to 69	65 to 95
14 mm bolt	65 to 87	90 to 120
Converter-to-transaxle case	27 to 40	37 to 55
Bearing housing-to-converter housing	14 to 19	19 to 26
Side bearing-to-transaxle case	14 to 19	19 to 26
Bearing cover-to-transaxle case	8 to 10	11 to 14
Oil pump-to-transaxle case	14 to 26	19 to 26
Governor cover-to-transaxle case	4 to 6	5 to 8
Oil pan	4 to 6	5 to 8
Anchor end bolt	9 to 11	12 to 15

9 General information

The automatic transaxle assembly combines a 3-speed automatic transmission and differential into one unit. Power from the engine passes through the torque converter and transmission to the differential and then to the drive axles and front wheels.

Due to the complexity of the automatic transaxle unit, it is recommended that any major fault diagnosis or repairs beyond those covered in this Chapter be left to a dealer or properly-equipped transmission shop.

10 Vacuum diaphragm – testing and replacement

1 Malfunctioning of the vacuum diaphragm can cause rough shifting and incorrect shift points.
2 Drain the transaxle (Chapter 1) and remove the diaphragm.
3 Check the diaphragm and rod for proper operation. Make sure there is no binding and that the rod is not bent.
4 Use a vacuum pump to check that the rod moves properly when vacuum is applied to the diaphragm.
5 Replace any suspect component and make sure that the new unit is the same as the old unit. Measure the new and old diaphragm rod to make sure they are the same length.
6 After installation, refill the transaxle to the proper level with the specified fluid.

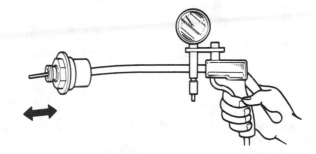

Fig. 7.7 Testing the vacuum diaphragm (Sec 10)

11 Kickdown solenoid – checking

1 A fault in the kickdown solenoid is indicated if the transaxle will not shift down when the throttle is depressed or the downshift is hesitant or rough.
2 Remove the solenoid switch.
3 Test the switch by applying battery power to the solenoid and making sure that the rod moves properly.
4 Install a new solenoid if there is any doubt about its condition.

7B

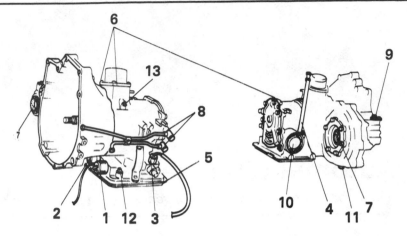

Fig. 7.8 Automatic transaxle components (Secs 9 through 14)

1	Kick-down solenoid
2	Vacuum diaphragm
3	Inhibitor switch
4	Oil level tube
5	Oil pan
6	Housing mating surface
7	Side oil seal
8	Oil pipe
9	Speedometer driven gear
10	Servo retainer
11	Drain plug
12	Fluid pressure sensor
13	Neutral switch

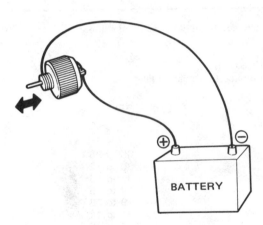

Fig. 7.9 Kick-down solenoid test (Sec 11)

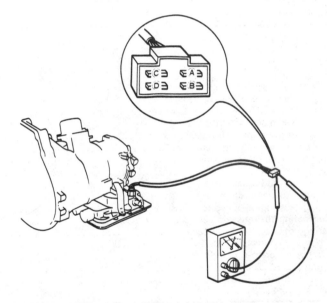

Fig. 7.10 Inhibitor switch test (Sec 12)

12 Inhibitor switch – testing

1   Check the inhibitor switch for proper operation by making sure that the engine starts only with the shifter in the Park and Neutral positions. The back-up lights should be on when the shifter is in the Reverse position.
2   Disconnect the switch and check the connector terminals for continuity. With the ignition on and the shifter in the noted positions, continuity should be between:

Park position	A – B
Reverse position	C – D
Neutral position	A – B

13 Shift control – checking and adjustment

1   Move the shifter through each position, making sure that the movement into each detent is positive and corresponds to the shifter plate.
2   The shifter should move between Drive and Neutral without the need to push in the button on the knob. The button must be depressed to shift between Drive and Reverse.
3   If the push button is loose on the shifter or the lever can be moved between Drive and Reverse without depressing it, adjust the shifter knob. Loosen the locknut, twist the shifter knob until proper operation is reached and then retighten the nut.

14 Automatic transaxle – removal and installation

1   Drain the transaxle fluid (Chapter 1).
2   Disconnect the battery negative cable.
3   Disconnect the speedometer cable, inhibitor switch, Neutral switch and kickdown solenoid couplers.
4   Disconnect the vacuum line from the diaphragm.
5   Raise the front end of the vehicle, support it securely and remove the front wheels.
6   Separate the lower balljoint (Chapter 11) and pull the drive axle from the transaxle (Chapter 8).
7   Remove the under-engine cover.
8   Support the engine with a jack.
9   Remove the front shift selector and counter rods.
10 Remove the crossmember.
11 Disconnect and plug the transaxle fluid lines.
12 Unbolt the Number 4 engine mount (Fig. 7.12) and separate it from the transaxle.
13 Remove the starter motor (Chapter 5) and the end cover.
14 Unbolt the torque converter from the drive plate.

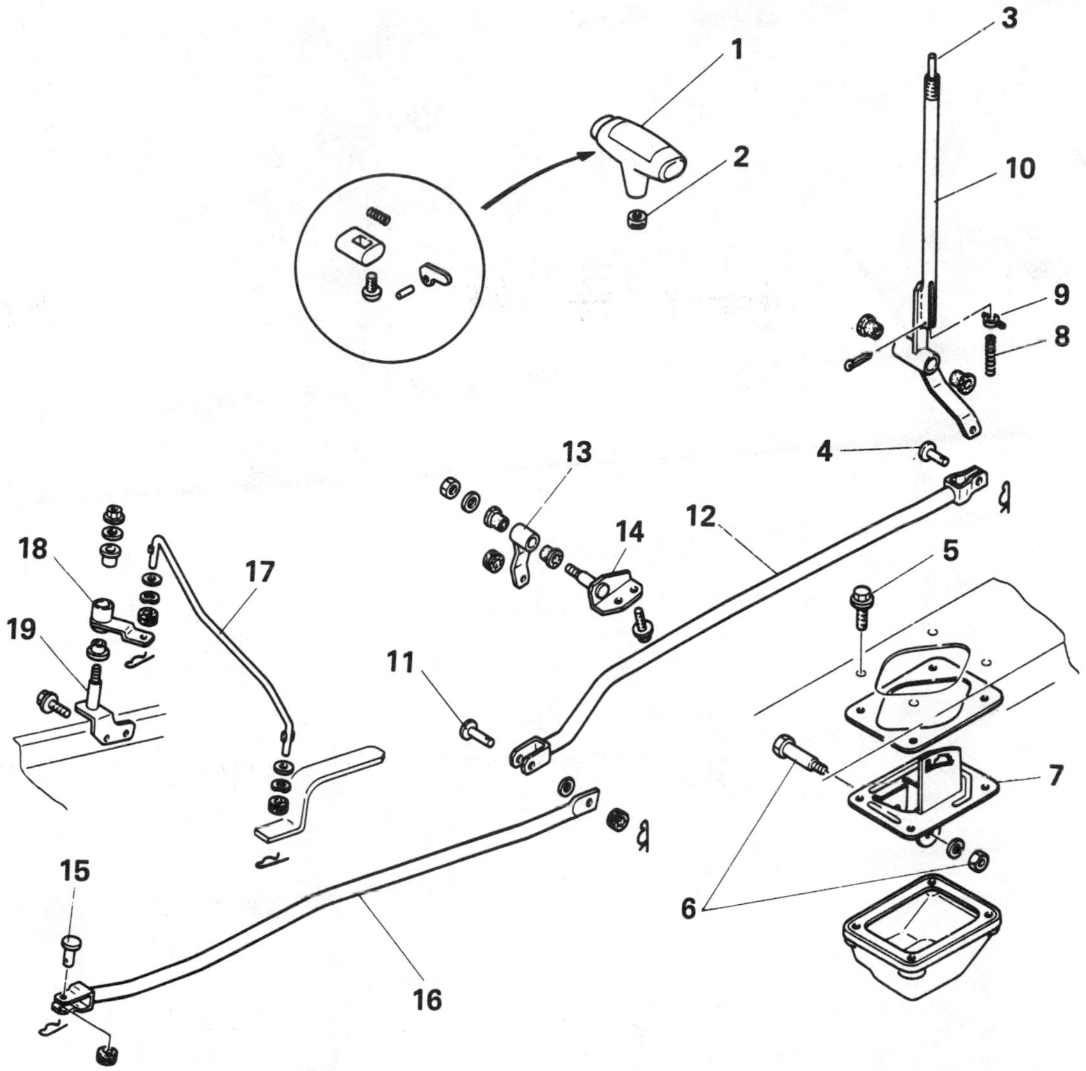

Fig. 7.11 Automatic transaxle shifter components (Secs 13 and 14)

1 Selector lever knob	6 Bolt and nut	11 Joint pin	16 Front selector rod
2 Lock nut	7 Selector lever bracket	12 Rear selector lever	17 Counter rod
3 Rod	8 Spring	13 Rear counter lever	18 Front counter lever
4 Joint pin	9 Guide pin	14 Rear counter bracket	19 Front counter bracket
5 Bolt	10 Selector lever	15 Joint pin	

15 Support the transaxle with a jack and remove the bolts retaining the converter housing to the engine.

16 Disconnect the transaxle from the engine and lower it from the engine compartment, taking care not to let the torque converter fall.

17 Installation is the reverse of removal with attention paid to the following:

Tighten all bolts to specification
Test the inhibitor switch (Section 12)
Check for fluid leaks
Check the manual shift and linkage (Section 13).

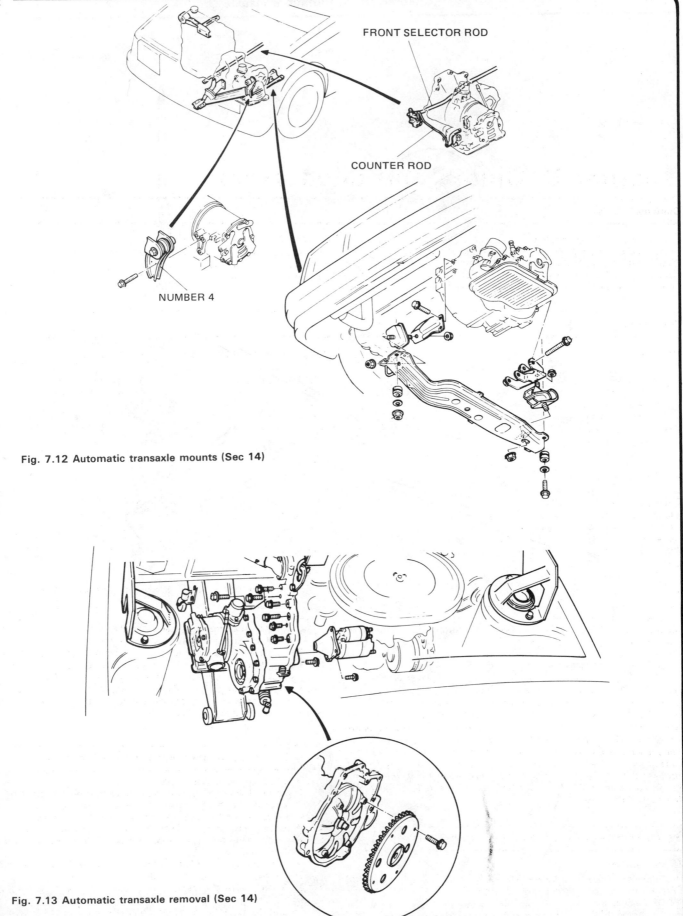

FRONT SELECTOR ROD

COUNTER ROD

NUMBER 4

Fig. 7.12 Automatic transaxle mounts (Sec 14)

Fig. 7.13 Automatic transaxle removal (Sec 14)

Chapter 8 Clutch and drive axles

Contents

Specifications

Clutch

	in	mm
Pedal		
Free play	0.43 to 0.67	11 to 17
Distance to floor	3.2 or more	80 or more
Height	9.05	230
Stroke	5.709	145
Disc		
Lining thickness	0.138	3.5
Service limit (from rivet head)	0.012	0.3
Runout limit	0.039	1.0
Pressure plate runout limit	0.0020	0.05

Torque specifications

	Ft-lb	Nm
Clutch pressure plate bolts	13 to 20	18 to 27
Clutch release lever and fork	13 to 20	18 to 27
Drive axle hub lock nut	116 to 174	160 to 240
Steering knuckle lower balljoint	33 to 40	44 to 55
Lower suspension arm balljoint	69 to 80	95 to 119

1 General information

The clutch disc is held in place against the flywheel by the pressure plate springs. During disengagement such as during gear shifting, the clutch pedal is depressed which operates a cable and pulls on the release lever so that the release bearing pushes on the pressure plate springs, thus disengaging the clutch.

Power from the engine is passed through the transaxle to the front wheels by two unequal length drive axles. The drive axles consist of three sections: the inner splined ends which are held in the differential by spring clips, two constant velocity (CV) joints and the outer splined ends which are held in the hub with a staked nut. The CV joints are internally splined and contain ball bearings because they operate at various lengths and angles as the driveshafts move through their full range of travel. The CV joints are lubricated with special grease and are protected by rubber boots which must be inspected periodically for cracks, tears or signs of leakage which could lead to damage and failure of the driveshaft.

2 Clutch pedal height and free play – checking and adjustment

Pedal height

1 Measure from the upper center of the clutch pedal pad to the firewall to determine pedal height. Check this measurement against specifications.
2 To adjust, remove the under dash cover, loosen the lock nut and rotate the clutch switch until the height measurement is within specifications.

3 Tighten the lock nut and reinstall the under dash cover.

Pedal free play

4 Press the clutch pedal with your hand and measure the free play. Check this measurement against specifications.
5 To adjust pedal free play, loosen the locknut on the clutch cable at the release lever. Turn the adjusting nut until the gap between the lever and roller is within specification with the clutch depressed.
6 Tighten the lock nut. After adjustment make sure that the measurement between the floor and the upper center of the pedal pad is within specification with the pedal down.

3 Clutch pedal – removal, inspection and installation

1 Remove the under dash cover.
2 Disconnect the return spring and remove the pedal-to-bracket clip.
3 Disengage the clutch cable and remove the pedal. It may be necessary to loosen the clutch switch to release the pedal.
4 Remove the bushing and inspect it for wear or damage. Check the pedal arm for distortion and the pad for wear. Replace any damaged or worn components.
5 Prior to installation, lightly lubricate the friction surfaces of the bushing, cable, cable hook and pedal arm.
6 To install, slide the pedal into position over the bushing and connect the return spring.
7 Engage the clutch cable bracket and retighten the clutch switch if necessary.
8 Replace the under dash cover.

4   Clutch cable – removal, inspection and installation

1   In the engine compartment, remove the nuts, washer, damper and pin from the end of the cable.

2   Pull the cable from the bracket on the transaxle.

3   In the passenger compartment, remove the under dash cover and disconnect the cable bracket from the pedal assembly.

4   Remove the clip and disengage the cable from the mounting bracket.

5   Remove the cable boot from the firewall and withdraw the cable from the vehicle.

6   Inspect the cable and boot for damage, replacing components as necessary.

7   Prior to installation, lightly lubricate the contact surfaces of the cable with chassis grease.

8   To install, insert the cable through the firewall from the passenger compartment and engage the boot, using a suitable sealant.

9   Engage the cable to the bracket and then hook it to the pedal arm.

10   In the engine compartment, insert the cable through the bracket and release arm. Install the pin, damper, washer and nuts.

11   Adjust the pedal free play (Section 2).

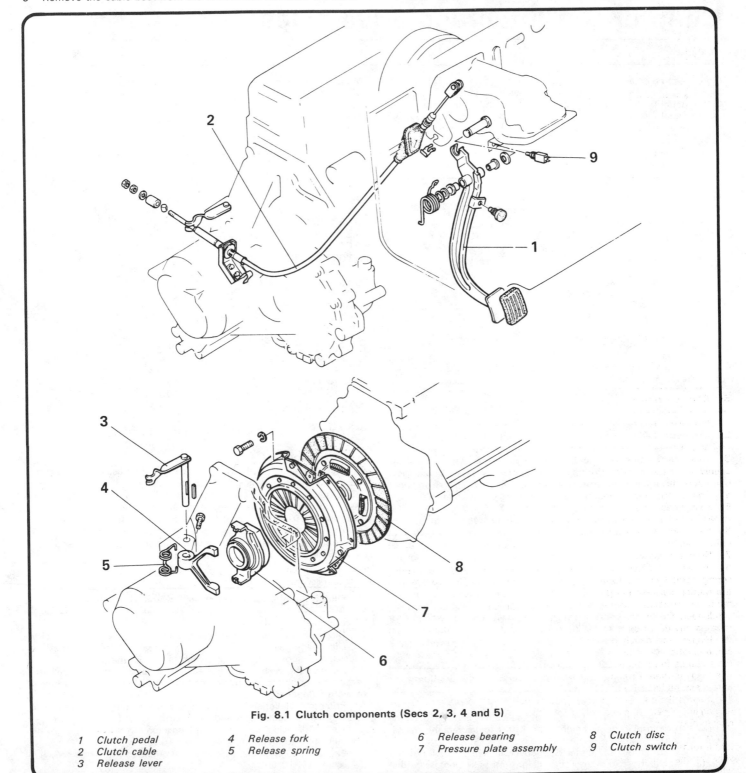

Fig. 8.1 Clutch components (Secs 2, 3, 4 and 5)

1 Clutch pedal	4 Release fork	6 Release bearing	8 Clutch disc
2 Clutch cable	5 Release spring	7 Pressure plate assembly	9 Clutch switch
3 Release lever			

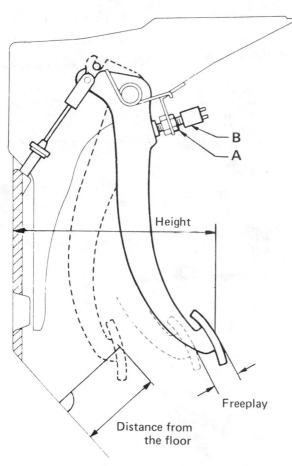

Fig. 8.2 Clutch pedal measurement (Sec 2)

A   Adjusting lock nut   B   Clutch switch

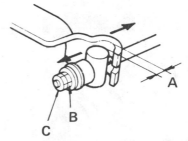

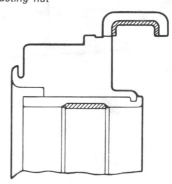

Fig. 8.3 Clutch pedal free play adjustment at the release lever
(Secs 2, 3 and 4)

A   Gap   C   Lock nut
B   Adjusting nut

Fig. 8.4 Clutch release bearing lubrication points (shaded areas)
(Sec 5)

5   Clutch – removal, inspection and installation

1   Remove the transaxle (Chapter 7).
2   Use a suitable tool, such as the proper size screwdriver handle, to center the clutch disc during removal of the pressure plate.
3   Lock the flywheel ring gear and loosen the pressure plate bolts evenly in a criss-cross fashion. Remove the bolts and lift the pressure plate away from the flywheel, taking care not to let the clutch disc fall.
4   Remove the pressure plate.
5   Disconnect the return spring from the release fork, twist the release lever and remove the release bearing.
6   Remove the release fork bolt and lift the fork and lever away as a unit.
7   Separate the return spring, key and fork.
8   Inspect the pressure plate for damage or wear of the diaphragm spring, scratches, scoring or color changes (indicating overheating) of the friction surface and damage or distortion of the cover. Although minor imperfections of the friction surface can be removed with fine sandpaper, the pressure plate should be replaced with a new unit if there is any doubt as to its condition.
9   Inspect the clutch disc friction material for cracks, loose rivets, contamination or signs of overheating. Check for wear by measuring the distance from the rivet head to the material surface and checking this measurement against specification. Replace the disc with a new unit if any faults are present.
10 Inspect the disc for distortion, wear, loose rivets, weak springs and damaged splines. Replace the disc with a new one if there is any question as to its condition.
11 Check the release bearing for wear and distortion and make sure that it turns and slides easily on the input shaft. Unless the vehicle has very low miles, it is a good idea to replace the bearing with a new one whenever the clutch is removed.

12 Inspect the clutch housing mounting surface, release lever, fork and return spring for wear, cracking, distortion, damage or fatigue, replacing as necessary.
13 Install the release lever, fork, spring and bearing.
14 Prior to installation, lubricate the release bearing input shaft and clutch disc splines lightly with moly-base grease.
15 Center the clutch disc (facing in the proper direction) with a suitable tool so that the splines will align properly with the input shaft and install the pressure plate, tightening the bolts to specification evenly in a criss-cross fashion.
16 Install the transaxle (Chapter 7).

6   Drive axles and constant velocity joints – inspection and fault diagnosis

1   The most common sign of drive axle or constant velocity joint failure is a knocking or clicking noise in turns.
2   Raise the vehicle and support it securely.
3   Inspect the constant velocity joint boots for signs of cracks, leaking lubricant or broken bands. Should lubricant leak from the constant velocity joint, it will wear prematurely and require replacement. Replace any damaged boots (Section 7).
4   Inspect along the length of each axle, checking for cracks, damage and signs of twisting or bending.
5   Grasp each axle and rotate in both directions as well as in and out to check for excessive movement, indicating worn splines or loose constant velocity joints.
6   Check the dynamic balancer on the right axle for damage, disintegration or signs that it has shifted.

7   Constant velocity joint dust boot – removal and installation

1   Remove the axle shaft (Section 8).
2   Place the axle in a vise, using blocks of wood to protect it from damage.
3   Insert a screwdriver into the boot retaining band locking clips and bend them outward (photo).
4   Remove the bands and discard them.

8

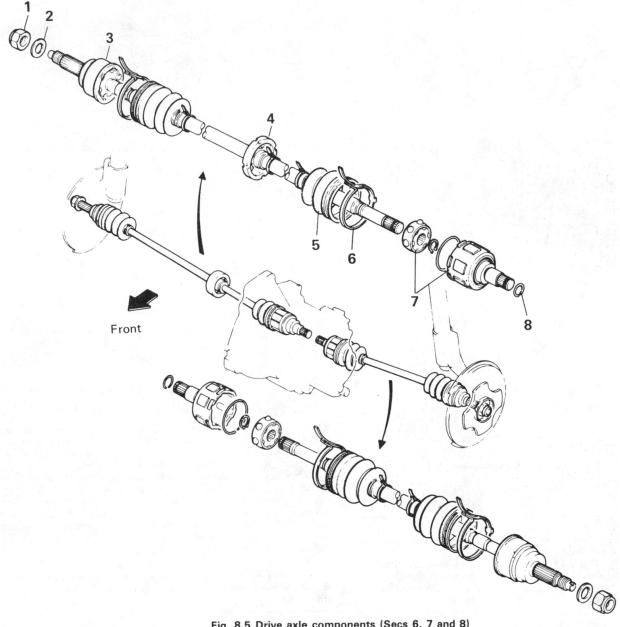

Fig. 8.5 Drive axle components (Secs 6, 7 and 8)

1 Lock nut	4 Dynamic dampener	5 Dust boot	7 Inner joint
2 Washer	(right axle only)	6 Boot band	8 Clip
3 Balljoint assembly			

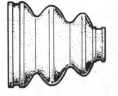 

Fig. 8.6 Inner (left) and outer dust boots (Sec 7)

5 Pry back the boot, working from the large end.
6 Use a screwdriver to remove the spring clip in the inner joint (photo).
7 Grasp the outer ring of the joint and pull it off (photo).
8 Clean the bearings carefully and inspect for damage, wear, galling and contamination by dirt.

9 Remove the snap-ring and slide the bearing inner ring, cage and ball assembly from the axle (photos).
10 Remove the inner boot from the shaft.
11 Remove the clamps and slide the outer boot off the shaft. On right shafts it will be necessary to remove the dynamic balancer after marking its position.
12 Obtain the necessary boot kits from your dealer. Due to the work involved, both dust boots should be replaced, even if only one is damaged. The boot kits contain the special lubricant required for use on constant velocity joints and no other type should be used.
13 To replace the outer boot, lightly lubricate the inside of the small end of the boot and slide it into place over the axle. To avoid damaging the sealing surface of the boot, place tape over the axle splines. On right axles, reinstall the dynamic balancer.
14 Pack the bearing cavity with the specified grease (photos).
15 Push the boot into position and seat it into the grooves.
16 Install the boot retaining bands so that the tightening tab folds in

7.3 Loosening the boot band retaining clips

7.6 Removing the outer constant velocity joint clip

7.7 Removing the outer ring

7.9a Removing the bearing snap-ring

7.9b Removing the bearing

7.14a Carefully pack grease into the cavity until the bearings are covered

8

7.14b Cover the bearing cavity

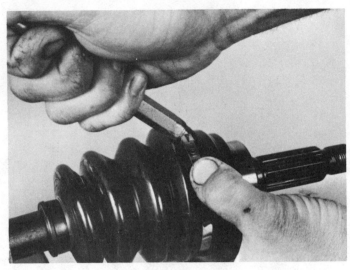

7.17 Bending the boot band locking clip

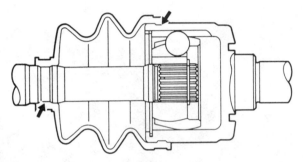

Fig. 8.7 Proper seating of the dust boot in the grooves (arrows) (Sec 7)

the opposite direction of shaft rotation when the vehicle is moving forward.

17 Bend the locking clips and secure them using a blunt tool such as a punch (photo).

18 To install the inner boot, lubricate the inner diameter and slide it onto the shaft, out of the way.

19 Place the bearing onto the shaft and install the snap ring.

20 Pack the bearing and cavity with grease as described in Step 14.

21 Install the outer ring onto the shaft and retain it with a new clip.

22 Install the boot and retaining clips.

23 Install the axle shaft (Section 8).

8   Drive axle – removal and installation

1   Remove the under-engine splash shield.

2   Drain the transaxle (Chapter 1).

3   Loosen the hub nut (Chapter 11).

4   Unbolt the lower balljoint and disconnect it from the hub.

5   While supporting the axle, pull the caliper and hub sharply outward to disengage the axle from the transaxle. Plug the axle opening in the transaxle with a clean, lint-free cloth.

6   Remove the hub nut.

7   Pull the caliper and hub toward the rear, separate the axle and remove it from the vehicle.

8   Installation is the reverse of removal. Prior to installation, lightly lubricate the axle spline for easier insertion into the transaxle and hub.

9   After installation, install a new hub nut and tighten all fasteners to specification.

Chapter 9 Braking system

Contents

Specifications

General

Brake fluid type	DOT type 3
Pedal free play	0.28 in to 0.35 in (6 mm to 9 mm)
Pedal height	8.46 in to 8.66 in (215 mm to 220 mm)
Depressed pedal height	3.27 in (83 mm)
Parking brake lever travel	5 to 9 notches

Drum brakes

	in	mm
Brake drums		
Diameter	7.09	180
Wear limit	7.13	181
Brake lining thickness		
Standard	0.16	4.0
Service limit	0.04	1.0
Wheel cylinders		
Bore diameter (standard)	11/16	17.46
Piston-to-bore clearance		
Standard	0.001 to 0.004	0.032 to 0.102
Service limit	0.006	0.15

Disc brakes

	in	mm
Pad linings		
Lining thickness		
Standard	0.39	10.0
Service limit	0.04	1.0
Disc		
Thickness		
Standard	0.43	11.0
Service	0.39	10.0
Runout limit	0.004	0.1
Caliper		
Bore diameter		
Standard	$2\frac{1}{8}$	53.97
Piston to bore clearance		
Standard	0.001 to 0.004	0.032 to 0.102
Service limit	0.006	0.15
Master cylinder		
Bore diameter	13/16	20.64
Piston-to-bore clearance		
Standard	0.002 to 0.005	0.04 to 0.125
Service limit	0.006	0.15
Piston-to-pushrod clearance	0.004 to 0.020	0.1 to 0.5

Torque specifications

	Ft-lb	Nm
Brake pedal-to-bracket	15 to 26	20 to 35
Slide pin bolt	33 to 40	45 to 55
Steering knuckle-to-chassis bolt	41 to 48	56 to 66
Brake hose-to-caliper	16 to 22	22 to 30
Wheel cylinder-to-backing plate	10 to 13	13 to 16
Backing plate-to-spindle	34 to 38	46 to 48
Brake line flare nut	10 to 16	13 to 22

1   General information

All models are equipped with disc-type front and self-adjusting rear hydraulically-operated brakes.

Front brakes are of the the sliding pin design featuring special bolts which both retain the caliper to the steering knuckle and locate it during movement. Rear brakes automatically adjust for wear when the vehicle is driven in reverse and the brakes applied.

Front drive vehicles tend to wear the front brake pads at a faster rate than a rear drive vehicle. Consequently it is important to inspect the pad linings frequently to make sure that they have not worn to the point where the disc itself is scored or damaged.

All models are equipped with power-assisted brakes and have a cable-actuated parking brake which operates the rear brakes only.

2   Hydraulic brake system bleeding

1   All air must be removed from the hydraulic fluid in the braking system in order to maintain proper operation. This must be done whenever a brake hose or component has been removed. On power brake models, apply the brakes with the engine off several times to remove the vacuum reserve.

2   Clean the area round the top of the master cylinder and remove the cap. Keep the master cylinder filled with the specified grade of brake fluid during the bleeding operation.

3   Obtain a clean jar and a piece of rubber tubing which will fit snugly over the bleed screw. Pour a sufficient amount of brake fluid in the jar to cover the end of the tubing. Place the other end of the tubing over the bleed screw fitting on the wheel to be bled. The dual diagonal brake system used on these models links opposite corners of the vehicles so the system must be bled in the following sequence: right rear, left front, left rear, right front brake. **Note:** *Always bleed the brake component with the longest line first.*

4   Remove the rubber dust cap from the bleeder screw, place a suitable end wrench on the bleeder fitting and install the rubber tubing around the fitting. Have an assistant slowly push down on the brake pedal as you release the bleed screw by turning the wrench approximately $\frac{3}{4}$ turn. Repeat this operation until no air bubbles are released into the brake fluid in the jar.

5   Repeat the bleeding operation on the other three wheels checking the fluid reservoir often. With the bleed screws closed, have an assistant apply the brakes several times to make sure the pedal is firm. During this operation, check to make certain that all brake pads and shoe assemblies are in proper position.

6   Install the rubber bleeder screw dust caps and check that the master cylinder is filled to within $\frac{1}{4}$ inch of the top edges.

7   Install the master cylinder gasket and cover.

3   Flexible hoses – inspection and replacement

1   Inspect the condition of the flexible brake hoses leading to each of the wheels. If they are swollen, chafed or damaged, they must be replaced.

2   Wipe off the top of the master cylinder reservoir and remove the cap. Place a sheet of suitable plastic over the top of the reservoir and replace the cap. This will stop the brake fluid from siphoning out during hose removal.

3   Clean around the hose flare nuts and using two suitable wrenches, remove the hose.

4   Install the new hose and bleed the system as described in Section 2. If only one hose has been replaced, it is only necessary to bleed that particular wheel.

5   Be sure to remove the plastic sheet from the master cylinder and check the fluid level.

4   Brake pedal height – measurement and adjustment

1   Use a straightedge to measure out from the firewall to a point directly above the center of the pedal pad to determine the pedal height. Check this measurement against Specifications.

2   If the pedal height is out of specification, remove the under dash cover and disconnect the brake light switch.

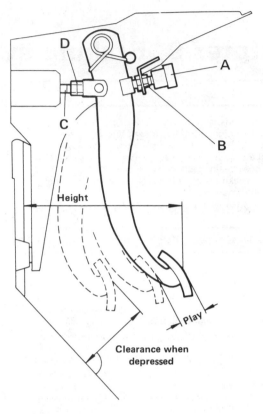

Fig. 9.1 Brake pedal measurement and adjustment (Sec 4)

A Brake pedal switch	C Brake rod
b Switch lock nut	D Rod lock nut

3   Loosen the light switch lock nut and move the switch away from the pedal arm.

4   Loosen the brake rod lock nut and turn the rod to adjust the pedal height.

5   When the height of the pedal is to specification, screw the brake light switch in until it touches the brake pedal. Turn the switch an additional $\frac{1}{2}$ turn and tighten the switch lock nut.

6   Press the brake pedal with your hand until resistance is felt or the power brake piston begins functioning. Check this distance against the free play measurement in Specifications.

7   Adjust the brake rod until the free play is within the specified limits and then tighten the lock nut.

8   Measure the depressed pedal height by pressing on the pedal and measuring the clearance between the pedal and the floor.

9   If there is too little clearance, bleed the brakes (Section 2). Should the clearance still be out of specification, adjust the brakes by applying them as you back up the vehicle. If the pedal is not brought up to the proper height, check the automatic adjustment mechanism for wear or damage.

5   Brake pedal – removal and installation

1   Remove the under dash panel.

2   Remove the cotter pin and then withdraw the clevis pin.

3   Remove the nut and washers and remove the brake pedal through-bolt.

4   Lift the brake pedal away from the brake bracket.

5   Installation is the reverse of removal. Prior to installation, lubricate the inner and outer contact points of the bushing and clevis pin.

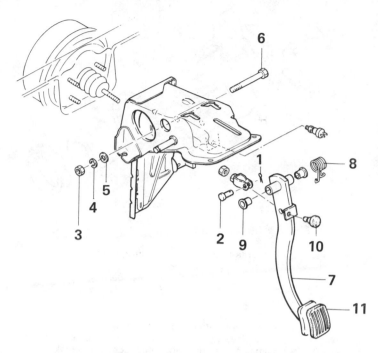

Fig. 9.2 Brake pedal components (Sec 5)

1 Cotter pin	7 Pedal assembly
2 Clevis pin	8 Return spring
3 Nut	9 Bushing
4 Lock washer	10 Stopper rubber
5 Plain washer	11 Pedal pad
6 Bolt	

6 Front disc brake pad – removal, inspection and installation

1 Raise the front of the vehicle, support it securely and remove the front wheels.
2 Remove the clip securing the brake line to the shock absorber strut and disconnect the line from the retainer.
3 Use a screwdriver to remove the pad return spring (photo).
4 Unscrew the lower slide pin and remove it.
5 Rotate the caliper upward and secure it out of the way with a piece of wire.
6 Remove the shim from the outer pad (photo).
7 Remove the pads from the caliper mounting bracket (photo).
8 Remove the anti-squeal springs from the pads.
9 Remove the shim from the inner pad.
10 Inspect the pads for signs of cracking, rust or overheating and measure pad thickness to determine wear. Inspect the brake disc

according to Section 8. If the disc needs to be re-surfaced, remove the front hub assembly (Chapter 11) and take the disc/hub units to a qualified shop.
11 Wipe the exposed portions of the caliper pistons with a clean lint-free cloth and then push the pistons back into the caliper if new, thicker pads are to be installed.
12 Inspect the springs and shims for damage or fatigue.
13 Prior to installation, lightly lubricate the backs of the pads, shims and contact surfaces of the caliper with lithium base grease.
14 To install, place the pads in position on the caliper mounting brackets with the shims and springs in place and rotate the caliper downward.
15 Install the return spring.
16 Install the caliper slide pin and tighten it to specification.
17 Install the brake line to the shock tower with the retaining clip.
18 Press on the brake pedal to seat the pads.
19 Install the wheels and lower the vehicle.

7 Disc brake caliper – removal, overhaul and installation

1 Raise the vehicle, support it securely and remove the front wheels.
2 Disconnect and plug the brake line at the caliper (photo).
3 Unbolt and remove the caliper slide pins.
4 Lift the caliper off the brake disc (photo).
5 Inspect the caliper for cracks, signs of overheating and leaking around the piston. Check the length of the brake hose for cracks or leaks.
6 Cut off the outer ends of the slide pin bushings and remove the bushings from the caliper.
7 Remove the caliper bleed screw.
8 Remove the piston by striking the caliper sharply on a block of wood. It may be necessary to repeat this procedure several times as the piston is a very tight fit. An alternative method is to reconnect the brake line to the caliper temporarily and have an assistant gently push on the brake pedal so that the piston is forced out.
9 Remove the dust seal from the piston.
10 Use a wood dowel to remove the piston seal.
11 Inspect the piston and bore for cracks and scoring and measure for wear.
12 Obtain a caliper rebuild kit from your dealer. Lubricate the piston bore with clean brake fluid or the assembly lube in the rebuild kit.
13 Install the piston seal in the caliper groove, using the assembly lube (photo).
14 Lubricate the dust boot lower inside diameter with the assembly lube.
15 Turn the top part of the dust seal inside out and insert it into the piston.
16 Lubricate the seal with assembly lube and insert it into its groove at the top of the bore.
17 Use both hands to push the piston into its bore (photo).
18 Install the bleed screw.
19 Install the brake pad shim, bottom edge first (photo).
20 Lubricate the caliper slide pin bushings with assembly lube and insert them into position, using the slide pins to guide them.
21 Lubricate the slide pins with assembly lube and the shims and

6.3 Pry the return spring loose with a screwdriver

6.6 Lift the shim from the outer pad

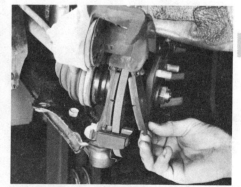
6.7 Remove the outer brake pad first

9

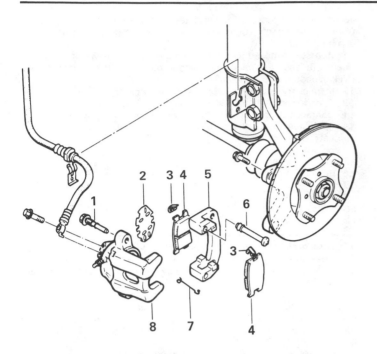

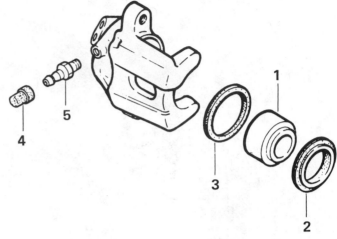

Fig. 9.3 Disc brake components (Secs 6, 7 and 8)

1   Slide pin   5   Mounting bracket
2   Shim   6   Bushing
3   Spring   7   Return spring
4   Pad   8   Caliper assembly

Fig. 9.4 Brake caliper components (Sec 7)

1   Piston   4   Rubber cap
2   Dust seal   5   Bleeder screw
3   Piston seal

backs of the brake pads with lithium base grease.
22 With the pads in place against the disc and the outer shim in place, install the caliper. Install the slide bolts loosely and make sure that the bushing bellows are not crimped.
23 Tighten the bolts to finger-tightness carefully, making sure that they are not cross-threaded. At this point tighten the bolts to specification.
24 Unplug the brake line and install it to the caliper, making sure that the gasket is in place.
25 Install the return springs to the pads.

7.2 Unbolt the brake line from the caliper

7.4 Lift the caliper from the brake assembly

7.13 Insert the piston seal into the groove in the caliper

7.17 Press the piston firmly into the caliper with both hands

7.19 Proper brake pad shim installation

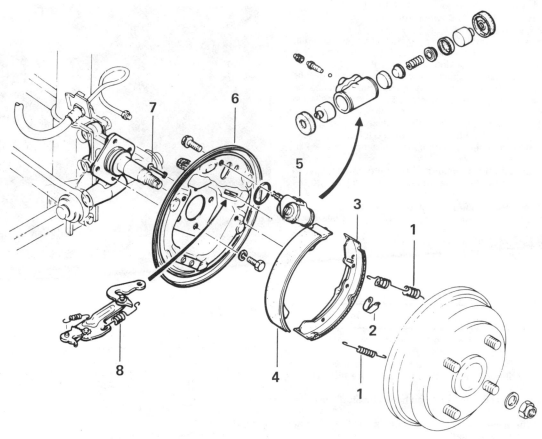

Fig. 9.5 Drum brake components (Secs 9, 10 and 11)

1	Return spring	3	Leading shoe
2	Holding spring	4	Trailing shoe

5	Wheel cylinder	7	Retaining pin
6	Backing plate	8	Anti-rattle spring

26 Press on the brake pedal to seat the pads and bleed the brakes (Section 2).
27 Install the wheels and lower the vehicle.

8 Brake disc – inspection

1   Because the front brakes of a front-drive vehicle are under considerable strain, it is important that the discs be periodically inspected for wear or damage.
2   Raise the front of the vehicle, support it securely and remove the front wheels.
3   Inspect the brake disc for cracking, scoring or rust damage.
4   Check the disc for runout and wear.
5   If the brake disc is worn or damaged, it should be either turned on a brake lathe (as long as it is still within specification) or replaced with a new one.
6   Remove the caliper (Section 7) and the front hub (Chapter 11).
7   Special tools are required to remove the disc from the hub. Consequently, the complete assembly should be taken to a properly-equipped shop to have the disc turned or replaced.
8   Reinstall the hub, caliper and wheel and lower the vehicle.

9 Rear drum brake linings – removal and installation

1   Raise the rear of the vehicle, support it securely and remove the wheel and hub (Chapter 11). Wipe the brake and backing plate clean with a rag, taking care not to breathe in any dust.
2   Measure the shoe lining thickness and check for cracking and signs of contamination by oil, grease or brake fluid.
3   Inspect the wheel cylinder for leakage.
4   Remove the front shoe retaining pin and spring assembly by

9.4 Removing the front shoe retaining pin

pushing inward and aligning the pin end with the slot (photo).
5   Disengage the lower end of the shoe from the anchor.
6   Unhook the spring and disengage the adjuster by pulling it off the pin.
7   Disengage the upper spring and remove the front shoe from the vehicle.

9

8   Remove the adjuster anti-rattle spring (photo).
9   Disengage the rear shoe pin and spring retainer.
10 Remove the rear shoe.
11 Inspect the adjuster assembly and spring for looseness or wear around the quadrant and knurled pin and for a bent or damaged spring.
12 Inspect the brake drum for cracking, scoring and wear.
13 Prior to installing the shoes, push forward and inward on the adjuster quadrant with a screwdriver so that the quadrant touches the backing plate. This will allow for more clearance during the installation of the shoes.
14 Lightly lubricate the contact points on the backing plate, adjuster, anchor and wheel cylinder with lithium base grease (photo).
15 Install the rear shoe retainer pin and spring assembly.
16 Install the adjuster-to-shoe spring.
17 Install the front shoe to the adjuster and anchor points and install the upper spring followed by the lower spring which attaches to the rear shoe.
18 Install the front shoe retaining pin and spring assembly.
19 Move the shoe assemblies so that the brake drum installs easily over them.
20 Install the hub assembly (Chapter 11).
21 Install the rear wheels and lower the vehicle.

10 Rear drum brake wheel cylinder – removal and installation

1   Raise the rear of the vehicle, support it securely and remove the rear wheels.
2   Remove the rear hub (Chapter 11) and brake shoes (Section 9).
3   Remove the upper rigid brake line flare nut and hose retainer clip and plug the hose.
4   Remove the two wheel cylinder retaining bolts and lift the cylinder from the backing plate.
5   To install, place the wheel cylinder in position, install the retaining bolts and tighten them to specification.
6   Install the brake line flare nut onto the wheel cylinder finger-tight.
7   Index the hose to the suspension strut tab and install the retaining clip.
8   Tighten the brake line flare nuts to specification.
9   Install the brake shoes, rear hub and wheel and lower the vehicle.

11 Rear drum brake wheel cylinder – overhaul

1   Remove the wheel cylinder (Section 10) and place it on a clean working surface.
2   Remove the bleeder screw and steel ball. It may be necessary to tap the wheel cylinder on a block of wood to dislodge the ball.
3   Remove the dust boots and pistons from the cylinder bore and then separate the boots from the pistons.
4   Push from one end of the piston to remove the rubber cups and spring assembly.
5   Remove the cylinder-to-backing plate gasket.
6   Clean all metal components in denatured alchohol or clean brake fluid.
7   Inspect the cylinder bore for wear, scoring, corrosion or pitting. If it is necessary to hone the piston bore, make sure that piston-to-bore clearance is still within specification.
8   Measure the bore to determine if the wear is within specification.
9   Check the spring to make sure it is not bent or fatigued.
10 Obtain a wheel cylinder rebuild kit from your dealer.
11 Lubricate the cylinder bore with assembly fluid (available at auto parts stores) or clean brake fluid.
12 Install the spring assembly into the bore.
13 Lubricate the cups and install them with the open ends toward the center of the cylinder.
14 Install new dust seals on the pistons.
15 Lubricate the pistons and install them into the piston bore and snap the dust seals firmly into the grooves.
16 Install the steel check ball and bleeder screw.
17 Install the cylinder-to-backing plate seal.
18 Install the cylinder to the backing plate (Section 10).

9.8 Hold the left side of the adjuster up and release the anti-rattle spring

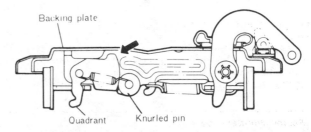

Fig. 9.6 Press on the brake adjuster quadrant (arrow) to provide clearance for installation of new shoes (Sec 9)

9.14 Lubricate all friction points on the backing plate

12 Master cylinder – removal and installation

1   Open the hood and use newspapers to form a catch basin below the master cylinder to catch leaking fluid which could damage the paint in the engine compartment.
2   Unplug the fluid level sensor connector.
3   Disconnect the two rigid lines from the master cylinder.
4   Remove the retaining nuts and washers and lift the master

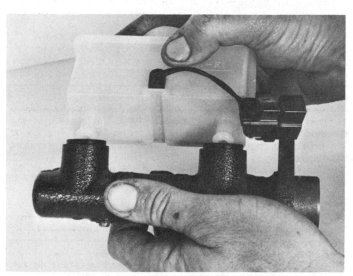

Fig. 9.7 Brake master cylinder components (Secs 12 and 13)

1 Cap assembly
2 Level sensor float
3 Reservoir
4 Bushing
5 Stopper bolt
6 Stop ring
7 Primary piston assembly
8 Secondary piston assembly

cylinder from the engine compartment, taking care not to leak any fluid on the paint.
5   To install, place the master cylinder on the power brake vacuum reservoir studs and then start the brake line flare nuts into the cylinder.
6   Install the master cylinder retaining nuts.
7   Tighten the flare nuts fully and plug in the level sensor connector.

13 Master cylinder – overhaul

1   Remove the master cylinder (Section 12).
2   Drain the fluid from the reservoir into a suitable container.
3   Hold the reservoir with one hand and the master cylinder with the other and rock the reservoir back and forth to remove it (photo).
4   Obtain a master cylinder overhaul kit from your dealer.
5   Place the master cylinder in the vertical position (with the front end down), depress the primary piston and remove the snap-ring.
6   Remove the primary piston and discard it. The overhaul kit will have a replacement unit.
7   Use a wooden dowel to depress the secondary piston. Remove the O-ring and retaining screw.
8   With the master cylinder in the vertical position with the rear end downward, tap it on a block of wood to remove the secondary piston.
9   Remove the spring from the front of the secondary piston.
10 From the secondary piston, remove the rear spreader and cylinder cup seal, the valve shims and the two seals from the rear of the piston.
11 From the reservoir, remove the cap, baffle and float. Remove the seal from the baffle.
12 Clean the master cylinder and inspect the bore for cracks, grooves or corrosion. Measure the bore for wear.
13 Inspect the reservoir for cracks, leaks or loose bushings.
14 Lubricate all components prior to assembly with clean brake fluid or assembly lube.
15 Install the valve shim on the front of the secondary piston. Place the seal (open end forward) onto the piston.
16 Install the center seal onto the secondary piston with the open end forward.
17 Install the rear secondary piston seal with the open end toward the rear.
18 Place the O-ring on the secondary piston retaining screw.
19 Lubricate the primary and secondary pistons with clean brake fluid or assembly lube.
20 Push the secondary piston assembly into the bore using a wooden dowel. Depress the spring slightly and insert the setscrew.
21 Insert the primary piston with the spring forward. Depress it slightly and then install the snap-ring.
22 Lubricate the reservoir bushings with brake fluid or assembly lube and install it to the master cylinder using a rocking motion to seat it.
23 Install the reservoir level float and baffle assembly and the cap.

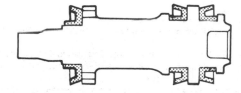

13.3 Grasp the master cylinder firmly and rock the reservoir from side to side to remove it

Fig. 9.8 Secondary piston seal installation (Sec 13)

9

24 Fill the reservoir with brake fluid and, holding your fingers over the ports, slowly push the piston one full stroke with a wood dowel and then release your fingers from over the ports. This will prime the master cylinder and make installation easier.
25 Place the master cylinder in position over the power brake reservoir studs and install the brake line flare nuts finger-tight.
26 Install the master cylinder retaining nuts.
27 Tighten the brake line flare nuts and plug in the level sensor connector.

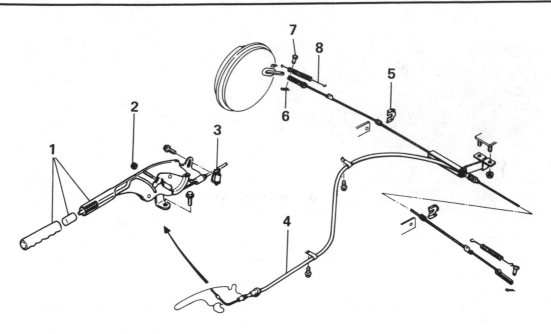

Fig. 9.9 Parking brake components (Secs 14, 15 and 16)

1   Parking lever assembly   3   Warning light switch   5   Clip   7   Clevis pin
2   Adjusting nut   4   Parking brake cable   6   Cotter pin   8   Return spring

14 Parking brake lever – adjustment

1   Pull upward on the parking brake lever and check that the specified number of notches are exposed.
2   If the lever is out of adjustment, release it and remove the console (if equipped).
3   Turn the adjuster nut on the end of the brake cable until the specified clearance is achieved.

15 Parking brake lever assembly – removal and installation

1   Remove the console (if equipped).
2   Remove the adjusting nut and unplug the warning light connector.
3   Unbolt and remove the parking brake lever assembly.

4   Installation is the reverse of removal.

16 Parking brake cable – removal and installation

1   Remove the console (if equipped), remove the adjusting nut and disengage the cable from the parking brake lever.
2   Raise the vehicle and support it securely.
3   From underneath the vehicle, remove the cotter pin and clevis pin and disengage the return spring at both rear wheels.
4   Remove the cable bracket-to-rear crossmember retaining clips and disengage the cable from the bracket.
5   Remove the cable hinges and the locking clip from the body.
6   Prior to installation, lubricate the inner cable and guide surfaces and the clevis pin with lithium base grease.
7   Installation is the reverse of removal and a new cotter pin should be used at each rear wheel.

Chapter 10 Chassis electrical system

Refer to Chapter 13 for specifications and information applicable to later USA models

Contents

Specifications

Lamp

	Watts
Headlight	65/55
Front parking light	3
Front turn signal light	27
Rear turn signal light	27
Taillight	8
Stoplight	27
Backup light	27
License light	8
Interior light	10
Map light	6

Indicator and warning lamps

Turn signal	1.4
High beam	3.4
Oil pressure	3.4
Alternator	3.4
Fuel	3.4
Stop	1.4
Rear window defroster	1.4
Brake	3.4

1 General information

The electrical system is of the 12 volt negative ground type.

Power for the lighting system and all electrical accessories is supplied by a lead/acid-type battery which is charged by an alternator. Circuits are protected from overload by a system of fuses and fuse links.

This Chapter covers repair and service procedures for various lighting and electrical components not associated with the engine. Information on the battery, alternator, voltage regulator and starter motor can be found in Chapter 5.

Note: *Whenever the electrical system is worked on, the negative battery cable should be disconnected to prevent electrical shorts and/or fires.*

2 Fuses and fusible links – replacement

Caution: *At no time should a fuse be bypassed by using metal or foil. Serious damage to the electrical system could result.*

1   The fuse block is located in the instrument panel to the left of the steering wheel behind a cover which also holds the fuse removal tool.
2   With the ignition off, remove each fuse in turn by grasping it with a tool and pulling outward. A blown fuse can be readily identified since the wire inside the glass fuse will be melted or burned. When a blown

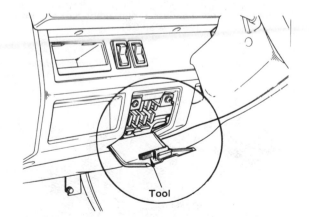

Fig. 10.1 Fuse panel location (Sec 2)

fuse is found, replace it with a new one of the same value by pushing it into place.
3   The fusible links are located in the engine compartment adjacent to the battery.
4   If the fuses in the fuse block are alright and the headlights or other

10

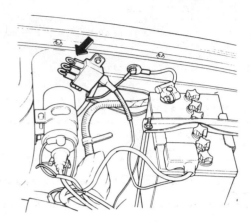

Fig. 10.2 Fusible link location (Sec 2)

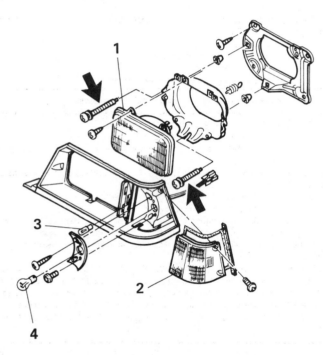

Fig. 10.3 Headlight components (adjustment screws arrowed)
(Secs 4 and 6)

1 Headlight	3 Parking lamp
2 Combination light	4 Turn signal light

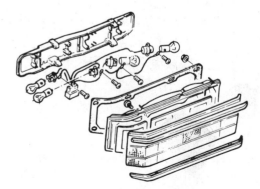

Fig. 10.4 Taillight components (Sec 6)

electrical components are inoperable, check the fusible links.
5   If one or more of the links are melted, disconnect the battery negative cable, make sure the links are cool to the touch and unplug both ends.
6   Obtain a replacement fusible link from your dealer, plug it in and reconnect the battery negative cable.
7   If the replacement fuse or fusible link immediately fails, do not replace it again until the cause of the problem is isolated and corrected. In most cases this will be a short circuit in the wiring system caused by a broken or deteriorated wire.

3   Horn – fault testing

1   If the horn does not work at all, check the fuse, horn switch, wiring and horn unit itself.
2   A vibrating or varying horn tone indicates loose connectors or damage to the horn unit main body.
3   If the sound from the horn is not of normal loudness, check the horn unit and the battery charge level.
4   Replace any suspect component.

4   Headlight sealed beam unit – removal and installation

1   Remove the radiator grille (Chapter 12).
2   Remove the screws retaining the turn signal light lens.
3   Remove the headlight retaining screws (not the adjustment screws). The retaining screws are smaller in size and pass through raised tabs in the light body. Unplug the headlight and remove it.
4   To install, plug the light into the connector and install the retaining screws.
5   Install the turn signal light lens and radiator grille.
6   Check the headlight alignment.

5   Headlight – alignment

1   It is always best to have the headlights aligned on the proper equipment but if this is not available the following procedure may be used.
2   Position the vehicle on level ground 10 feet (3.048 meters) in front of a dark wall or board. The wall or board must be at right angles to the center-line of the vehicle.
3   Draw a vertical line on the wall or board in line with the center-line of the vehicle.
4   Bounce the vehicle on its suspension to ensure that it settles at the proper level and check the tires to make sure that they are at the proper pressure. Measure the height between the ground and the center of the headlights.
5   Draw a horizontal line across the board or wall at this measured height. Mark a cross on the horizontal line on either side of the vertical center-line at the distance between the center of the light and the center-line of the vehicle.
6   Turn the headlights on and switch them to high beam.
7   Use the adjusting screws to align the centers of each beam onto the crosses which were marked on the horizontal line.
8   Bounce the vehicle on its suspension again to make sure the beams return to the correct position. Check the operation of the dimmer switch.
9   The headlights should be adjusted with the proper equipment at your earliest convenience.

6   Bulb replacement – front parking and turn signal lights

1   Remove the lens cover screws and lift the lens cover away.
2   Grasp the parking light bulb firmly and pull it from the socket to remove it.
3   To remove the turn signal bulb, push it in, turn it counterclockwise and withdraw it.
4   Reinstall the lens cover.

7 Bulb replacement – rear

Side marker light

1 Remove the two securing screws and lift the lens away.
2 Grasp the bulb firmly and pull it from its socket. Press the new bulb into the socket and replace the lens.

Tail and backup lights

3 Remove the rear trim panel cover.
4 Squeeze the four retaining clips and pull the bulb retainer from the light housing.
5 The bulbs are removed by pushing in and rotating counter-clockwise.
6 Install the new bulb(s) and replace the retainer by pushing it in place until it clicks.
7 Replace the trim panel.

License plate light

8 Remove the trim panel and from inside the vehicle, remove the two nuts retaining the light housing.
9 Withdraw the housing and replace any burned out bulbs by pushing in, rotating counterclockwise and releasing from the socket.
10 Installation is the reverse of removal.

8 Bulb replacement – interior

Dome lamp

1 Grasp the lens firmly and pull it from the housing.
2 Expand the retainers at the ends of the bulb and remove the bulb.
3 Install the new bulb and snap the lens in place.

Instrument panel lights

4 The instrument cluster bulbs are accessible after the cluster has been removed (Section 14).
5 The bulbs are removed by rotating the sockets counterclockwise to release them. Pull the bulb from the socket and press the new one in place.
6 The heater control lamp is accessible after removing the heater control (Chapter 3). Rotate the socket counterclockwise, withdraw the socket and pull the bulb out to remove it.

9 Radio – removal and installation

1 Disconnect the battery negative cable.
2 Remove the radio switch knobs.
3 Remove the retaining nuts and pull the radio outward.
4 Disconnect the antenna and electrical wiring connectors and remove the radio from the dash panel.
5 Installation is the reverse of removal.
6 Reconnect the battery negative cable.

10 Antenna – removal and installation

1 Disconnect the battery negative cable.
2 Remove the radio (Section 9).
3 Unplug the antenna wire from the radio and disengage it from the clip on the underside of the dash.
4 Remove the screws attaching the antenna to the body and pull the antenna upward.
5 Withdraw the antenna wire carefully through the antenna mounting hole.
6 To install, feed the antenna wire through the mounting hole, place the antenna in position in the mounting hole and install the mounting screws.
7 Engage the antenna wire to the underside of the dash and then plug it into the radio.
8 Install the radio.
9 Reconnect the battery negative cable.

11 Combination switch – removal and installation

1 Disconnect the battery negative cable.
2 Remove the steering wheel (Chapter 11).
3 Remove the steering column shrouds (three screws and one retaining bolt).
4 Loosen the screw retaining the switch to the column and rotate the switch.
5 Unplug the four connectors from the switch.
6 Withdraw the switch from the shaft.
7 To install, place the switch in position and align the tab on clamp with the notch in the steering column and tighten the screw.
8 Install the right half of the steering column cover, followed by the left half.
9 Install the steering wheel temporarily and make sure a gap exists between the wheel hub and steering column hub so that it does not rub. If it is necessary to adjust the gap, loosen the upper column bolts, slide the cover up or down for clearance and re-tighten the bolts.
10 Install the steering wheel and reconnect the battery negative cable.

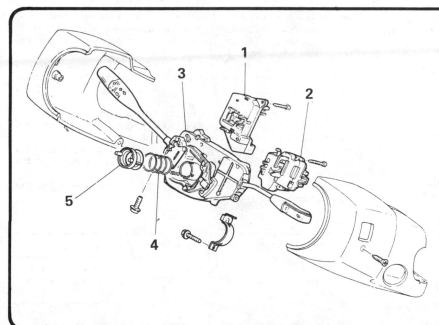

**Fig. 10.5 Combination switch components
(Sec 11)**

1 *Light and dimmer switch assembly*
2 *Wiper/washer switch assembly*
3 *Combination switch*
4 *Spring*
5 *Cancel cam*

10

12 Combination switch – testing

1   Remove the switch (Section 11).
2   Disassemble the switch by releasing the clips. Inspect for broken or corroded contacts and lubricate lightly with conductive silicone

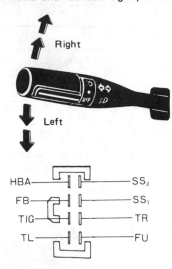

Fig. 10.6 Turn signal positions (top) and turn signal and hazard switch connector (Sec 12)

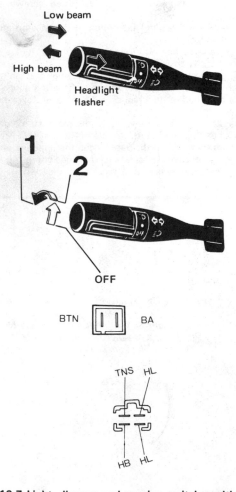

Fig. 10.7 Light, dimmer and passing switch positions and connector (Sec 12)

grease prior to reassembly. When reassembling, make sure that the alignment pins on the control levers are in their proper positions.
3   Test the combination switch with an ammeter/ohmmeter by making contact with the probes at the specified connectors terminal to make sure there is continuity.

Turn signal
Fig. 10.6
4   With the lever in the positions shown, there should be continuity between:

    Left turn position : FU – TL
    Neutral position : TIG – HBA – FB
    Right turn position : FU – TL – TR

Hazard switch
Fig. 10.6
5   The hazard switch is located at the base of the turn signal lever. Continuity should be:

    On position : FU – TL – TR, HBA – FB, SS₁ – SS₂

Light, dimmer and passing switch
Fig. 10.7
6   With the switch in the positions shown, continuity should be between:

Low beam	HB – HL
	HL – BA
High beam	HB – HL
	HU – BA
Passing On	HU – BA

Wiper and washer switch
Fig. 10.8
7   In the positions shown, the continuity on the switch terminals should be:

Wiper
Off position	AS – SWL
On position	SWL – E
1 (int.)	AS – SWL
	INT – E
2 (low)	SWL – E
3 (high)	SWH – E

Washer
On	SW – E

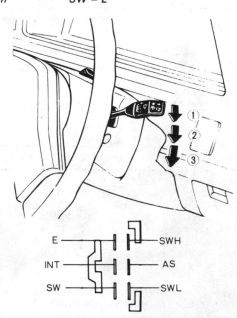

Fig. 10.8 Wiper/washer switch and connector (Sec 12)

13 Ignition switch – removal and installation

1   Disconnect the battery negative cable.
2   Making sure that it is centered in the straight-ahead position, remove the steering wheel (Chapter 11).
3   Remove the combination switch (Section 11).
4   Remove the screw from the ignition switch and remove the electrical connector (photo).
5   Remove the two wires from the tab of the lock mechanism.
6   Trace the wires from the switch to the connector under the dash and unplug it.
7   Remove the steering column (Chapter 11).
8   Place the steering column in a vise, protecting it from damage with wood blocks in the vise jaws.
9   Use a chisel and hammer to make indentations across the heads of the break-off type bolts retaining the switch to the column. Unscrew the retaining bolts with a screwdriver inserted into the indentations (photo).
10 Remove the switch from the steering column.
11 With the key removed and the locking lug extended, install the switch by inserting the lug into the steering column.
12 Install new break-off bolts finger-tight and then cycle the switch several times to check for proper operation.
13 Tighten the special bolts until the heads break off.
14 Carefully insert the steering column into position under the dash, making sure not to snag any wires.
15 Insert the ignition switch wires into the switch and align the tab on the steering column with the recess in the switch.
16 Install the screw in the ignition wire connector, feed the wire down along the steering column and plug in the connector under the dash.
17 Fasten the wires to the switch with the tab.
18 Install the steering column (Chapter 11) and combination switch.
19 Install the steering wheel (Chapter 11).
20 Reconnect the battery negative cable and check the ignition switch for proper operation.

14 Instrument cluster – removal and installation

1   Disconnect the battery negative cable.
2   Remove the instrument cluster finish panel (Chapter 12).
3   Remove the lower ventilator vent from under the dash.
4   Reach up under the dash panel and disconnect the speedometer cable connector by pressing on the protruding release pin and then withdrawing it.
5   Remove the four instrument cluster retaining screws.
6   Pull the cluster out of the dash and disconnect the wiring plugs (photo).
7   Remove the cluster from the vehicle.
8   To install, reconnect the wiring plugs and place the cluster in position.
9   From under the dash, insert the speedometer connector into place until it clicks.
10 Install the cluster retaining screws.
11 Install the cluster finish panel and reconnect the battery negative cable.

15 Instrument cluster gauges – removal and installation

1   Disconnect the battery negative cable.
2   Remove the instrument cluster (Section 14).
3   Remove the meter cover retaining screws. Remove the meter top piece (photo).
4   Remove the meter cover.
5   Remove the gauge retaining nut at the rear of the cluster and lift the gauge from the cluster.
6   Installation is the reverse of removal.

16 Printed circuit board – removal and installation

1   Disconnect the battery negative cable.
2   Remove the instrument cluster (Section 14).

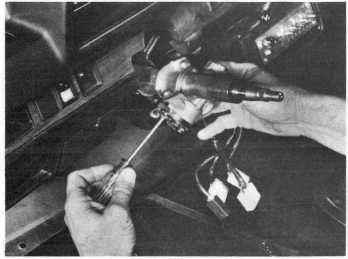

13.4 The ignition switch connector retaining screw location

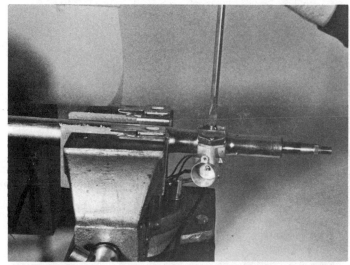

13.9 Unscrew the break-off head bolts in a counterclockwise direction

14.6 Instrument cluster wiring plug release lever (arrow)

10

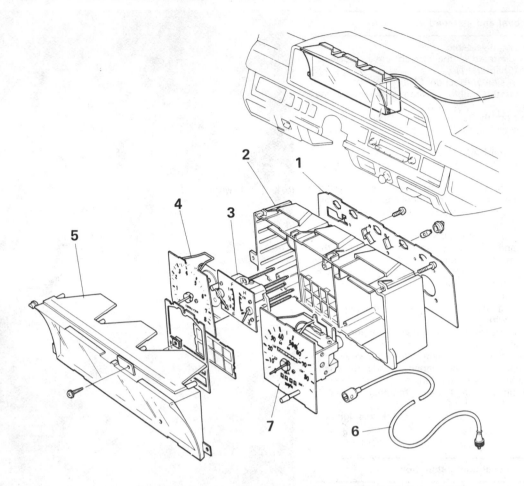

Fig. 10.9 Instrument cluster components (Secs 14 through 16)

1	*Printed circuit board*	3	*Fuel and water*	4	*Tachometer*
2	*Meter top piece*		*temperature meter*	5	*Meter cover*

6	*Speedometer cable*
7	*Speedometer*

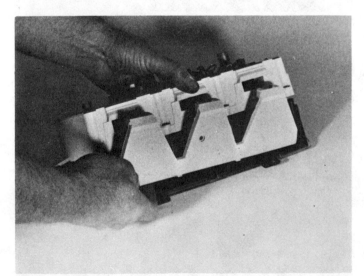

15.3 Remove the meter top piece retaining screw and then disengage it from the cover

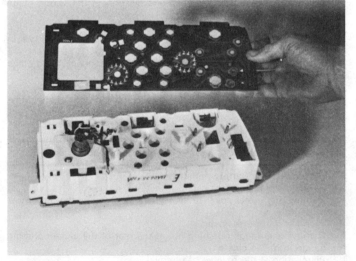

16.3 Handle the circuit board carefully when lifting it from the instrument cluster

3   Remove the nuts on the back of the instrument cluster retaining the circuit board and lift the board away (photo).
4   To install, place the circuit board carefully into position and install

the retaining nuts.
5   Install the instrument cluster and reconnect the battery negative cable.

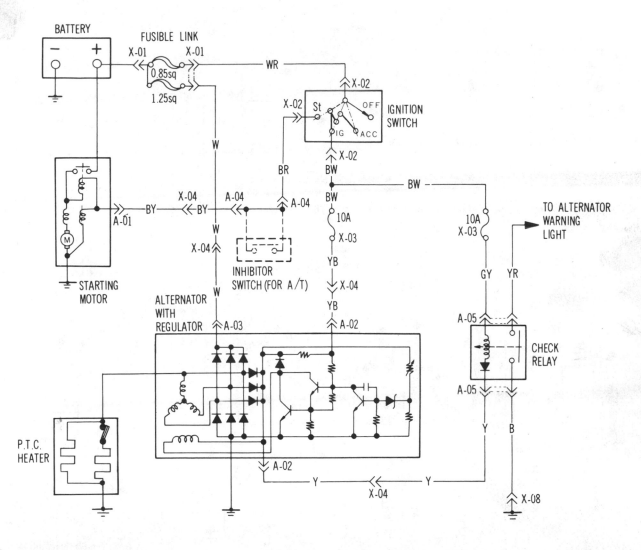

CODE	COLOR	CODE	COLOR
B	Black	Lg	Light green
Br	Brown	O	Orange
G	Green	R	Red
Gy	Gray	W	White
L	Blue	Y	Yellow
Lb	Light blue		

Fig. 10.10 Charging and starting system wiring diagram (1981 models)

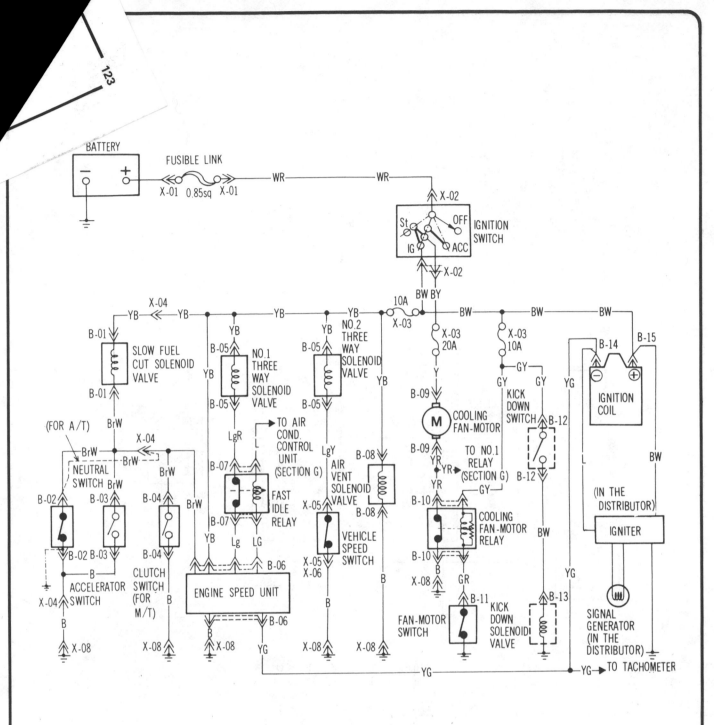

Fig. 10.11 Emissions, ignition, cooling fan and automatic transaxle kickdown systems wiring diagram (1981 models)

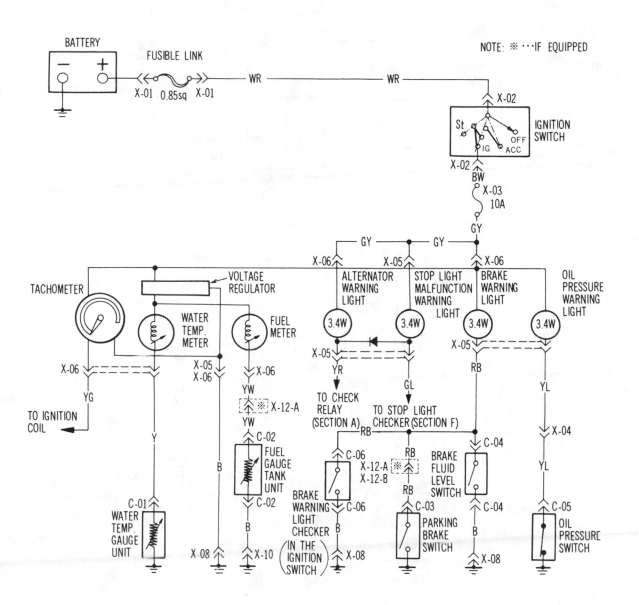

Fig. 10.12 Meter and warning light wiring diagram (1981 models)

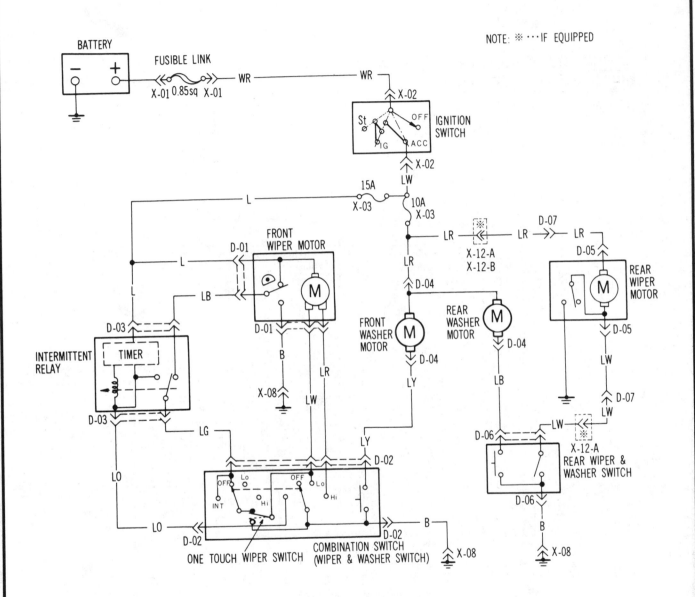

Fig. 10.13 Front and rear wiper and washer wiring diagram (except sedans) (1981 models)

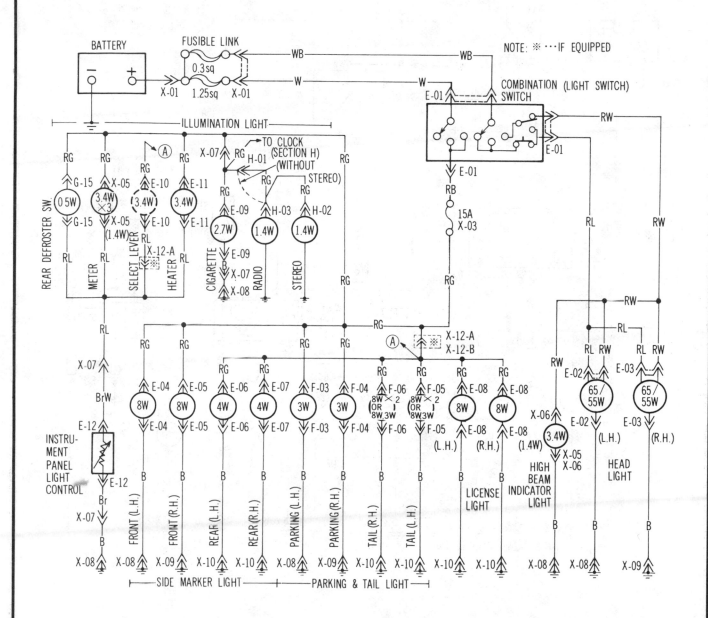

Fig. 10.14 Headlight, side marker lights, parking, tail, license and illumination light system wiring diagram (1981 models)

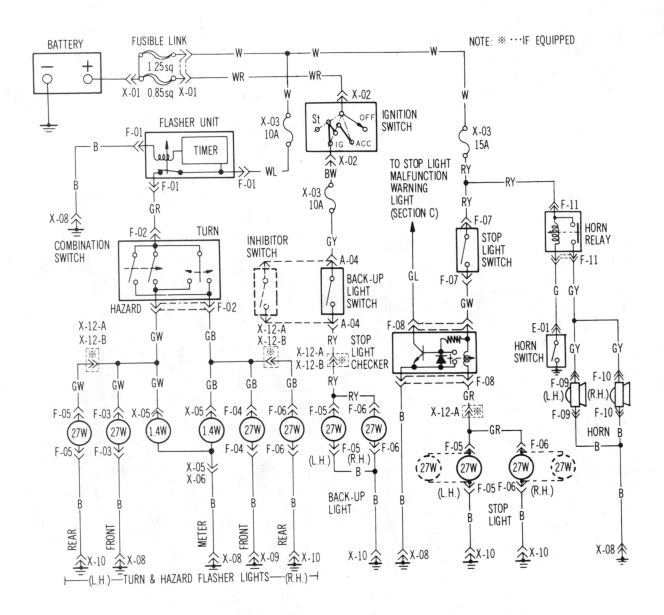

Fig. 10.15 Turn and hazard, back up and stop lights and horn wiring diagram (1981 models)

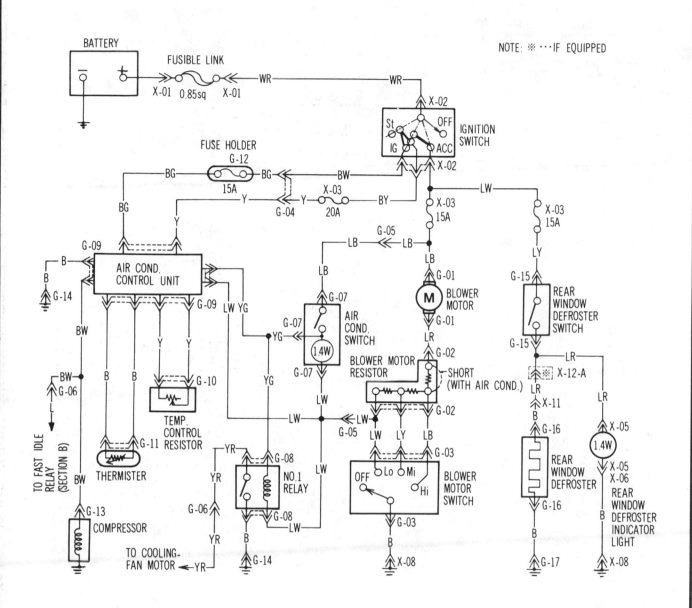

Fig. 10.16 Heater, air conditioner and rear window defroster wiring diagram (1981 models)

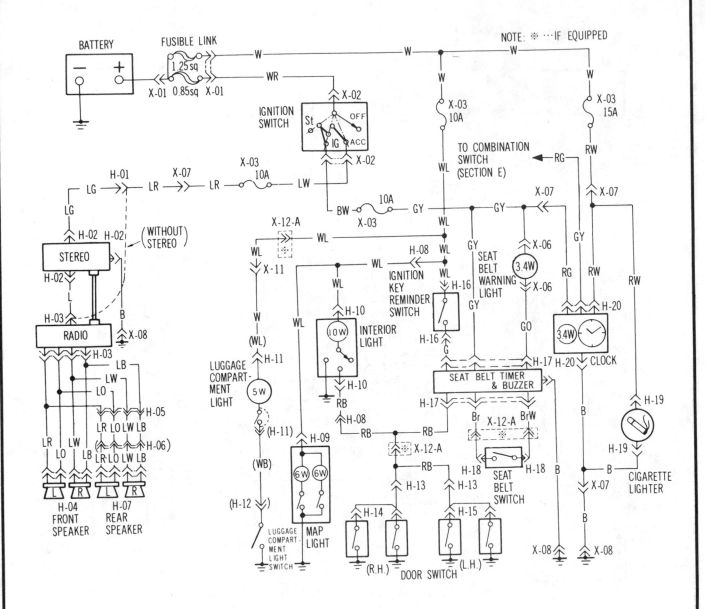

Fig. 10.17 Radio and stereo, luggage compartment light, map lights, interior lights, seat belt warning buzzer, ignition key buzzer, lighter and clock wiring diagram (1981 models)

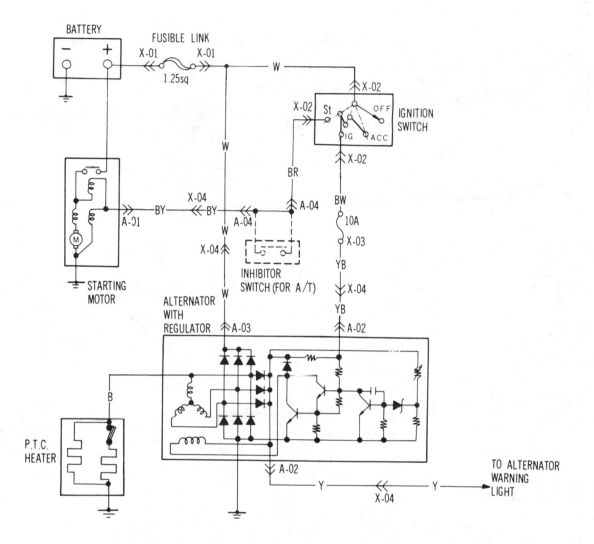

CODE	COLOR	CODE	COLOR
B	Black	Lg	Light green
Br	Brown	O	Orange
G	Green	R	Red
L	Blue	Y	Yellow
Lb	Light blue	W	White

Fig. 10.18 Charging and starting system wiring diagram (1982 models)

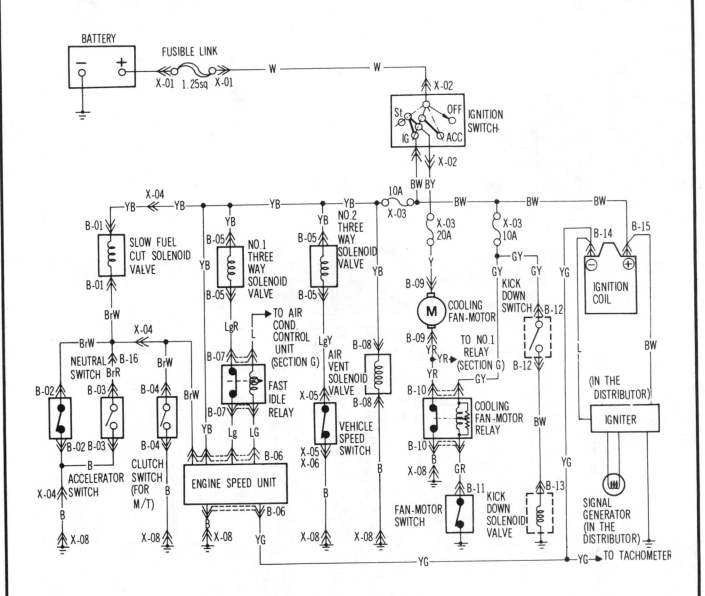

Fig. 10.19 Emissions, ignition, cooling fan and automatic transaxle kickdown system wiring diagram (1982 models)

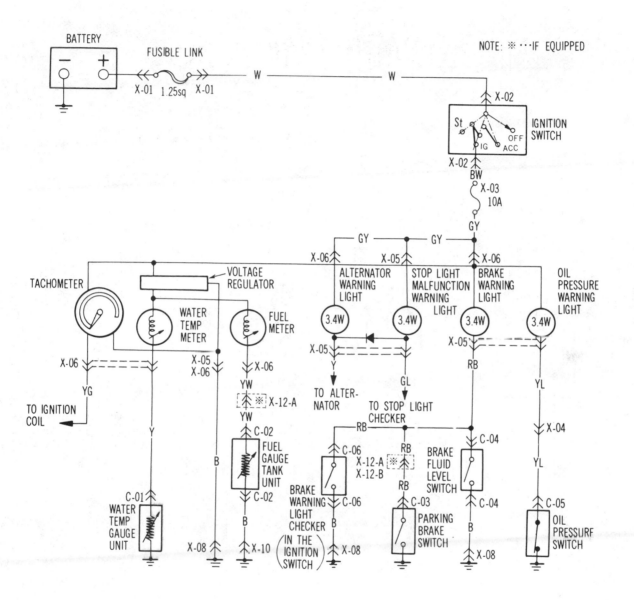

Fig. 10.20 Meter and warning light wiring diagram (1982 models)

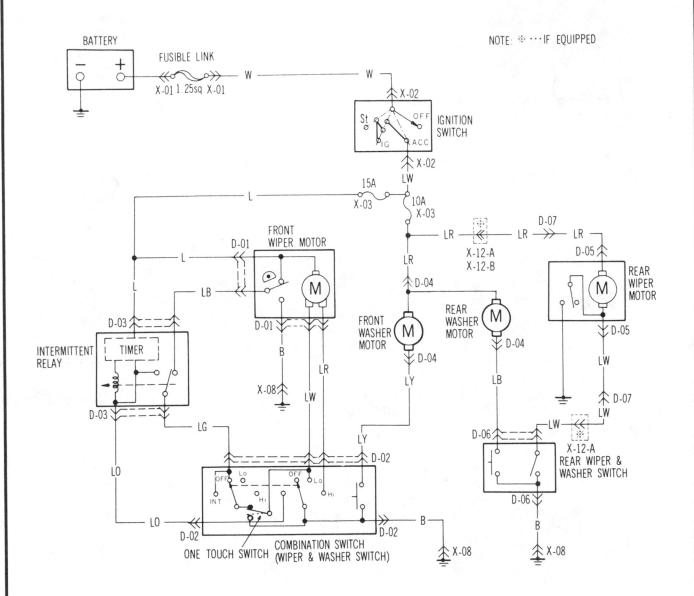

Fig. 10.21 Front and rear wiper and washer wiring diagram (except sedan) (1982 models)

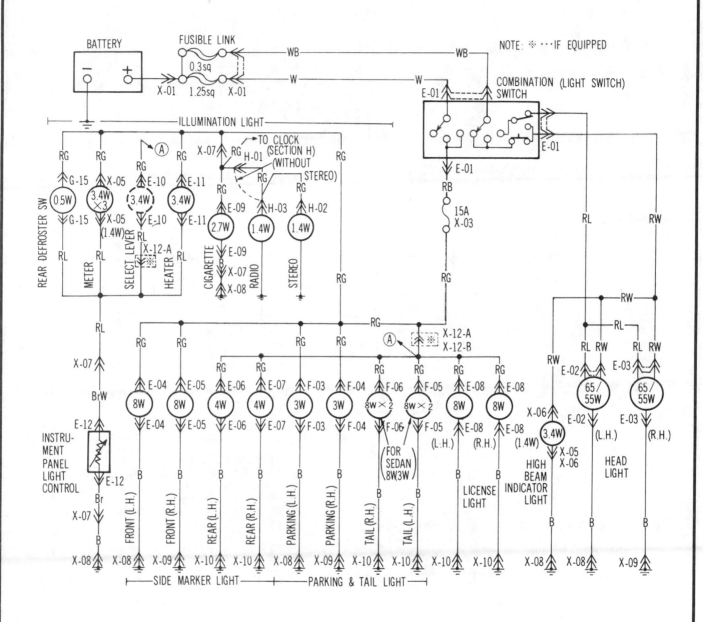

Fig. 10.22 Headlight, side marker lights, parking, tail, license and illumination light system wiring diagram (1982 models)

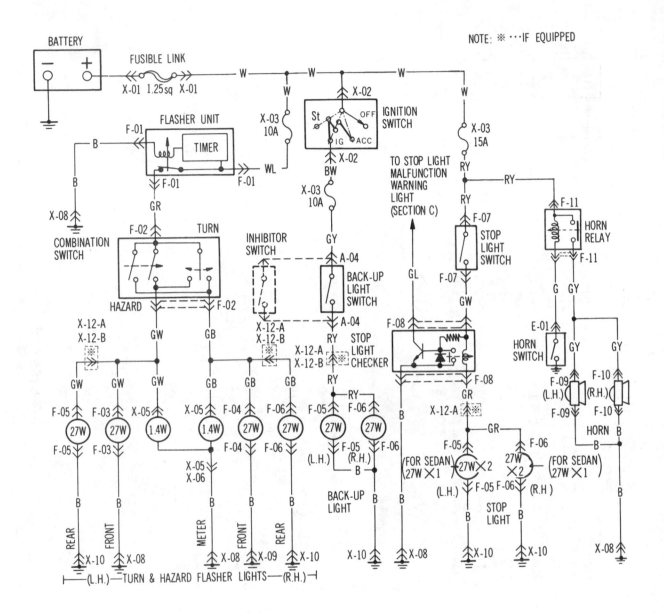

Fig. 10.23 Turn and hazard, backup and stop and horn wiring diagram (1982 models)

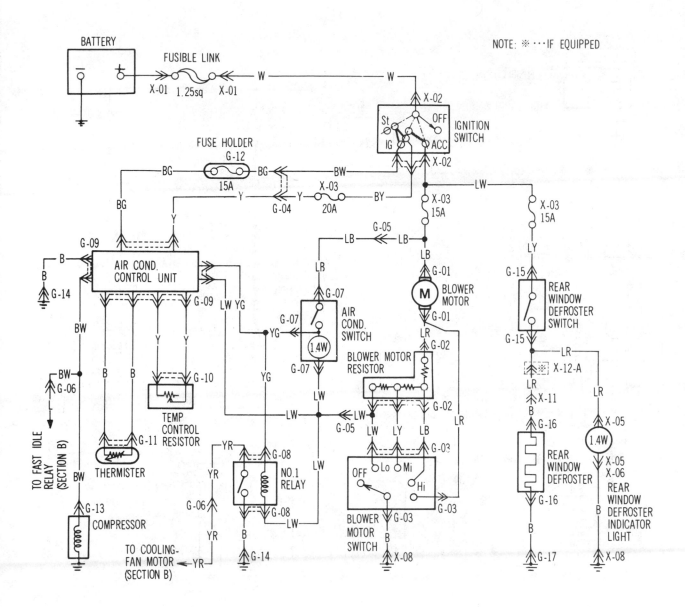

Fig. 10.24 Heater, air conditioner and rear window defroster wiring diagram (1982 models)

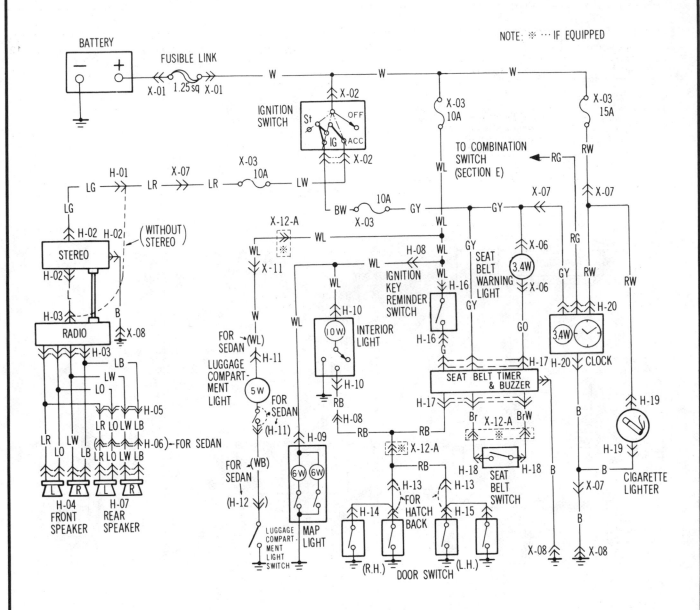

Fig. 10.25 Radio and stereo, luggage compartment system, map lights, interior lights, seat belt warning buzzer, lighter and clock wiring diagram (1982 models)

Chapter 11 Suspension and steering

Refer to Chapter 13 for specifications and information applicable to later USA models

Contents

Specifications

Front suspension

Type	MacPherson strut
Spring free length	14.92 in (379 mm)
Spring diameter	5.20 in (132.2 mm)
Toe-in	0.12 in (3 mm)

Rear suspension

Type	Independent strut
Spring free length	14.35 in (364 mm)
Spring diameter	4.49 in (114 mm)
Toe-in	0 in (0 mm)
Wheel bearing preload	0.2 to 2.2 lb (0.4 to 1.0 kg)

Steering

Type	Rack-and-pinion
Maximum steering wheel free play	1.18 in (30 mm)

Wheels and tires

Wheel size	
Standard	4½ in x 13 in
Optional	5 in x 13 in
Wheel runout limit	0.04 in (1 mm)
Tire size	
Standard	155-13
Optional	155SR-13, 175/70 SR-13
Tire runout limit	0.10 in (2.5 mm)

Torque specifications

Steering	Ft-lb	Nm
Steering wheel nut	29 to 36	40 to 50
Steering gear box-to-frame	23 to 34	32 to 47
Steering bracket	12 to 17	16 to 23
Steering balljoint	13 to 20	18 to 27
Tie-rod lock nut	26 to 29	35 to 40
Tie-rod end-to-steering knuckle	22 to 33	30 to 45
Steering rack-to-tie-rod	43 to 58	60 to 80

Front suspension	Ft-lb	Nm
Steering knuckle-to-shock absorber	58 to 86	80 to 119
Knuckle-to-lower arm balljoint	33 to 40	44 to 55
Lower arm-to-lower arm balljoint	69 to 86	95 to 119
Steering knuckle-to-brake assembly	41 to 48	56 to 66
Upper mounting nuts	17 to 22	23 to 30
Driveaxle lock nut	116 to 174	160 to 240
Steering knuckle-to-tie-rod end	22 to 33	30 to 45
Brake disc-to-hub	33 to 40	45 to 55

11

Rear suspension

	Ft-lb	Nm
Hub spindle-to-shock absorber	69 to 86	95 to 116
Hub spindle-to-brake backing plate	33 to 50	46 to 68
Lateral link through-bolt	46 to 55	64 to 76
Upper mounting nuts	16 to 20	21 to 27
Rear hub lock nut initial torque (see Section 10, Steps 18 thru 22)		
1981 and 1982 models	16 to 19	21 to 28
1983 and later models	18 to 22	24 to 30
Wheel lug nuts	65 to 80	88 to 108

1 General information

The front suspension on all models is of the MacPherson strut type which features a shock absorber strut and spring mounted on top of the steering knuckle. The steering knuckle is located by the lower suspension arm and some models are equipped with a stabilizer bar.

The rear suspension is a modified MacPherson strut design consisting of a shock absorber strut and spring attached to the spindle which is mounted to the ends of the parallel lower links. The assembly is located by a rubber-bushed trailing link.

The shock absorbers on the front and rear suspension struts are integral and can be replaced only by disassembling the strut assemblies.

Steering is of the rack-and-pinion type and the steering column is designed to collapse in the event of an accident.

2 Front stabilizer bar – removal and installation

1 Raise the vehicle and support it securely.
2 Hold the stabilizer bar-to-lower control arm bolt with a wrench and remove the two nuts. Withdraw the bolt and remove the bushings, retainer and spacer.
3 Remove the brackets, bushings and plates retaining the stabilizer bar to the chassis and remove the bar.
4 Installation is a reversal of removal. After installation, the stabilizer-to-lower control arm bolt end must extend $\frac{1}{4}$ inch (6.3 mm) beyond the nuts.

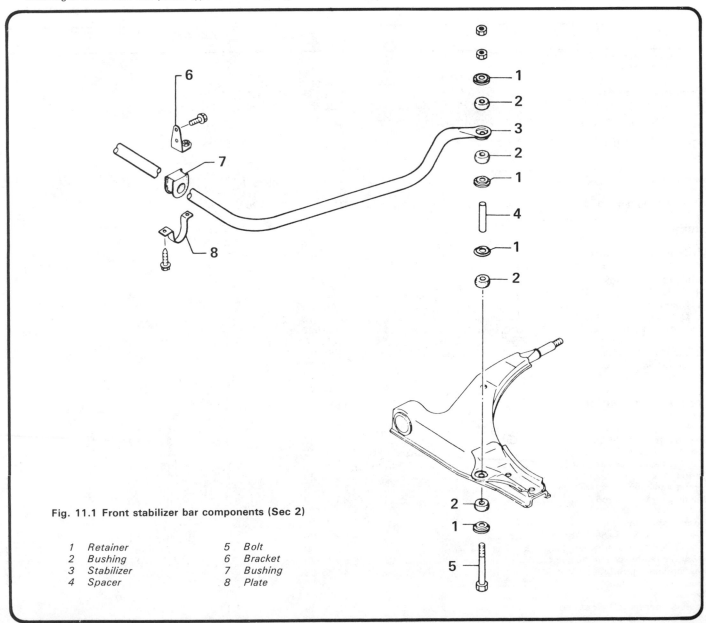

Fig. 11.1 Front stabilizer bar components (Sec 2)

1	Retainer	5	Bolt
2	Bushing	6	Bracket
3	Stabilizer	7	Bushing
4	Spacer	8	Plate

3 Lower control arm – removal and installation

1   Raise the vehicle and support it securely. Remove the front wheels and the lower splash shields.

2   Remove the nuts and bolts from the lower balljoint (photo).
3   Remove the two bolts retaining the rear support of the control arm (photo).
4   Remove the nut and bolts attaching the lower control arm spindle to the chassis (photo).

3.2 Remove the lower balljoint nut while holding the bolt with another wrench

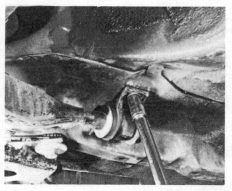

3.3 Remove the lower control arm rear support U-clamp and nuts

3.4 Remove the lower control arm spindle nut and bolts

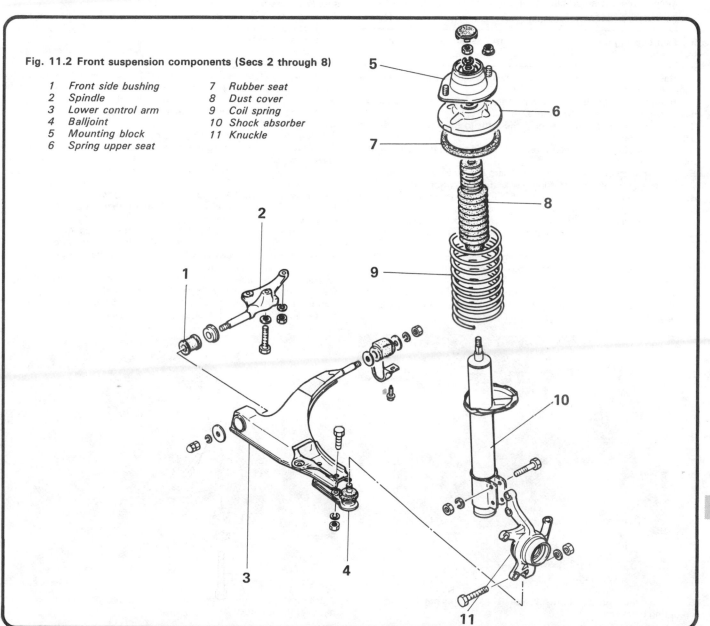

Fig. 11.2 Front suspension components (Secs 2 through 8)

1   Front side bushing
2   Spindle
3   Lower control arm
4   Balljoint
5   Mounting block
6   Spring upper seat
7   Rubber seat
8   Dust cover
9   Coil spring
10   Shock absorber
11   Knuckle

11

5   Disengage the balljoint from the steering knuckle and remove the lower control arm from the vehicle.
6   Installation is the reverse of removal. The lower control arm spindle bolts should not be tightened to specification until the vehicle weight has been lowered onto the suspension.

4   Lower control arm bushings – removal and installation

1   The front side bushing in the control arm can be removed only with special tools. If the bushing is worn, remove the control arm (Section 3), have the bushing pressed out and replaced with a new one.
2   To replace the rear bushing, raise the vehicle and support it securely.
3   Remove the bolts retaining the U-clamp which attaches the control arm to the chassis.
4   Remove the nut from the rear of the control arm and slide the bushing from the arm.
5   Install the new bushing, place the U-clamp into position and install the bolts snugly.
6   Install the nut on the rear of the control arm and tighten to specification.
7   Tighten the U-clamp bolts to specification and lower the vehicle.

5   Front spring and shock absorber strut assembly – removal and installation

1   Raise the vehicle, support it securely, remove the front wheels and open the hood.
2   Remove the spring clip retaining the brake hose, using a pair of pliers to release it from the hole in the bracket.
3   Remove the two nuts retaining the strut to the knuckle and then extract the bolts.
4   In the engine compartment, remove the cap from the center of the rubber strut cover.
5   Loosen the two strut tower nuts. There should be a mark denoting the outside edge of the mounting block. If there is not, mark the side of the block which faces toward the fender with a dab of white paint for ease of installation (photo).
6   With an assistant supporting the weight of the shock tower, remove the strut tower nuts and then withdraw the shock assembly from the vehicle.
7   To install, position the strut assembly with the studs protruding through the fender tower and the marked edge of the mounting block outward.
8   Install the mounting bolts and nuts snugly.
9   Place the brake hose in position and install the retaining clip.
10 Tighten the nuts and bolts to specification.

11 Install the cap in the rubber strut cover, install the front wheels and lower the vehicle.

6   Balljoint – removal and installation

1   Raise the front of the vehicle, support it securely and remove the front wheels.
2   Remove the nut and bolt retaining the balljoint to the steering knuckle.
3   Unbolt the balljoint from the lower control arm (two bolts).
4   Remove the balljoint from the steering knuckle. It may be necessary to tap lightly on the knuckle to release the balljoint.
5   To install, place the balljoint in position, install the retaining nuts and bolts and tighten to specification.
6   Install the wheels and lower the vehicle.

7   Spring and shock absorber assembly – dismantling, inspection and reassembly

Caution: *During certain portions of this procedure, the coil spring will be under pressure. Care should be exercised and only proper tools should be used.*
1   Remove the shock absorber strut (Sections 5 and 9).
2   Place the strut assembly in a vise, using two blocks of wood to protect the strut tube.
3   Loosen (but do not remove) the nut at the top of the spring tower (photo).
4   Install a suitable spring compressor. Make sure that the bottom of the compressor seats securely at the base of the spring tower and the jaws have a tight grip on the top coil (photo).
5   Slowly and carefully apply pressure with the compressor until the spring insulator and collar are loose.
6   Remove the nut and lift off the collar assembly.
7   Slowly release the spring tension and lift the spring from the tower. The spring should be kept in the vertical position during this operation because if it tips over and slips from the compressor it could be ejected with great force and cause injury. It is a good idea to mark the top and bottom locations of the spring ends prior to removal.
8   Remove the dust cover and inspect the shock strut rod for grooves, wear or signs that the plating is flaking off.
9   Remove the shock absorber and pump it in complete strokes several times to check for smooth and uniform action throughout the stroke. Check to make sure there is no lag in the smooth operation when the direction of travel is changed in mid stroke and that the resistance on extension and compression is uniform. Inspect the seals for signs of excessive leakage, a small amount of oil around the seal is normal. The shock absorber unit is not rebuildable. A faulty unit must be replaced with a new one from your dealer or a replacement

5.5 Loosen the strut tower nuts. White paint denotes outside edge of mounting block (arrow)

7.3 With the strut unit in the horizontal position, loosen (but do not remove) the top nut

7.4 Proper installation of the spring compressor

cartridge available at auto parts stores.
10 Place the shock absorber unit in the vise and install the spring to the tower. Slowly apply spring pressure with the compressor until the insulator, metal collar and rubber cover can be installed.
11 Install the nut and washer, tightening the nut snugly.
12 Remove the spring compressor carefully, making sure that the nut is holding the assembly together.
13 Place the strut assembly in the vise horizontally and tighten the nut to specification.
14 Install the spring and shock absorber assembly to the vehicle (Sections 5 and 9).

8 Front hub – removal and installation

1 Raise the front of the vehicle, support it securely and remove the front wheels.
2 Use a drift punch and a hammer to drive up the portion of the hub nut collar which has been peened into the spindle groove so that the nut can be removed. An alternative method is to grind a small bolt into a chisel shape to use as a tool which can be driven along the groove to bend the nut collar upward evenly (photo).
3 Remove the hub nut.
4 Disconnect the steering tie-rod by removing the cotter key and nut

8.2 Drive the nut collar clear of the groove

and then pressing the tie-rod from the knuckle with a suitable tool.
5 Disconnect the brake hose from the caliper and plug it.
6 Unbolt the caliper and use a piece of wire to retain it out of the way.
7 Remove the lower balljoint retaining nut and bolt.
8 Remove the two strut-to-steering knuckle bolts. It may be necessary to lift up on the hub to relieve pressure so that the bolts can be withdrawn.
9 Carefully withdraw the hub from the axle splines and the vehicle.
10 Inspect the hub splines and grease seal for damage or leaking. Special tools are required to disassemble the hub so if any faults are detected it should be taken to your dealer or a properly equipped shop for further dismantling and inspection.
11 Prior to installation apply a thin coat of wheel bearing grease to the spline and grease seal.
12 To install, place the hub in position, install the bolts and tighten them to specification.
13 Install a new hub nut, tighten it to specification and peen it in place in the groove with a hammer and suitable rounded punch.
14 Install the brake caliper and hose and bleed the brakes (Chapter 9).
15 Install the front wheels and lower the vehicle.

9 Rear spring and shock absorber assembly – removal and installation

1 Raise the rear of the vehicle, support it securely and remove the rear wheels.
2 From inside the vehicle, remove the trim panel (Chapter 12) and remove the top shock absorber mounting nuts.
3 From underneath the vehicle, disconnect the brake hose from the strut, unscrew it from the rigid brake line and plug it.
4 Disconnect the parking brake cable at the brake backing plate.
5 Unbolt the trailing arm from the lower side of the strut.
6 Unbolt and disconnect the lateral link from the strut and remove the strut and brake assembly as a unit.
7 Remove the nuts and bolts retaining the brake assembly to the strut and remove the brake. Refer to Section 7 for further disassembly and inspection.
8 To install, place the brake assembly in position on the strut, install the nuts and bolts and tighten them to specification.
9 Install the strut assembly to the vehicle, tightening the nuts and bolts snugly. Unplug the brake line and connect it to the brake and reconnect the parking brake cable.
10 Install the wheels and lower the vehicle onto the suspension.
11 Tighten the suspension bolts to specification.
12 Inside the vehicle, tighten the upper mounting nuts to specification and install the trim panel.

10 Rear hub and bearings – removal, inspection, lubrication and installation

1 Raise the rear of the vehicle, support it securely and remove the rear wheels.
2 Loosen the grease cap by working around its circumference with a screwdriver or chisel to pry it loose. Remove the grease cap (photo).
3 Use a drift punch or a $\frac{1}{4}$ inch or larger bolt which has been ground to a chisel point to drive upward the peened portion of the hub nut collar.
4 Remove the hub nut.
5 Retain the outer bearings while removing the hub (photo).
6 Wipe the spindle with a clean rag and inspect for cracks and signs of overheating.
7 Inspect the brake drum for damage (Chapter 1).
8 Pry the inner bearing seal carefully from the hub with a screwdriver or equivalent (photo).
9 Use a suitable drift punch to drive out the outer bearing, using the indentations in the hub. Discard the seals (photo).
10 Clean the bearings in a suitable solvent. If compressed air is available, blow the bearing dry taking care not to spin it.
11 Inspect the bearings for looseness, scoring or signs that the bearing race has spun.
12 If the bearing races are scored, rusted or damaged, drive them out using a suitable drift punch and replace them with new ones as a set.

11

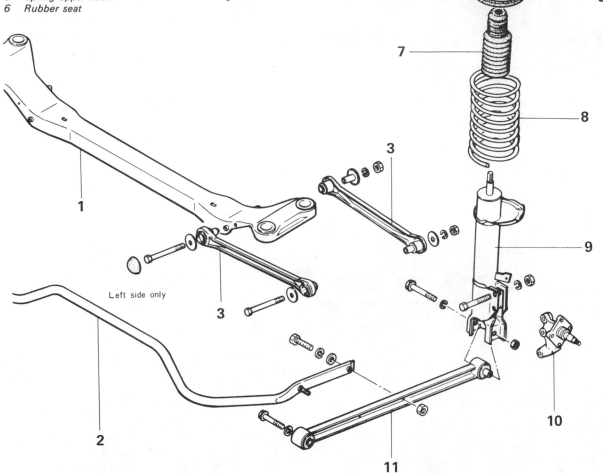

Fig. 11.3 Rear suspension components – left side (Secs 9, 11, 13, 12 and 14)

1 Crossmember
2 Stabilizer bar
3 Lateral link
4 Mounting block
5 Spring upper seat
6 Rubber seat
7 Dust cover
8 Coil spring
9 Shock absorber
10 Rear hub spindle
11 Trailing link

Left side only

10.2 Loosen the grease cap by working around its circumference with a chisel

10.5 Hold the wheel bearings in place while sliding the hub off the spindle

10.8 Pry the bearing seal from the hub

13 Lubricate the bearings, using the specified grease (see Chapter 1 specifications) (photo).
14 Install the outer bearing in position and tap it into place using a brass drift and a hammer until it is seated.
15 Pack the space in the hub between the inner and outer races with the specified grease.
16 Install the inner bearing.
17 Tap a new grease seal into place and lubricate the outer lip.
18 Install the hub on the spindle, followed by the washer and a *new* lock nut. Tighten the lock nut to the initial torque specification (16 to 19 ft-lbs for 1981 and 1982 models/18 to 22 ft-lbs for 1983 and later models).
19 Turn the hub two or three revolutions to seat the bearings, then loosen the lock nut slightly (until it can be turned with your fingers).
20 Attach a spring scale to one of the lug nut studs and pull on the scale to see how much force (in pounds) is required to just start turning the hub. Add the force required to turn the hub to the standard bearing preload (0.9 to 2.2 lb) and record the figure for future reference.
21 Slowly turn the hub with the scale, while tightening the lock nut, until the figure determined in Step 20 is reached on the scale — DO NOT TIGHTEN THE LOCK NUT ANY FARTHER!
22 Stake the lock nut collar into the spindle keyway (photo 10.21) so the nut cannot turn.
23 Install the wheel and tighten the lug nuts evenly and securely.

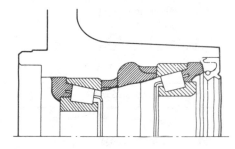

Fig. 11.4   Rear hub bearing grease packing locations (Sec 10)

Fig. 11.5   Checking rear wheel bearing preload (Sec 10)

10.9 Drive the inner bearing race out of the hub with a drift punch

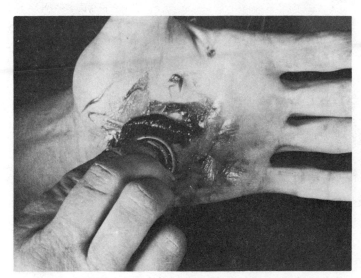

10.13 Work the grease into the bearings from the back of the rollers

10.21 Stake the hub nut collar into the spindle groove

11

11 Rear stabilizer bar – removal and installation

1   Raise the rear of the vehicle, support it securely and remove the
rear wheels.
2   Remove the nuts and bolts retaining the stabilizer bar to the
trailing links.
3   Remove the stabilizer bar from the vehicle.
4   Installation is the reverse of removal, however, the vehicle weight
should be lowered onto the suspension before the stabilizer nuts and
bolts are tightened to specification.

12 Rear trailing link – removal and installation

1   Raise the rear of the vehicle, support it securely and remove the
wheels.
2   Unbolt the stabilizer bar and remove it (Section 11).
3   Remove the bolts at either end of the trailing link and remove the
link from the vehicle.
4   To install, place the front end of the link in position, install the
sway bar without the bolts and then insert and start to thread in the
front bolt.
5   Install the rear end of the link to the shock absorber. Use a plastic
hammer to tap on the link so that the bolt can be inserted.
6   Install the stabilizer bar bolts.
7   Install the wheels and lower the vehicle weight onto the suspension before tightening the bolts to specification.

13 Rear lateral link – removal and installation

1   Raise the rear of the vehicle, support it securely and remove the
wheels.
2   Remove the spindle-to-lateral link through-bolt.
3   Mark the position of the toe-in adjustment mounting bolt.
4   Remove the nut from the through-bolt of the crossmember.
5   Place a jack under the center of the crossmember.
6   Remove the four nuts retaining the crossmember to the body.
7   To remove the left side lateral link, disconnect and plug the brake
lines at the junction block on the crossmember.
8   Remove the two nuts retaining the parking brake cable to the fuel
tank.
9   Lower the jack until the crossmember through-bolt can be
removed.
10   Remove the left side lateral link.
11   To remove the right side lateral link it will first be necessary to
remove the muffler rubber isolator. It will then be possible to lower the
crossmember, remove the through-bolts and remove the lateral link.
12   Installation is the reverse of removal. Install the crossmember
bolts and tighten to specification but all nuts and bolts pertaining to
the suspension should be installed snugly. After vehicle weight has
been lowered onto the suspension, tighten these bolts to specification.
Have the toe-in checked by a dealer or qualified specialist as soon as
possible.

14 Rear spindle — removal and installation

1   Raise the vehicle, support it securely and remove the wheels.
2   Remove the rear hub (Section 10).
3   Disconnect the brake hose from the shock absorber strut.
4   Disconnect and plug the brake hose at the flex line.
5   Disconnect the parking brake spring from the cable.
6   Remove the pin and disconnect the parking brake cable.
7   Unbolt the backing plate assembly (four bolts) (photo).
8   Remove the lower shock absorber strut bolt.
9   Remove the lateral link through-bolt by lifting up on the spindle
and then working the bolt out (photo).
10   Remove the two strut-to-spindle bolts and remove the spindle.
11   Installation is a reversal of removal. All nuts and bolts related to
the suspension should not be tightened to specification until the ve-
icle weight has been lowered onto the suspension.

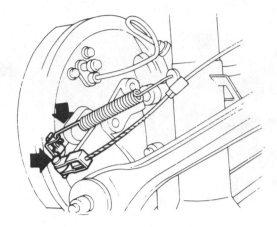

Fig. 11.6 Parking brake spring and pin (arrows) (Sec 14)

14.7 Unbolt and remove the backing plate

14.9 Remove the nut, then pull the bolt out while lifting
the spindle

15 Steering – general information

All models are equipped with rack-and-pinion steering. The steering unit is bolted to the chassis behind the engine and operates the steering arms by way of tie-rods. The inner ends of the tie-rods are protected by rubber boots which should be inspected periodically for looseness, cuts and leaking lubricant.

The steering wheel operates the steering shaft which actuates the steering unit through universal joints. Looseness in the steering can be caused by wear in the steering shaft universal joints, the rack-and-pinion unit, the tie-rod and rod ends or loose steering unit retaining bolts.

16 Steering wheel – removal and installation

1 Disconnect the battery negative cable.
2 Grasp the horn cover at the upper edge and snap it rearward to remove it.
3 Remove the wheel retaining nut.
4 Mark the relationship of the wheel and hub for ease of installation.
5 Use a suitable wheel puller to draw the wheel off the steering shaft (photo). **Note:** *Do not strike the end of the steering shaft.*

16.5 Pull in and then out on the rim to remove the steering wheel

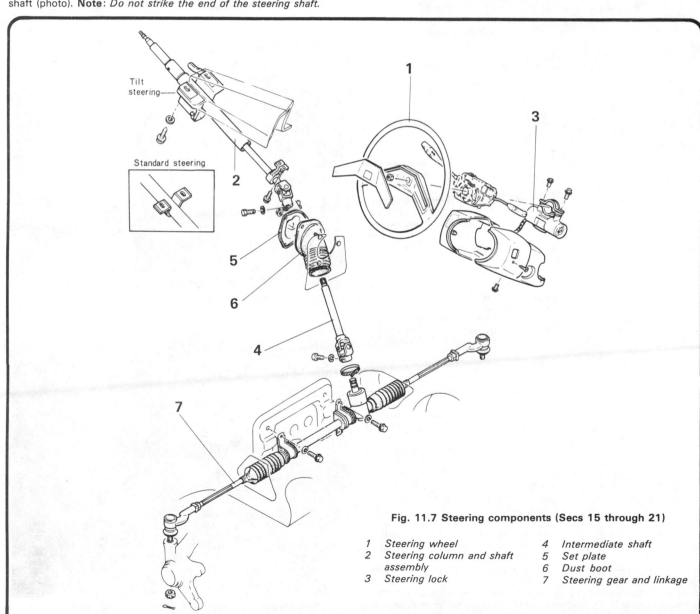

Fig. 11.7 Steering components (Secs 15 through 21)

1	Steering wheel	4	Intermediate shaft
2	Steering column and shaft assembly	5	Set plate
3	Steering lock	6	Dust boot
		7	Steering gear and linkage

11

6   To install, place the wheel on the shaft and align the marks made during removal.
7   Install the hub nut and tighten to specification.

17 Steering column – removal, inspection and installation

1   Disconnect the battery negative cable.
2   Mark the relationship of the hub and wheel and remove the steering wheel (Section 16).
3   Unplug the combination switch.
4   Remove the underdash cover for access.
5   Remove the lock pin from the steering shaft coupler retaining bolt and remove the bolt.
6   Remove the upper and lower steering column support bolts and slide the column upward (photo).
7   Unplug the ignition switch.
8   Withdraw the steering column from the vehicle.
9   Inspect the steering column and shaft for damage and free movement of the steering shaft. Check the steering column bearings for binding (Section 18).
10   To install, carefully insert the steering column into position under the dash, making sure not to snag any wires.
11   Place the splines of the steering column universal joint over the steering shaft splines.
12   Install the upper steering column support bolts finger-tight.
13   Install the lower steering column support bolts and tighten them.
14   Tighten the top column support bolts at this time.
15   Install the steering shaft universal joint bolts. Install the retaining clip through the end of the bolt.
16   Plug in the ignition switch connector and fasten the wires to the switch with the tab.
17   Install the underdash cover.
18   Install the steering wheel (Section 16).
19   Connect the battery negative cable.

18 Steering column bearings – removal, inspection and replacement

1   Remove the steering column (Section 16) and place it securely in a vise using wood blocks to protect from damage by the vise jaws.
2   Turn the steering shaft to determine if the bearings are dry or causing binding. In either case, replace the bearings with new ones rather than attempt to lubricate them.
3   Remove the upper bearing by prying it from the column tube (photo).
4   Remove the bottom bearing using a slide hammer.
5   To remove the lower steering shaft bearing, slide it up the shaft (away from the universal joint) and then off the shaft (photo).
6   Slide the new bearings into position and then temporarily install the steering wheel to check for proper operation prior to installing the column to the vehicle.
7   Reinstall the steering column (Section 16).

19 Steering gear boot – removal and installation

1   The boot should be replaced with a new one if it is cut, loose or leaking lubricant.
2   Raise the front of the vehicle, support it securely and remove the wheels.
3   Mark the location of the boot.
4   Remove the outer (smaller) boot band with a pair of pliers.
5   Remove the inner boot band by cutting it.
6   Disconnect the tie-rod end (Section 20).
7   Slide the boot off the tie-rod and remove it from the vehicle.
8   Prior to installing a new boot, clean the length of the tie-rod and lubricate the steering gear joint with the specified lubricant (Chapter 1).
9   Slide the new boot into position along the tie-rod to the marked position.
10   Install the large boot band supplied with the replacement kit by pulling it tight with a pair of pliers. The band must be installed with the groove facing inward.
11   Install the outer boot band.

17.6 When removing the steering column, make sure that it is not entangled under dash wires

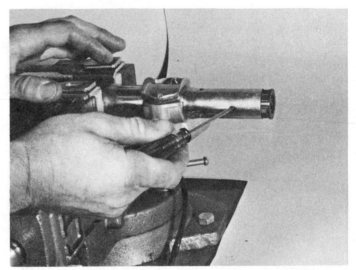

18.3 Removing the upper steering column bearing with a screwdriver

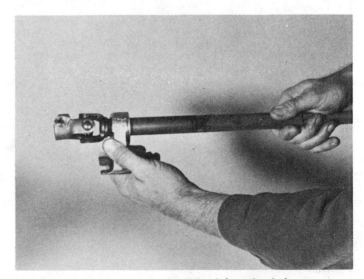

18.5 Remove the lower bearing by sliding it from the shaft

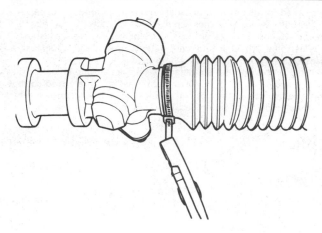

Fig. 11.8 Inner steering boot band installation (Sec 19)

12 Connect the tie-rod end.
13 Install the wheels and lower the vehicle.

20 Tie-rod end – removal and installation

1   The tie-rod end should be replaced if wear causes excessive
looseness or the rubber boot is cut or leaking lubricant.
2   Raise the front of the vehicle, support it securely and remove the
front wheels.
3   Remove the tie-rod end nut (photo).
4   Use a suitable tool to disconnect the rod end from the steering
arm (photo).
5   Mark the location of the rod end lock nut.
6   Loosen the lock nut and unscrew the rod end from the tie-rod.
7   Thread the new rod end into the tie-rod to the position marked
prior to removal and tighten the lock nut to specification.
8   Install the toe-rod end to the steering arm, install the nut and
tighten to specification.
9   Install the front wheels and lower the vehicle.
10 It is a good idea to have the front end suspension alignment
checked after the replacement of any steering component.

21 Steering gear – removal and installation

1   Raise the vehicle, support it securely and remove the front wheels.
2   Disconnect the tie-rod end from the steering arm (Section 20).
3   Cut and remove the strap retaining the steering shaft dust boot to
the steering gear housing and pull back the boot for access.
4   Remove the steering shaft-to-gear retaining bolt.
5   Unbolt the steering gear and withdraw the assembly complete
with the tie-rod assemblies through the tie-rod hole in the chassis.
6   Installation is the reverse of removal. Make sure the steering
wheel and the front wheels are in the straight-ahead position when
inserting the steering gear splines to the steering shaft. Have the front
end alignment checked by a dealer or qualified specialist.

22 Steering angles and wheel alignment

1   Proper wheel alignment is essential to proper steering and even tire
wear. Symptoms of alignment faults are pulling of the steering to one
side or the other and uneven tire wear.
2   If these symptoms are present, check for the following before
having the alignment adjusted:

   Loose steering gear bolts
   Damaged or worn steering gear mounts
   Improperly adjusted wheel bearings
   Bent tie-rods.
   Worn balljoint
   Insufficient steering gearbox lubricant
   Improper tire pressure
   Mixing tires of different construction

20.3 Remove the tie-rod end cotter pin and nut

20.4 Press the rod end out of the knuckle

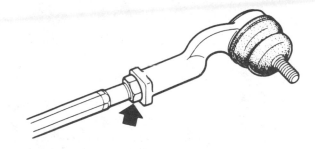

Fig. 11.9 Tie-rod lock nut marking location (Sec 20)

11

3   Alignment faults in the rear suspension are manifest in uneven tire
wear or uneven tracking of the rear wheels. This can be easily checked
by driving the vehicle straight across a puddle of water onto a dry
patch of pavement. If the rear wheels do not follow the fronts almost
exactly, the alignment should be adjusted.
4   Front or rear wheel alignment should be left to your dealer or a
properly-equipped shop.

23 Wheels and tires

1   Check the tire pressure (cold) weekly.
2   Inspect the sidewalls and treads periodically for damage and signs of abnormal or uneven wear.
3   Make sure the wheel lug nuts are properly tightened.
4   Do not mix tires of dissimilar construction or tread pattern on the same axle.
5   Never include the temporary spare in the tire rotation pattern as it is designed for use only until a damaged tire is repaired or replaced.
6   Periodically inspect the wheels for elongated or damaged lug holes, distortion or nicks on the rim. Replace any suspect wheel.
7   Clean the wheel inside and outside and inspect for rust and corrosion which could lead to wheel failure.
8   If the wheel and tire are balanced on the car, one wheel stud and lug hole should be marked whenever the wheel is removed so that it can be reinstalled in the original position. If balanced on the vehicle, the wheel should not be moved to a different axle position.

Chapter 12 Bodywork

Contents

1   General information

Models are available in 2-door hatchback, 4-door hatchback and 4-door sedan body styles.

The body is of unitized construction and certain components which are vulnerable to accident damage can be unbolted and replaced with new units. Among these are the front fenders, grille, hood, doors, trunk and bumpers.

2   Maintenance – body and frame

1   The condition of your vehicle's body is very important, as it is on this that the second hand value will mainly depend. It is much more difficult to repair a neglected or damaged body than it is to repair mechanical components. The hidden areas of the body, such as the fender wells, the frame, and the engine compartment, are equally important, although obviously not requiring as frequent attention as the rest of the body.

2   Once a year, or every 12 000 miles, it is a good idea to have the underside of the body and the frame steam cleaned. All traces of dirt and oil will be removed and the underside can then be inspected carefully for rust, damaged brake lines, frayed electrical wiring, damaged cables, and other problems. The front suspension components should be greased upon completion of this job.

3   At the same time, clean the engine and the engine compartment using either a steam cleaner or a water soluble degreaser.

4   The fender wells should be given particular attention, as undercoating can peel away and stones and dirt thrown up by the tires can cause the paint to chip and flake, allowing rust to set in. If rust is found, clean down to the bare metal and apply an antirust paint.

5   The body should be washed once a week (or when dirty). Thoroughly wet the vehicle to soften the dirt, then wash it down with a soft sponge and plenty of clean soapy water. If the surplus dirt is not washed off very carefully, it will in time wear down the paint.

6   Spots of tar or asphalt coating thrown from the road surfaces are best removed with a cloth soaked in solvent.

7   Once every six months, give the body and chrome trim a thorough wax job. If a chrome cleaner is used to remove rust on any of the vehicle's plated parts, remember that the cleaner also removes part of the chrome so use it sparingly.

3   Maintenance – upholstery and carpets

1   Every three months, remove the carpets or mats and thoroughly clean the interior of the vehicle (more frequently if necessary). Vacuum the upholstery and carpets to remove loose dirt and dust.

2   If the upholstery is soiled, apply an upholstery cleaner with a damp sponge and wipe it with a clean, dry cloth.

4   Body repair – minor damage

See color photo sequence on pages 158 and 159.

Repair of minor scratches

If the scratch is very superficial, and does not penetrate to the metal of the bodywork, repair is very simple. Lightly rub the area of the scratch with a fine rubbing compound to remove loose paint from the scratch and to clear the surrounding paint of wax buildup. Rinse the area with clean water.

Apply touch-up paint to the scratch using a small brush. Continue to apply thin layers of paint until the surface of the paint in the scratch is level with the surrounding paint. Allow the new paint at least two weeks to harden, then blend it into the surrounding paint by rubbing with a very fine rubbing compound. Finally, apply a coat of wax to the scratch area.

Where the scratch has penetrated the paint and exposed the metal of the body, causing the metal to rust, a different repair technique is required. Remove any loose rust from the bottom of the scratch with a pocket knife, then apply rust inhibiting paint to prevent the formation of rust in the future. Using a rubber or nylon applicator, coat the scratched area with glaze type filler. If required, this filler can be mixed with thinner to provide a very thin paste which is ideal for filling narrow scratches. Before the glaze filler in the scratch hardens, wrap a piece of smooth cotton cloth around the top of a finger. Dip the cloth in thinner and then quickly wipe it along the surface of the scratch. This will ensure that the surface of the filler is slightly hollowed. The scratch can now be painted over as described earlier in this Section.

Repair of dents

When deep denting of the vehicle's bodywork has taken place, the first task is to pull the dent out until the affected area nearly attains its

12

original shape. There is little point in trying to restore the original shape completely as the metal in the damaged area will have stretched on impact and cannot be reshaped fully to its original contours. It is better to bring the level of the dent up to a point which is about $\frac{1}{8}$ in below the level of the surrounding metal. In cases where the dent is very shallow, it is not worth trying to pull it out at all.

If the underside of the dent is accessible, it can be hammered out gently from behind using a mallet with a wooden or plastic head. Whilst doing this, hold a suitable block of wood firmly against the metal to absorb the hammer blows and thus prevent a large area of the metal from being stretched out.

If the dent is in a section of the body which has double layers, or some other factor making it inaccessible from behind, a different technique is in order. Drill several small holes through the metal inside the damaged area, particularly in the deeper sections. Screw long self-tapping screws into the holes just enough for them to get a good grip in the metal. Now the dent can be pulled out by pulling on the protruding head of the screws with a pair of locking pliers.

The next stage of the repair is the removal of the paint from the damaged area and from an inch or so of the surrounding 'sound' metal. This is accomplished most easily by using a wire brush or sanding disk in a drill motor, although it can be done just as effectively by hand with sandpaper. To complete the preparation for filling, score the surface of the bare metal with a screwdriver or the tang of a file (or drill small holes in the affected area). This will provide a really good 'key' for the filler material. To complete the repair, see the Section on filling and painting.

Repair of rust holes or gashes

Remove all paint from the affected area and from an inch or so of the surrounding 'sound' metal using a sanding disk or wire brush mounted in a drill motor. If these are not available a few sheets of sandpaper will do the job just as effectively. With the paint removed you will be able to determine the severity of the corrosion and therefore decide whether to replace the whole panel if possible, or to repair the affected area. New body panels are not as expensive as most people think and it is often quicker and more satisfactory to install a new panel than to attempt to repair large areas of rust.

Remove all trim pieces from the affected area (except those which will act as a guide to the original shape of the damaged body ie. headlamp shells etc). Then, using metal snips or a hacksaw blade, remove all loose metal and any other metal that is badly affected by rust. Hammer the edges of the hole inwards to create a slight depression for the filler material.

Wire brush the affected area to remove the powdery rust from the surface of the metal. If the back of the rusted area is accessible, treat it with rust-inhibiting paint.

Before filling can be done it will be necessary to block the hole in some way. This can be accomplished with sheet metal riveted or screwed into place, or by stuffing the hole with wire mesh.

Once the hole is blocked off the affected area can be filled and painted (see the following section on filling and painting).

Filling and painting

Many types of body fillers are available, but generally speaking, body repair kits which contain filler paste and a tube of resin hardener are best for this type of repair work. A wide, flexible plastic or nylon applicator will be necessary for imparting a smooth and contoured finish to the surface of the filler material.

Mix up a small amount of filler on a clean piece of wood or cardboard (use the hardener sparingly). Follow the maker's instructions on the package, otherwise the filler will set incorrectly.

Using the applicator, apply the filler paste to the prepared area. Draw the applicator across the surface of the filler to achieve the desired contour and to level the filler surface. As soon as a contour that approximates the correct one is achieved, stop working the paste. If you continue, the paste will begin to stick to the applicator. Continue to add thin layers of filler paste at 20-minute intervals until the level of the filler is just proud of the surrounding metal.

Once the filler has hardened, excess can be removed using a body file. From then on, progressively finer grades of sandpaper should be used, starting with a 180-grit paper and finishing with 600-grit wet-or-dry paper. Always wrap the sandpaper around a flat rubber or wooden block, otherwise the surface of the filler will not be completely flat. During the sanding of the filler surface the wet-or-dry paper

should be periodically rinsed in water. This will ensure that a very smooth finish is produced in the final stage.

At this point, the repair area should be surrounded by a ring of bare metal, which in turn should be encircled by the finely feathered edge of the good paint. Rinse the repair area with clean water until all of the dust produced by the sand operation has gone.

Spray the entire area with a light coat of primer. This will reveal any imperfections in the surface of the filler. Repair these imperfections with fresh filler paste or glaze filler and once more smooth the surface with sandpaper. Repeat this spray-and-repair procedure until you are satisfied that the surface of the filler and the feathered edge of the paintwork are perfect. Rinse the area with clean water and allow it to dry completely.

The repair area is now ready for painting. Paint spraying must be carried out in a warm, dry, windless and dustfree atmosphere. These conditions can be created if you have access to a large indoor working area, but if you are forced to work in the open, you will have to pick your day very carefully. If you are working indoors, dousing the floor in the work area with water will help to settle the dust which would otherwise be in the air. If the repair area is confined to one body panel, mask off the surrounding panels. This will help to minimise the effects of a slight mis-match in paint color. Trim pieces such as chrome strips, door handles, etc., will also need to be masked off or removed. Use masking tape and several thicknesses of newspaper for the masking operations.

Before spraying, shake the paint can thoroughly, then spray a test area until the technique is mastered. Cover the repair area with a thick coat of primer. The thickness should be built up using several thin layers of primer rather than one thick one. Using 600-grit wet-or-dry sandpaper, rub down the surface of the primer until it is very smooth. While doing this, the work area should be thoroughly rinsed with water, and the wet-or-dry sandpaper periodically rinsed as well. Allow the primer to dry before spraying additional coats.

Spray on the top coat, again building up the thickness by using several thin layers of paint. Begin spraying in the center of the repair area and then, using a circular motion, work out until the whole repair area and about two inches of the surrounding original paint is covered. Remove all masking material 10 to 15 minutes after spraying on the final coat of paint. Allow the new paint at least two weeks to harden, then using a very fine rubbing compound, blend the edges of the paint into the existing paint. Finally, apply a coat of wax.

---

5   Body repair – major damage

1   Major damage must be repaired by an auto body/frame repair shop with the necessary welding and hydraulic straightening equipment.
2   If the damage has been serious, it is vital that the frame be checked for correct alignment, as the handling of the vehicle will be affected. Other problems, such as excessive tire wear and wear in the transmission and steering may also occur.

---

6   Maintenance – hinges and locks

Once every 3000 miles, or every three months, the door and hood hinges and locks should be given a few drops of light oil or lock lubricant. The door striker plates can be given a thin coat of grease to reduce wear and ensure free movement.

---

7   Weatherstripping – maintenance and replacement

1   The weatherstripping should be kept clean and free of contaminants such as gasoline or oil. Spray the weatherstripping periodically with silicone lubricant to reduce abrasion and cracking.
2   To remove the weatherstripping, pull it from around the door or trunk lid and disengage it from the retaining clips.
3   Use pliers to remove the retaining clips and install them in the new weatherstripping.
4   Install the new weatherstripping by placing it in position and pushing the retainers into the door or trunk lid.

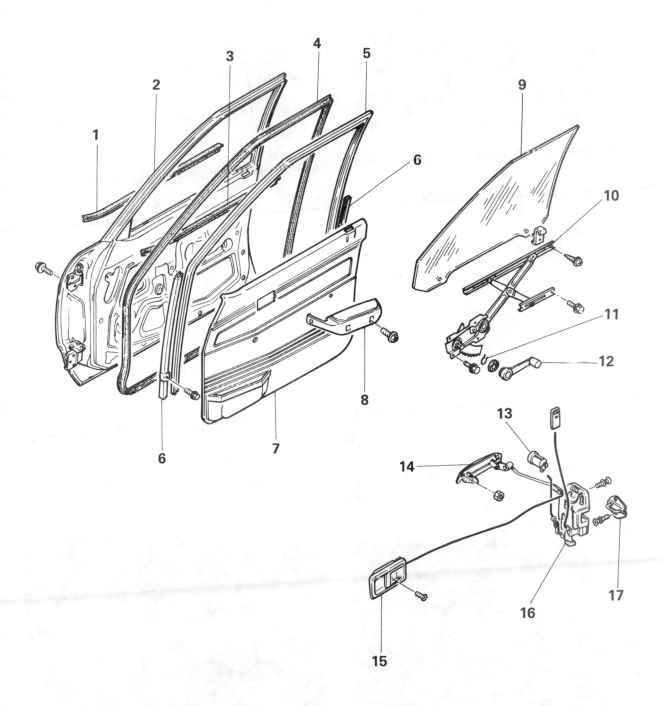

Fig. 12.1 Front door components (Secs 7, 8, 9, 10, 11 and 13)

1 Outer weatherstripping	6 Glass guide	10 Regulator	14 Outer door handle
2 Door	7 Door trim	11 Horseshoe clip (snap-ring)	15 Inner door handle
3 Inner weatherstripping	8 Armrest		16 Door lock (latch)
4 Weatherstripping	9 Glass	12 Regulator handle	17 Latch striker
5 Glass run channel		13 Lock cylinder	

12

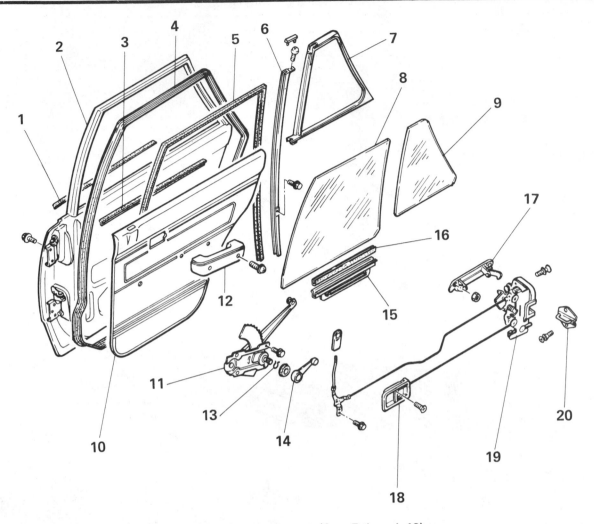

Fig. 12.2 Rear door components (Secs 7 through 13)

1	Outer weatherstripping	7	Quarter window weatherstrip
2	Door	8	Glass
3	Inner weatherstripping	9	Quarter window glass
4	Weatherstripping	10	Door trim
5	Glass run channel	11	Regulator
6	Center channel	12	Armrest
		13	Snap-ring
		14	Regulator handle
		15	Lift bracket
		16	Rubber strip
		17	Outer handle
		18	Inner handle
		19	Door lock
		20	Latch striker

8.2 Loosen the striker and adjust for the proper closing action

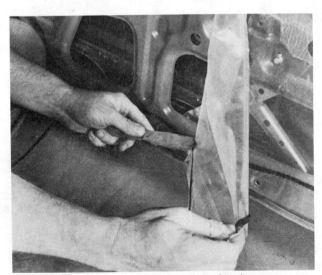

9.5 Scrape along the adhesive when removing the watershield, taking care not to tear it

8 Door striker adjustment

1   If the door does not close smoothly, the door striker should be adjusted.
2   Loosen the mounting screw, adjust the striker and retighten the screws (photo).
3   Repeat the procedure until the door closes properly.

9 Door trim panel – removal and installation

1   Remove the armrest (two screws).
2   Remove the door handle by removing the screw and disengaging the handle from the control rod.
3   Remove the window crank by inserting a screwdriver or hooked piece of wire behind the handle to extract the horseshoe clip.
4   Carefully insert a screwdriver between the door panel and door and pry the plastic retaining pins out, working around the circumference until the panel can be removed.
5   Carefully remove the watershield using a scraper or putty knife. Do not damage the watershield as it can be re-used (photo).
6   To install, place the watershield in position and press into place, using the adhesive as a guide. Install the door trim panel and push inward on the retaining and alignment pins to secure it in place. Install the armrest, window crank and door handle.

10 Door latch assembly – removal and installation

1   Remove the door trim panel (Section 9) and glass (Sections 11 and 12).
2   Remove the window glass retainer.

3   Disconnect the outer door lock linkage.
4   Disconnect the rear inner door handle lock link retainer and remove the lock rod through the access hole.
5   Disconnect the outer door latch linkage from the outer door handle.
6   Remove the three latch retaining screws and the bolts attaching the outer door handle in place.
7   Withdraw the latch assembly from the door.
8   To install, place the assembly in the door in the vertical position and then rotate it into place. Install the retaining screws.
9   Reconnect the inside rod to the mechanism.
10 Reinstall the glass retainer by aligning it with the guide and sliding it into place.
11 Reinstall the outside door handle.
12 Install the glass and door trim panel.

11 Front door glass – removal and installation

1   Remove the door trim panel (Section 9).
2   Install the window crank temporarily to raise the glass to sufficient clearance to gain access to the window regulator-to-glass screws.
3   Remove the two retaining screws (photo).
4   Remove the chrome outer strip at the top of the door (photos).
5   Pry the end of the rubber stripping loose and remove it (photo).
6   Lift the glass up and out of the door channel (photo).
7   To install, lower the glass into the door and install the clips and retaining screws at the bottom. It may be necessary to lift up on the glass so that the screws can be tightened properly.
8   Lay the runner weatherstripping in position and, working from the middle, press it in place.
9   Install the outer chrome strip and corner piece.
10 Install the door trim panel.

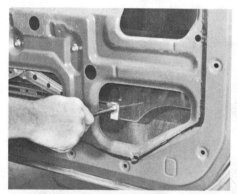
11.3 With the window glass partially raised, remove the retaining screws

11.4a Prying the rear of the front door outer weatherstripping loose

11.4b Remove the front door outer weatherstripping by removing the corner piece

11.5 Remove the window glass weatherstripping by pulling it loose, starting at the rear end

11.6 Lift the glass upward and inward to remove

12 Rear door glass – removal and installation

1   Remove the door trim panel and watershield (Section 9).
2   Remove the center channel screws and lift the channel from the door.
3   Remove the quarter window and glass assembly.
4   Remove both the inner and outer weatherstrips.
5   Install the window crank temporarily and lower the door glass to gain access to the retaining screws. Remove the screws and remove the glass by lowering the rearward side, disengaging it from the roller and holder sliding it upward.
6   To install, lower the glass into position, engage it to the roller and holder and install the retaining screws.
7   Install the inner and outer weatherstrips and quarter glass assembly.
8   Install the center channel and retaining screws.
9   Install the watershield and door trim panel.

13 Window regulator – removal and installation

1   Remove the door trim panel (Section 9) and glass (Sections 11 and 12).
2   Mark the position of the regulator attaching bolts prior to removal for ease of installation.

3   Temporarily install the window crank and move the mechanism to the closed position.
4   Remove the bolts and lift the mechanism from the vehicle through the access hole (photo).
5   To install, place the mechanism in position and install the bolts in the marked position until they are finger-tight.
6   Tighten the bolts in a criss-cross pattern.
7   Install the glass and door trim panel.

14 Rear quarter window – removal and installation

1   Pry the covers from the hinges with a screwdriver (photo).
2   Loosen (but do not remove) the front hinge-to-body screws (photo).
3   Partially open the latch and loosen the screw (photo).
4   Open the window and have an assistant hold the weight of the glass.
5   Remove the retaining screws and have the assistant lift the window from the vehicle.
6   To install, have an assistant hold the window in position and install the retaining screws.
7   Open and close the window several times to check for proper operation, adjusting as necessary. Install the hinge covers.

13.4 Remove the window regulator mechanism through the access hole. Note the white paint marking the bolt locations for easier installation (arrows)

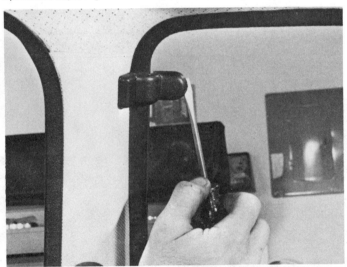

14.1 Remove the quarter window front hinge cover with a screwdriver

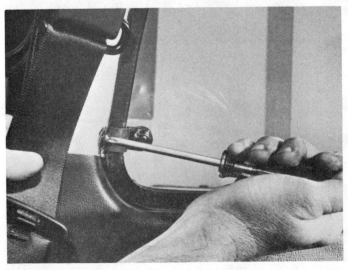

14.2 Loosen the front quarter window retaining screws

14.3 Open the quarter window latch and loosen the retaining screw

15 Rear hatchback – removal and installation

1   With an assistant supporting the weight of the lid, remove the attaching bolts.
2   Remove the gas strut support-to-body bolts and lift the hatchback away from the vehicle.
3   To install, have the assistant hold the hatchback in place, install the attaching bolts followed by the strut bolts.

16 Windshield, stationary quarter window and rear glass – removal and installation

The windshield, stationary quarter window and rear glass on all models are sealed in place with a special compound. Removal of the existing sealant requires the use of special equipment, making glass replacement a complex operation.

In view of this, it is not recommended that stationary glass removal be attempted by the home mechanic. If replacement is necessary due to breakage or leakage, the work should be referred to your dealer or a qualified shop.

17 Hood – removal and installation

1   Mark the location of the hood brace (photo).
2   Have an assistant hold the hood in an upright position and remove the hood brace bolts.
3   Remove the C-clips from the hood hinges.
4   Grasp the hood hinge pins with pliers and work them out of the

17.1 Mark the hood brace location (arrow) prior to removal

hinges, taking care not to lose the washers.
5   Lift the hood from the vehicle.
6   Installation is the reverse of removal, using needle-nosed pliers to install the nine pin C-clips and installing the hood brace at the marked location.

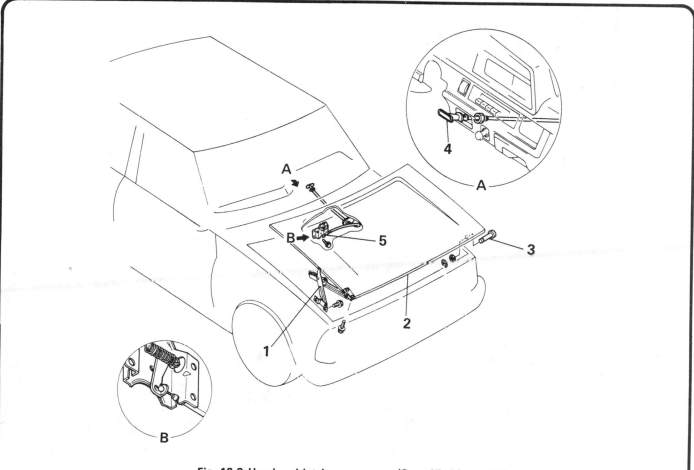

Fig. 12.3 Hood and latch components (Secs 17, 18 and 19)

1 Hood stay	3 Hinge pin	4 Hood release lever	5 Hood latch
2 Hood			

12

These photos illustrate a method of repairing simple dents. They are intended to supplement *Body repair - minor damage* in this Chapter and should not be used as the sole instructions for body repair on these vehicles.

1   If you can't access the backside of the body panel to hammer out the dent, pull it out with a slide-hammer-type dent puller. In the deepest portion of the dent or along the crease line, drill or punch hole(s) at least one inch apart . . .

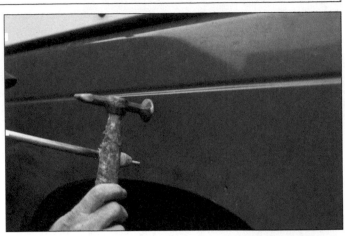

2   . . . then screw the slide-hammer into the hole and operate it. Tap with a hammer near the edge of the dent to help 'pop' the metal back to its original shape. When you're finished, the dent area should be close to its original contour and about 1/8-inch below the surface of the surrounding metal

3   Using coarse-grit sandpaper, remove the paint down to the bare metal. Hand sanding works fine, but the disc sander shown here makes the job faster. Use finer (about 320-grit) sandpaper to feather-edge the paint at least one inch around the dent area

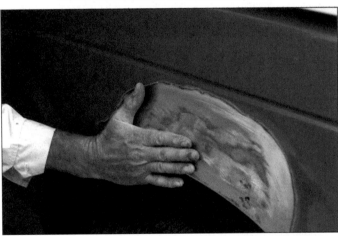

4   When the paint is removed, touch will probably be more helpful than sight for telling if the metal is straight. Hammer down the high spots or raise the low spots as necessary. Clean the repair area with wax/silicone remover

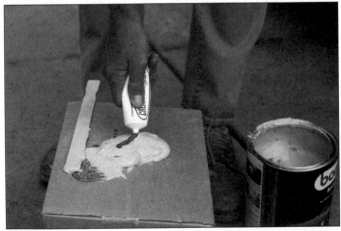

5   Following label instructions, mix up a batch of plastic filler and hardener. The ratio of filler to hardener is critical, and, if you mix it incorrectly, it will either not cure properly or cure too quickly (you won't have time to file and sand it into shape)

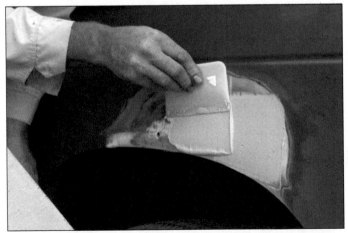

6   Working quickly so the filler doesn't harden, use a plastic applicator to press the body filler firmly into the metal, assuring it bonds completely. Work the filler until it matches the original contour and is slightly above the surrounding metal

7   Let the filler harden until you can just dent it with your fingernail. Use a body file or Surform tool (shown here) to rough-shape the filler

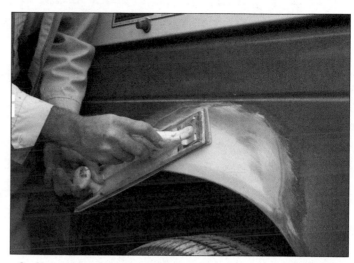

8   Use coarse-grit sandpaper and a sanding board or block to work the filler down until it's smooth and even. Work down to finer grits of sandpaper - always using a board or block - ending up with 360 or 400 grit

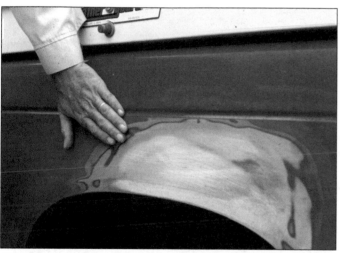

9   You shouldn't be able to feel any ridge at the transition from the filler to the bare metal or from the bare metal to the old paint. As soon as the repair is flat and uniform, remove the dust and mask off the adjacent panels or trim pieces

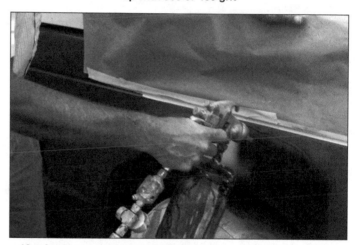

10   Apply several layers of primer to the area. Don't spray the primer on too heavy, so it sags or runs, and make sure each coat is dry before you spray on the next one. A professional-type spray gun is being used here, but aerosol spray primer is available inexpensively from auto parts stores

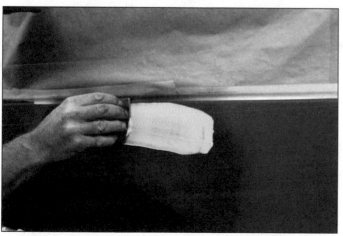

11   The primer will help reveal imperfections or scratches. Fill these with glazing compound. Follow the label instructions and sand it with 360 or 400-grit sandpaper until it's smooth. Repeat the glazing, sanding and respraying until the primer reveals a perfectly smooth surface

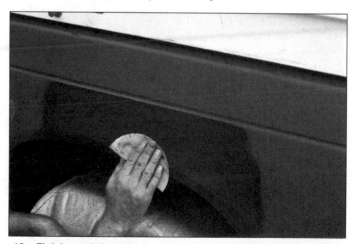

12   Finish sand the primer with very fine sandpaper (400 or 600-grit) to remove the primer overspray. Clean the area with water and allow it to dry. Use a tack rag to remove any dust, then apply the finish coat. Don't attempt to rub out or wax the repair area until the paint has dried completely (at least two weeks)

18 Hood latch – adjustment

1   If the hood does not close satisfactorily, loosen the retaining bolts, move the latch up or down as required and tighten the bolts.
2   Check for proper operation and repeat the procedure until the proper closing action is achieved.

19 Hood latch cable – removal and installation

1   Open the hood and disengage the cable from the latch assembly.
2   From inside the vehicle, disconnect the cable from the hood release control and pull the cable through the firewall to remove it.
3   To install, push the cable through the retaining bracket under dash and then through the firewall.
4   Engage the cable to the hood latch mechanism in the engine compartment.
5   Connect the cable to the hood release control in the passenger compartment and check for proper operation.

20 Instrument cluster finish panel – removal and installation

1   Pull off the heater blower knob (photo).

2   Remove the four screws which retain the finish panel.
3   Remove the panel by pushing down on the right side bottom edge and pulling outward (photo).
4   To install, place the finish panel in position and press it until it snaps into place.
5   Install the retaining screws and press the heater blower knob in place.

21 Rear shock absorber tower cover – removal and installation

1   Open the trunk or hatchback for access.
2   On some models it may be necessary to remove the rear interior taillight cover to gain access to the rear of the tower cover.
3   Remove the tower cover screws and plastic retainers and remove the cover.
4   Installation is the reverse of removal.

22 Radiator grille – removal and installation

1   Insert a screwdriver into the center of the grille retaining clip and pry the clip apart as you pull outward on the grille. Work around the grille until all of the clips are released and it can be lifted away.

20.1 Grasp the heater blower knob and pull it straight off to remove

20.3 Remove the finish panel by pushing downward on the right side and pulling outward

23.1 The bumper is retained by two nuts located at the reinforcement plate

24.2 An extension and socket are necessary to remove the bumper end cap retaining nut

2   To install, place the grille in position and push inward until it snaps into place.

23 Bumpers – removal and installation

1   Remove the nuts retaining the bumper bracket to the reinforcement (photo).
2   Lift the bumper away from the vehicle.
3   To install, insert the bumper shock absorbers into the chassis and install the retaining nuts.

24 Bumper end cap – removal and installation

1   Remove the bumper from the vehicle (Section 23).
2   Remove the two bolts and one nut retaining the end cap to the bumper. To remove the retaining nut it will be necessary to pry out the plastic cover on the back of the bumper and then use a socket and extension (photo).
3   Installation is the reverse of removal.

12

Chapter 13 Supplement:
Revisions and information on later USA models

Contents

1 Introduction

This supplement contains specifications and service procedure changes that apply to later GLC front wheel drive models produced for sale in the US. Also included is information related to previous models that was not available at the time of the original publication of this manual.

Where no differences (or very minor differences) exist between the later models and previous models, no information is given. In such instances, the original material included in Chapters 1 through 12 should be used.

2 Specifications

Note: *The specifications listed here include only those items which differ from those listed in Chapters 1 through 12. For information not specifically listed here, refer to the appropriate Chapter.*

Tune-up and routine maintenance

Power steering fluid type	ATF type F
Power steering drivebelt deflection	
New belt	5/16 to 25/64 in (8 to 10 mm)
Used belt	25/64 to 1/2 in (10 to 12 mm)
Ignition timing	6° BTDC

Cooling system
Thermostat lift (fully open) . . . .   11/32 in (8.5 mm) or more

Fuel system
Fuel pump discharge pressure (1984 and 1985 models) . . . . .   4.27 to 5.97 psi

Engine electrical system
Alternator output voltage . . . .   14.4 ± 0.3 V at 2000 to 2500 rpm

Suspension and steering

Torque specifications	Ft-lbs
Power steering pump pulley nut	22 to 29
Front strut mounting nuts/bolts	
Upper mount.	17 to 22
Lower mount	58 to 86
Rear strut lower mounting bolt	
Early models	23 to 34
Later models	40 to 50
Rear suspension lateral link bolts	69 to 86
Rear suspension trailing link-to-body bolts	
Early models	23 to 34
Later models	43 to 54
Automatic transaxle cable-type shifter locknuts	8.0

3   Tune-up and routine maintenance

Introduction
The following checks/adjustments should be done in addition to the ones outlined in the maintenance schedule in Chapter 1.

Weekly or every 250 miles (400 Km)
Check the power steering fluid level (if applicable)
Check/adjust the power steering pump drivebelt

Every 7500 miles (12000 Km) or 7.5 months
Inspect the rack seal boots
Inspect the transaxle change rod boot

Every 15000 miles (24000 Km) or 15 months
Check the power steering system
Check the operation of the choke

Power steering fluid level check
1   This check must be done when the engine is *cold*, so let the vehicle sit several hours (or overnight) before proceeding.
2   The reservoir for the power steering pump is located near the front of the engine, on the right side.
3   Use a rag to clean the reservoir cap and the area around the cap.

This will help to prevent foreign material from falling into the reservoir when the cap is removed.
4   Twist and pull on the reservoir cap, which has a built-in dipstick attached to it. Once the cap is removed, wipe off the fluid at the end of the dipstick with a clean rag. Now reinstall the dipstick/cap assembly to get a fluid level reading. Remove the dipstick again and note the fluid level. It should be up to the line on the dipstick.
5   If additional fluid is required, pour the specified type directly into the reservoir using a funnel to prevent spills. *Do not overfill the reservoir.*
6   If the reservoir requires frequent fluid additions, all power steering hoses, hose connections, the power steering pump and the steering box should be carefully checked for leaks.

Power steering pump drivebelt — check and adjustment
7   The drivebelt check is covered in detail in Chapter 1.
8   To adjust the belt, loosen the mounting and adjusting bar bolts approximately 1/2-turn, then tighten or loosen the adjusting bolt until the specified drivebelt deflection is obtained. Don't forget to tighten the mounting and adjusting bar bolts when the adjustment is complete.

Rack seal boot — inspection
9   If the steering rack (gearbox) seal rubber boots are damaged or

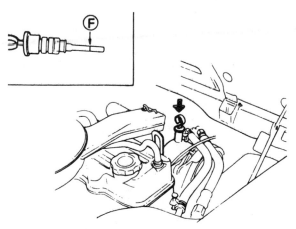

Fig. 13.1   The power steering fluid dipstick (arrow) is attached to the top of the pump reservoir (the level should be up to the F mark on the dipstick)

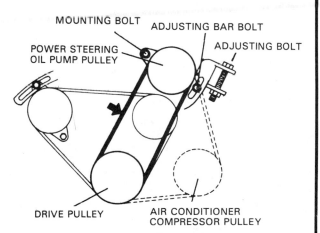

Fig. 13.2   Power steering system drivebelt adjustment details

13

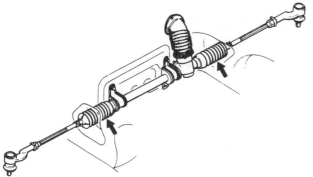

Fig. 13.3 Rack seal rubber boot locations (do not confuse them with the driveaxle boots)

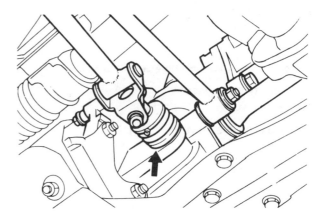

Fig. 13.4 Transaxle change rod rubber boot location

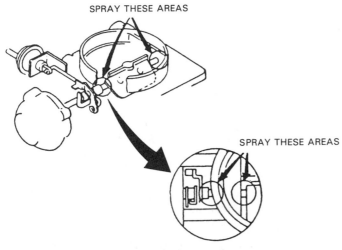

Fig. 13.5 Choke shaft/linkage lubrication points

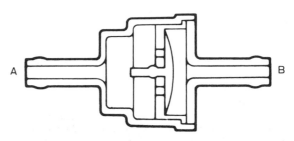

Fig. 13.6 Fuel check valve port locations

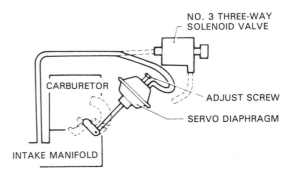

13.7 Throttle opener system component layout

deteriorated, serious and costly damage can occur to the steering joints and seals the rubber boots are designed to protect. Therefore, the boots should be inspected very carefully at the recommended intervals.

10 Raise the front of the vehicle and support it securely on jackstands. Block the rear tires and apply the parking brake to keep the vehicle from rolling.

11 Crawl under the vehicle and check the two boots (one on each side of the steering gear) very carefully for cracks, tears, holes, deteriorated rubber and loose or missing clamps. If the boots are dirty, wipe them clean before beginning the inspection.

12 If damage or deterioration is evident, have the boots replaced with new ones by a dealer service department or auto repair shop.

Transaxle change rod boot inspection

13 Refer to the *Rack seal boot — inspection* procedure outlined above, but note that the transaxle change rod is equipped with only one boot (see accompanying illustration).

Power steering system — inspection

14 Raise the front of the vehicle and support it securely on jackstands. Block the rear tires and apply the parking brake to keep the vehicle from rolling.

15 Crawl under the vehicle and check for fluid leaks at each of the power steering system hose and line connections. Tighten any connections that are leaking.

16 Check the rubber hoses for leaks as well.

Choke — inspection

17 The choke only operates when the engine is cold, so this check can only be performed before the vehicle has been started for the day.

18 Open the hood and remove the top cover of the air cleaner assembly. It is held in place by a wing nut and/or spring-type clips. Place

the cover and wing nut aside, out of the way of moving engine components.

19 Look at the top of the carburetor at the center of the air cleaner housing. You will notice a flat plate at the carburetor opening. **Note:** *Do not allow anything to drop down into the carburetor opening while the air cleaner top is off.*

20 Have an assistant press the accelerator pedal to the floor. the plate should close completely. **Note:** *Do not position your face directly over the carburetor during the next step, as the engine could backfire, causing serious burns.*

21 Have your assistant start the engine while you observe the plate at the carburetor. When the engine starts, the choke plate should open slightly.

22 Allow the engine to continue running at an idle speed. As the engine warms up to operating temperature, the plate should slowly open, allowing more air to enter through the top of the carburetor. After a few minutes, the choke plate should be completely open to the vertical position.

23 If the choke plate, shaft and linkage are covered with dirty looking deposits, they should be cleaned with an aerosol carburetor cleaner (available at auto parts stores). Lubricate the shaft and linkage pivots with spray lubricant after they have been cleaned thoroughly.

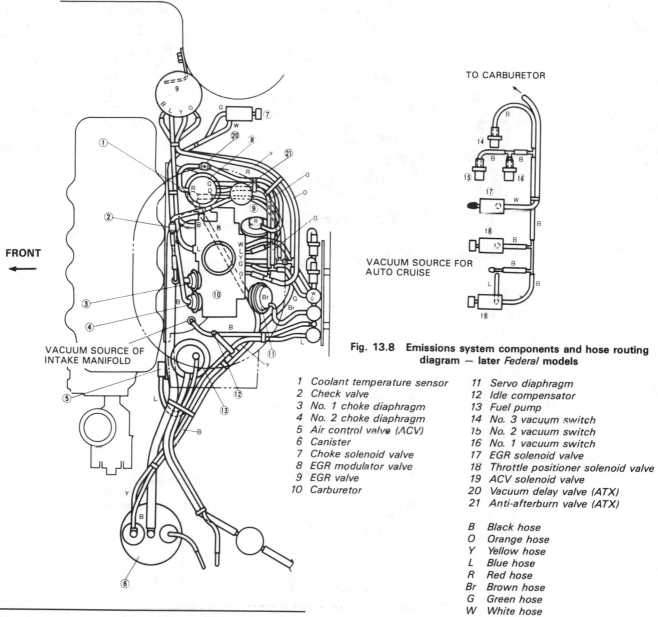

Fig. 13.8 Emissions system components and hose routing diagram — later *Federal* models

1	Coolant temperature sensor	11	Servo diaphragm
2	Check valve	12	Idle compensator
3	No. 1 choke diaphragm	13	Fuel pump
4	No. 2 choke diaphragm	14	No. 3 vacuum switch
5	Air control valve (ACV)	15	No. 2 vacuum switch
6	Canister	16	No. 1 vacuum switch
7	Choke solenoid valve	17	EGR solenoid valve
8	EGR modulator valve	18	Throttle positioner solenoid valve
9	EGR valve	19	ACV solenoid valve
10	Carburetor	20	Vacuum delay valve (ATX)
		21	Anti-afterburn valve (ATX)

B	Black hose
O	Orange hose
Y	Yellow hose
L	Blue hose
R	Red hose
Br	Brown hose
G	Green hose
W	White hose

4 Fuel and exhaust systems

General information

Later models are equipped with an electronically-controlled carburetor which is significantly different than the carburetor covered in Chapter 4. Servicing and adjustment must be done by a Mazda dealer service department.

Carburetor — disassembly, inspection and reassembly

Because of the complexity of this particular carburetor and the need for special tools and equipment to overhaul and adjust it, major repair work should be left to a Mazda dealer service department or carburetor repair specialist.

Fuel check valve — inspection

1   Some later models have a check valve installed in the fuel return line between the carburetor and tank.
2   To remove the valve, slide back the hose clamps and detach the fuel lines.
3   To check the valve for proper operation, blow into port A (see accompanying illustration) — air should come out port B.
4   Next, blow into port B — no air should come out port A. If the valve is defective, it should be replaced with a new one or carburetor

flooding could occur.
5   When reinstalling the valve, make sure that the carburetor fuel line is attached to port A and be sure to reposition the hose clamps.

Throttle opener system

6   Later models equipped with both air conditioning and power steering use a throttle opener system to maintain the proper idle speed when these two accessories are in use.
7   To check the throttle opener system, start the engine and apply vacuum to the servo diaphragm. The engine speed should increase to about 1200 rpm.
8   If the engine speed does not increase to between 1400 and 1900 rpm, adjust by turning the adjust screw.

5 Emissions control systems

Air injection system — description and testing

1   The air injection system on these models has no air pump. It consists of a reed valve, mounted on the air cleaner housing, and air lines which connect the reed valve to the exhaust manifold. Federal models

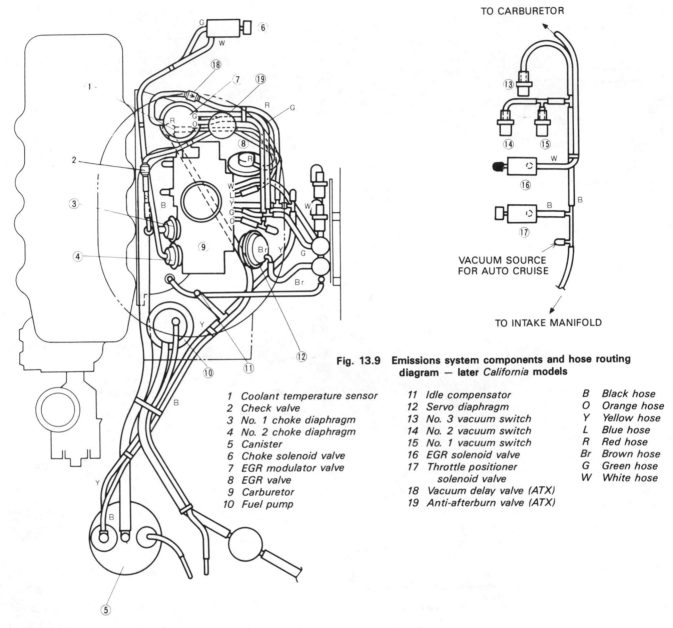

Fig. 13.9 **Emissions system components and hose routing diagram — later *California* models**

1 Coolant temperature sensor	11 Idle compensator	B Black hose
2 Check valve	12 Servo diaphragm	O Orange hose
3 No. 1 choke diaphragm	13 No. 3 vacuum switch	Y Yellow hose
4 No. 2 choke diaphragm	14 No. 2 vacuum switch	L Blue hose
5 Canister	15 No. 1 vacuum switch	R Red hose
6 Choke solenoid valve	16 EGR solenoid valve	Br Brown hose
7 EGR modulator valve	17 Throttle positioner	G Green hose
8 EGR valve	solenoid valve	W White hose
9 Carburetor	18 Vacuum delay valve (ATX)	
10 Fuel pump	19 Anti-afterburn valve (ATX)	

also utilize a coolant temperature sensor, air control valve (ACV), solenoid valve and electronic control unit.

2   The reed valve supplies outside air to the exhaust system to promote oxidation (complete burning) of any unburned fuel that may be present in the exhaust gases. It is actuated by negative pressure exhaust gas pulsations in the manifold. Air is drawn through the air cleaner and directed to the exhaust manifold by the valve motion corresponding to the exhaust pulses.

Reed valve testing

3   Remove the air cleaner cover and filter element. Be careful not to drop anything down into the carburetor.

4   Start the engine and allow it to idle.

5   Hold a thin piece of paper over the reed valve inlet port as shown in the accompanying illustration. If the reed valve is operating properly, the paper should be drawn to the port by the exhaust gas pulsations.

ACV (Federal models only) testing

6   Remove the air cleaner cover and filter element.

7   Disconnect the vacuum line from the ACV, then start the engine and let it idle.

8   Apply a vacuum to the ACV port with a hand pump (or attach an intake manifold vacuum line to the port) and check the reed valve operation as described in Paragraph 5.

9   Release the vacuum and try to determine if the air flow through

the reed valve decreases.

10   If the ACV does not function as described, replace it with a new one.

ACV solenoid valve testing

11   Mark the vacuum lines so they can be reattached to the correct ports, then disconnect them from the solenoid valve.

12   Attach a separate section of vacuum line to one of the ports and blow into the line; air should come out the other port.

13   Disconnect the wires from the valve and apply battery voltage to the valve terminals with jumper wires. **Caution:** *Be very careful — do not cause a short circuit!*

14   Blow into the vacuum line again; air should now exit the valve air filter.

15   If the solenoid valve does not function as described, replace it with a new one.

Coolant temperature sensor testing

16   The engine must be completely cool when this test is begun (coolant temperature approximately 68°F). The sensor is attached to the intake manifold just to the rear of and below the EGR valve.

17   Disconnect the wires from the sensor, then check the resistance by attaching the leads of an ohmmeter to the sensor wire terminals. With the coolant at approximately 68°F, the resistance should be about 2.45 K ohms.

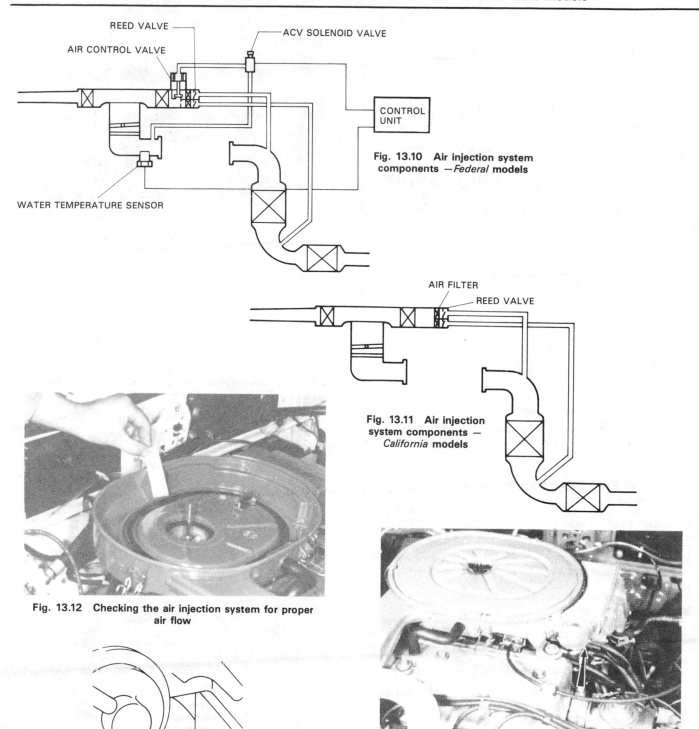

Fig. 13.10 Air injection system
components —*Federal* models

Fig. 13.11 Air injection
system components —
California models

Fig. 13.12 Checking the air injection system for proper
air flow

Fig. 13.13 The ACV (arrow) is attached to the reed
valve housing

Fig. 13.14 Coolant temperature sensor location

18 Start the engine and allow it to warm up to operating temperature. As the coolant temperature increases, the resistence of the temperature sensor should *decrease* (when the coolant temperature is approximately 176°F, the resistance should be about 0.32 K ohms).

19 If the sensor does not function as described, replace it with a new one.

Evaporative emissions system — description and testing

20 The system used on later models is unchanged from 1982 models except for the addition of a coolant temperature sensor.

Coolant temperature sensor check

21 Disconnect the vacuum line from the No. 1 purge control valve on top of the canister.

22 Run the engine at 1500 rpm. When the engine is cold (coolant below 122°F), no vacuum should be felt at the vacuum line. When the engine warms up (coolant above 122°F), vacuum should be felt at the line. If not, replace the sensor with a new one. *See Paragraphs 16 through 18 for additional, more detailed coolant temperature sensor tests.*

13

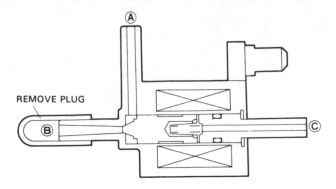

Fig. 13.15   EGR solenoid valve port locations

Fig. 13.16   EGR modulator valve location (disconnect hose A from the modulator port)

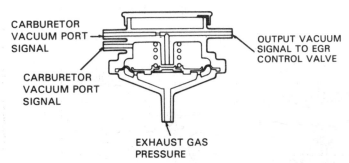

Fig. 13.17   Suction should be felt at the port labelled *output vacuum signal to EGR control valve*

Fig. 13.18   Vacuum switch locations

Exhaust Gas Recirculation (EGR) system — description and testing

23   The EGR system used on later models is nearly identical to the system described in Chapter 6. The major differences in the systems are the number and type of components which control vacuum to the EGR valve itself. Later models are equipped with an EGR solenoid valve, a water thermo-switch, an EGR modulator valve, an EGR thermo valve, vacuum switches and a vacuum delay valve (not all models).

EGR valve testing
24   Refer to Chapter 6 for this test.

EGR solenoid valve testing
25   Mark the vacuum lines so they can be reattached to the correct ports, then disconnect them from the solenoid valve. Attach a separate section of vacuum line to port A (see accompanying illustration) and remove the plug cap from port B.
26   Blow into the line attached to port A and make sure air comes out of port B.
27   Disconnect the wires from the valve and apply battery voltage to the valve terminals with jumper wires. **Caution:** *Be very careful — do not cause a short circuit!*
28   Blow into the vacuum line again; air should now come out of port C.

Water thermo-switch testing
29   The engine must be completely cold when this test is performed. Locate the thermo-switch (it is threaded into the radiator) and disconnect the wires.
30   Attach the leads of an ohmmeter to the switch terminals. When the coolant temperature is *below* 62°F, the ohmmeter should indicate *no continuity*.
31   Start the engine and allow it to idle. Watch the ohmmeter as the engine warms up. When the coolant temperature exceeds 65°F, the ohmmeter should indicate continuity.
32   Replace the valve with a new one if it does not function as described.

EGR modulator valve testing
33   With the engine idling at normal operating temperature, disconnect the EGR valve-to-modulator vacuum line from the modulator port.
34   Increase engine speed to 2000 rpm and check for suction at the

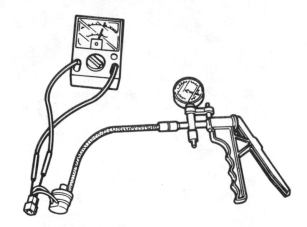

Fig. 13.19   Checking a vacuum switch for proper operation

modulator port. If no suction is felt, replace the modulator valve with a new one.

EGR thermo valve testing
35   This test should be done by a Mazda dealer service department.

Vacuum switch testing
36   Mark the vacuum lines so they can be reattached to the correct ports, then disconnect them from the vacuum switch being tested. Also, disconnect the wires from the switch.
37   Attach the leads of an ohmmeter to the vacuum switch terminals and apply vacuum to one of the ports with a hand-type vacuum pump.
38   Refer to the accompanying illustration to determine if the switch is operating properly.

	Connector	Terminal	Calibration
No. 1 & No. 3 Vacuum switch	LR —[ ]— LW / GY	LR ~ GY (+) (−)	Within 20mm-Hg OFF ON −120 ± 10mm-Hg
		LW ~ GY (+) (−)	Within 25mm-Hg OFF ON −200 ± 10mm-Hg
No. 2 vacuum switch	YG B	YG ~ B (+) (−)	Within 30mm-Hg OFF ON −370 ± 20mm-Hg

Fig. 13.20   Vacuum switch calibration — 1983 models

	Connector	Terminal	Calibration
No. 1 vacuum switch	L —[ ]— R / B	L ~ B (+) (−)	Within 20mm-Hg open closed −120 ± 10mm-Hg
No. 2 vacuum switch		R ~ B (+) (−)	Within 25mm-Hg open closed −200 ± 10mm-Hg
No. 3 vacuum switch	L B	L ~ B (+) (−)	Within 30mm-Hg open closed −370 ± 20mm-Hg

Fig. 13.21   Vacuum switch calibration — 1984 models

13

Vacuum delay valve testing

39 Remove the vacuum delay valve (see the accompanying illustration).

40 Attach the vacuum delay valve to a hand-type vacuum pump with a piece of vacuum line 29-inches long (see illustration).

41 Close off the vacuum delay valve with your thumb, then apply a vacuum of 20 in-Hg with the pump.

42 Release your thumb, then check the time required for the vacuum reading to decrease from 15.7 in-Hg to 3.9 in-Hg. It should take 2.3 ± 1.0 seconds. If not, replace the valve with a new one.

High altitude compensator (Federal models only) — description and testing

43 This system is nearly identical to the system described in Chap-

ter 6, but note that air should *not* pass through the valve at altitudes *below 3608 feet.*

Slow fuel cut system — description and testing

44 The system used on these models is identical to the one described in Chapter 6, but note that when testing the accelerator switch for continuity, the ohmmeter leads should be attached to terminals C and D of the carburetor wiring harness (see accompanying illustration).

Throttle positioner solenoid valve

45 On later models the deceleration control system incorporates a solenoid valve for the throttle positioner.

46 To check the deceleration control system on these models, start

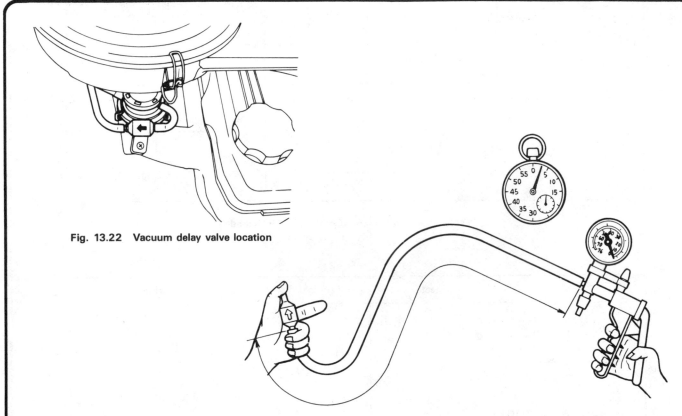

Fig. 13.22   Vacuum delay valve location

Fig. 13.23   Checking the vacuum delay valve (note the direction of the arrow on the valve)

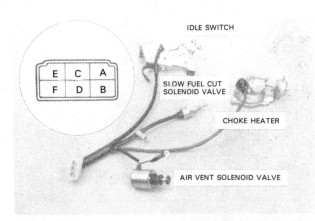

Fig. 13.24   Accelerator switch wire terminal locations

13.25   The throttle positioner solenoid valve (arrow) used on later model deceleration systems

the engine and run it at idle.
47 Connect a tachometer to the engine and increase the speed gradually to check that the servo diaphragm operates within the specified
engine speed.
48 To check the solenoid valve, disconnect the vacuum tube (A in
the accompanying illustration) from the solenoid valve and the electrical connector from the solenoid valve.
49 Blow air through Port A of the solenoid valve, making sure the air
exits through Port B.
50 Apply battery power to the solenoid valve and repeat the test. The
air should now come out through the valve air filter.
51 Replace the valve with a new one if it fails either test.

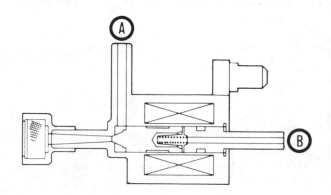

**13.26 The deceleration system throttle positioner
solenoid valve**

---

6 Chassis electrical system

Cruise control — general information

Some later models are equipped with an electronic cruise control
system. Due to the complexity of the system and the special tools and
expertise required to service it, any malfunctions should be diagnosed
and repaired by a Mazda dealer service department.

Wiring diagrams

The wiring diagrams on the following pages cover the circuits in later
models which differ significantly from the ones included in Chapter 10.

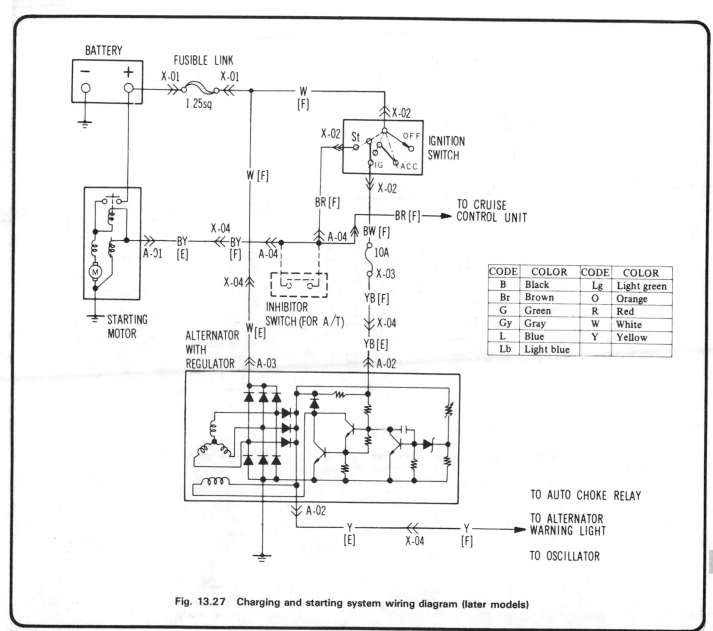

CODE	COLOR	CODE	COLOR
B	Black	Lg	Light green
Br	Brown	O	Orange
G	Green	R	Red
Gy	Gray	W	White
L	Blue	Y	Yellow
Lb	Light blue		

Fig. 13.27 Charging and starting system wiring diagram (later models)

13

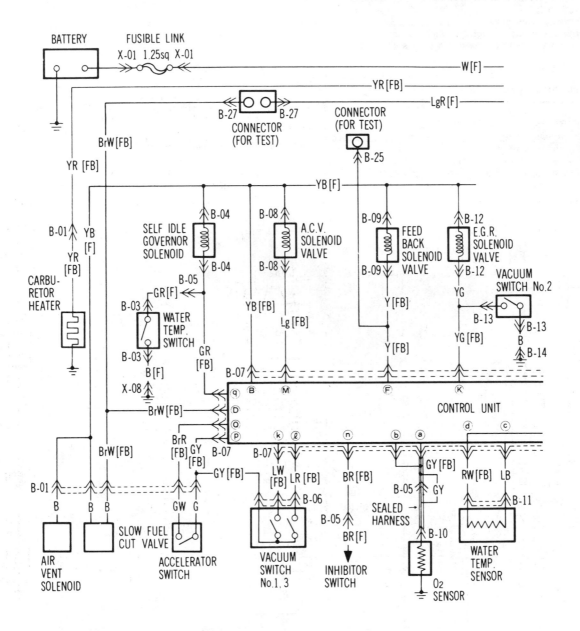

Fig. 13.28 Emissions, ignition, cooling fan and automatic transaxle kickdown system wiring diagram (later models)

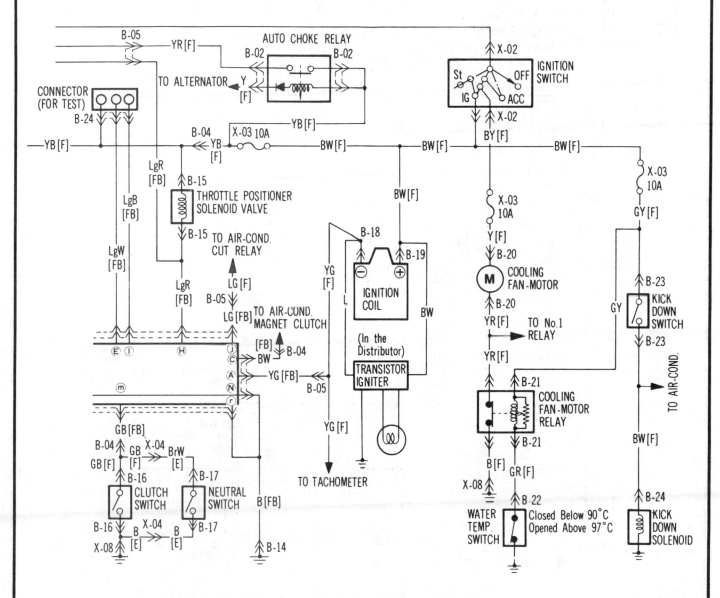

Fig. 13.28 Emissions, ignition, cooling fan and automatic transaxle kickdown system wiring diagram (later models) (continued)

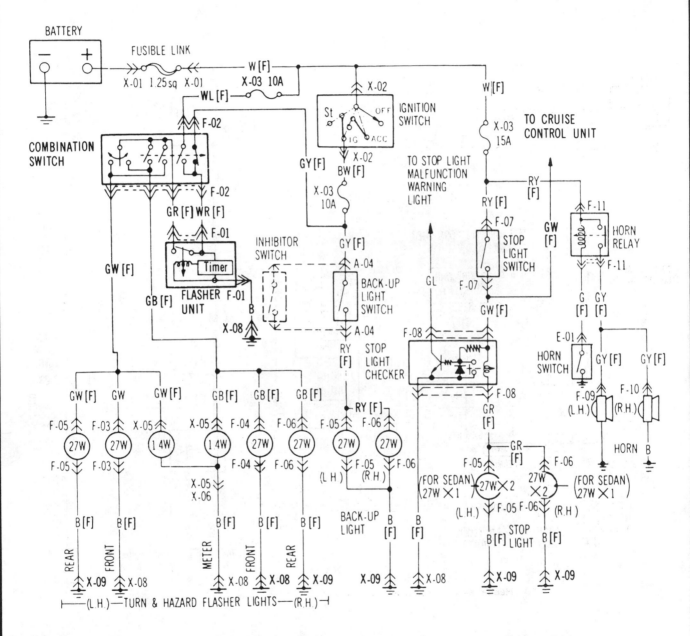

Fig. 13.29 Turn signal, hazard, back up, stop light and horn wiring diagram (later models)

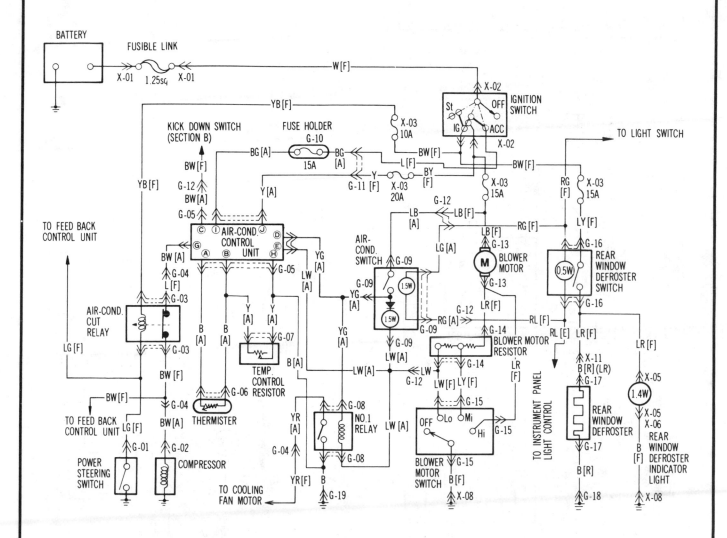

Fig. 13.30 Heater, air conditioner and rear window defroster wiring diagram (later models)

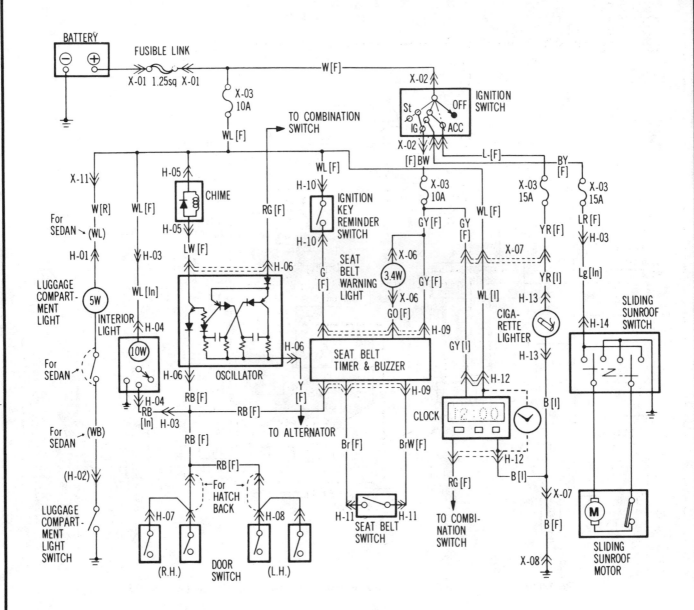

Fig. 13.31 Luggage compartment, sunroof and interior lights; lights off, ignition key and seat belt reminders; clock wiring diagram (later models)

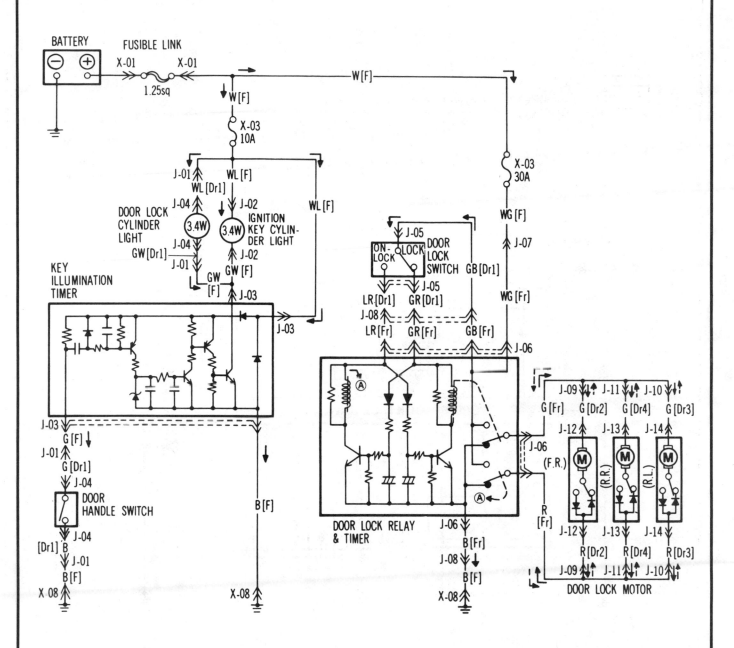

Fig. 13.32 Ignition and door lock lights; power door lock wiring diagram (later models)

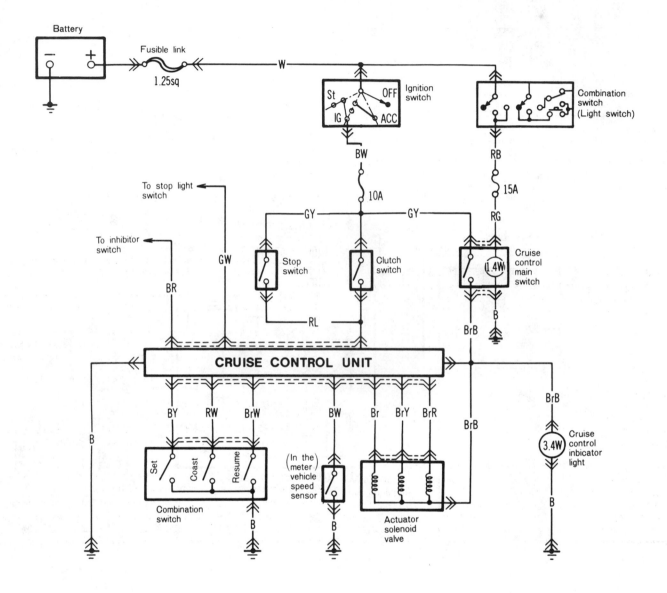

Fig. 13.33 Cruise control wiring diagram (later models)

Fig. 13.34   Power steering system pressure switch location

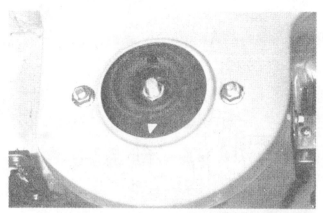

Fig. 13.35   On later models, the triangular mark on the
upper strut mount must face *in*

7   Suspension and steering

Power steering system pressure switch — check

1   Disconnect the wire lead from the pressure switch on the power steering pump. Position the wheels straight-ahead.
2   Connect the positive lead of an ohmmeter (or circuit tester) to the switch terminal and ground the other lead on the body. *No continuity* should exist.
3   Turn the steering wheel in either direction and see if continuity is indicated. If not, replace the switch with a new one.

Power steering pump — removal and installation

4   Remove the air cleaner duct if it is in the way.
5   Push on the drivebelt to keep the pulley from moving and loosen the pulley locknut.
6   Loosen the pump mounting bolts and adjusting bolt, then remove the drivebelt.
7   Disconnect the wire lead from the pressure switch on the pump body.
8   Position a drain pan under the fittings, then disconnect the hoses from the pump. Use flare-nut wrenches, if possible, to avoid damaging the fittings. Plug the hose ends.
9   Remove the pump mounting bolts and lift out the pump.
10   Installation is the reverse of removal. Refer to the drivebelt adjustment procedure in Section 3 and bleed the system as described later in this Section.

Power steering gear — removal and installation

11   The removal procedure for the power steering gear is identical to the procedure outlined in Chapter 11, but note that the fluid lines must be disconnected from the power steering gear and plugged before removing the mounting bolts (Step 5). Also, hold the steering gear assembly with the line fittings up to prevent fluid from leaking all over.

12   When installing the power steering gear, tighten the mounting bracket bolts *after* the steering shaft is attached. Also, the notches in the mounting brackets must face *down*.
13   Bleed the system as described below.

Power steering system — bleeding procedure

14   The power steering system should be bled whenever any of the hose fittings are loosened (such as when replacing the pump or steering gear), if air bubbles appear adhering to the dipstick or if the pump makes a rattling or buzzing noise.
15   Raise the front of the vehicle and support it on jackstands. Block the rear wheels and apply the parking brake to keep the vehicle from rolling.
16   Turn the steering wheel from lock-to-lock several times, then check the fluid level. Add fluid if necessary. Repeat the procedure until the fluid level stabilizes.
17   Start the engine and allow it to idle, then turn the steering wheel from lock-to-lock several times. Check the fluid level and add more as required. Repeat the procedure until the fluid level stabilizes and no bubbles appear on the dipstick.
18   Lower the vehicle.

Front spring and shock absorber strut assembly — removal and installation

19   The procedure outlined in Chapter 11 is correct, but note that on later models, the triangular mark on the upper mount must face *in* rather than out.

8   Automatic transaxle cable-type shifter

1   Later models use a cable-type control between the shifter and the transaxle instead of the rod-type used on earlier models.

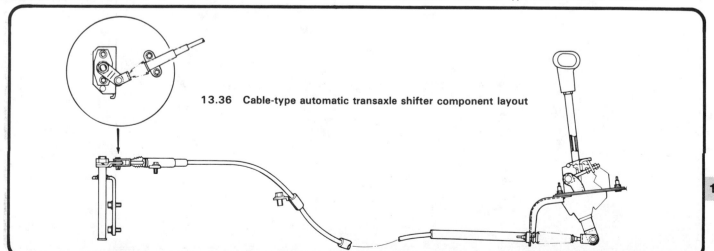

13.36   Cable-type automatic transaxle shifter component layout

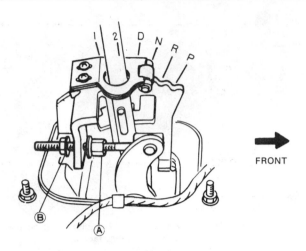

13.37   Cable type shifter locknuts (A and B)

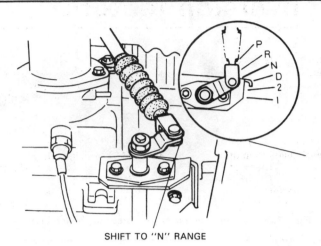

SHIFT TO "N" RANGE

13.38   Shifting the cable-type shifter into Neutral
at the transaxle

Adjustment

2   Apply the parking brake and pry the console cover off for access to the shifter mechanism.
3   To adjust the shifter detents, loosen the adjusting locknuts (A and B in the accompanying illustration).
4   Shift the selector into Neutral (making sure the detent roller is in Neutral as well).
5   Place the selector lever at the transaxle in Neutral.
6   Tighten locknut A at the shifter mechanism until it just contacts the T-joint and then tighten locknut B to the specified torque.

7   Depress the button on the shift lever and push the lever toward the Park position until the selector lever on the transaxle side begins to move and check the distance the lever has moved.
8   Move the lever toward the Drive position and check the distance it moves before the lever begins to operate on the transaxle side.
9   If the lever movement toward Park and Drive are not even, adjust the locknuts until it is.
10   After the locknuts have been adjusted, tighten them to the specified torque and check the shift cable mechanism for proper operation.

Conversion factors

Length (distance)

	X	factor	=	unit	X	factor	=	unit
Inches (in)	X	25.4	=	Millimetres (mm)	X	0.0394	=	Inches (in)
Feet (ft)	X	0.305	=	Metres (m)	X	3.281	=	Feet (ft)
Miles	X	1.609	=	Kilometres (km)	X	0.621	=	Miles

Volume (capacity)

	X	factor	=	unit	X	factor	=	unit
Cubic inches (cu in; in³)	X	16.387	=	Cubic centimetres (cc; cm³)	X	0.061	=	Cubic inches (cu in; in³)
Imperial pints (Imp pt)	X	0.568	=	Litres (l)	X	1.76	=	Imperial pints (Imp pt)
Imperial quarts (Imp qt)	X	1.137	=	Litres (l)	X	0.88	=	Imperial quarts (Imp qt)
Imperial quarts (Imp qt)	X	1.201	=	US quarts (US qt)	X	0.833	=	Imperial quarts (Imp qt)
US quarts (US qt)	X	0.946	=	Litres (l)	X	1.057	=	US quarts (US qt)
Imperial gallons (Imp gal)	X	4.546	=	Litres (l)	X	0.22	=	Imperial gallons (Imp gal)
Imperial gallons (Imp gal)	X	1.201	=	US gallons (US gal)	X	0.833	=	Imperial gallons (Imp gal)
US gallons (US gal)	X	3.785	=	Litres (l)	X	0.264	=	US gallons (US gal)

Mass (weight)

	X	factor	=	unit	X	factor	=	unit
Ounces (oz)	X	28.35	=	Grams (g)	X	0.035	=	Ounces (oz)
Pounds (lb)	X	0.454	=	Kilograms (kg)	X	2.205	=	Pounds (lb)

Force

	X	factor	=	unit	X	factor	=	unit
Ounces-force (ozf; oz)	X	0.278	=	Newtons (N)	X	3.6	=	Ounces-force (ozf; oz)
Pounds-force (lbf; lb)	X	4.448	=	Newtons (N)	X	0.225	=	Pounds-force (lbf; lb)
Newtons (N)	X	0.1	=	Kilograms-force (kgf; kg)	X	9.81	=	Newtons (N)

Pressure

	X	factor	=	unit	X	factor	=	unit
Pounds-force per square inch (psi; lbf/in²; lb/²)	X	0.070	=	Kilograms-force per square centimetre (kgf/cm²; kg/cm²)	X	14.223	=	Pounds-force per square inch (psi; lbf/in²; lb/²)
Pounds-force per square inch (psi; lbf/in²; lb/in²)	X	0.068	=	Atmospheres (atm)	X	14.696	=	Pounds-force per square inch (psi; lbf/in²; lb/in²)
Pounds-force per square inch (psi; lbf/in²; lb/in²)	X	0.069	=	Bars	X	14.5	=	Pounds-force per square inch (psi; lbf/in²; lb/in²)
Pounds-force per square inch (psi; lbf/in²; lb/in²)	X	6.895	=	Kilopascals (kPa)	X	0.145	=	Pounds-force per square inch (psi; lbf/in²; lb/in²)
Kilopascals (kPa)	X	0.01	=	Kilograms-force per square centimetre (kgf/cm²; kg/cm²)	X	98.1	=	Kilopascals (kPa)
Millibar (mbar)	X	100	=	Pascals (Pa)	X	0.01	=	Millibar (mbar)
Millibar (mbar)	X	0.0145	=	Pounds-force per square inch (psi; lbf/in²; lb/in²)	X	68.947	=	Millibar (mbar)
Millibar (mbar)	X	0.75	=	Millimetres of mercury (mmHg)	X	1.333	=	Millibar (mbar)
Millibar (mbar)	X	0.401	=	Inches of water (inH₂O)	X	2.491	=	Millibar (mbar)
Millimetres of mercury (mmHg)	X	0.535	=	Inches of water (inH₂O)	X	1.868	=	Millimetres of mercury (mmHg)
Inches of water (inH₂O)	X	0.036	=	Pounds-force per square inch (psi; lbf/in²; lb/in²)	X	27.68	=	Inches of water (inH₂O)

Torque (moment of force)

	X	factor	=	unit	X	factor	=	unit
Pounds-force inches (lbf in; lb in)	X	1.152	=	Kilograms-force centimetre (kgf cm; kg cm)	X	0.868	=	Pounds-force inches (lbf in; lb in)
Pounds-force inches (lbf in; lb in)	X	0.113	=	Newton metres (Nm)	X	8.85	=	Pounds-force inches (lbf in; lb in)
Pounds-force inches (lbf in; lb in)	X	0.083	=	Pounds-force feet (lbf ft; lb ft)	X	12	=	Pounds-force inches (lbf in; lb in)
Pounds-force feet (lbf ft; lb ft)	X	0.138	=	Kilograms-force metres (kgf m; kg m)	X	7.233	=	Pounds-force feet (lbf ft; lb ft)
Pounds-force feet (lbf ft; lb ft)	X	1.356	=	Newton metres (Nm)	X	0.738	=	Pounds-force feet (lbf ft; lb ft)
Newton metres (Nm)	X	0.102	=	Kilograms-force metres (kgf m; kg m)	X	9.804	=	Newton metres (Nm)

Power

	X	factor	=	unit	X	factor	=	unit
Horsepower (hp)	X	745.7	=	Watts (W)	X	0.0013	=	Horsepower (hp)

Velocity (speed)

	X	factor	=	unit	X	factor	=	unit
Miles per hour (miles/hr; mph)	X	1.609	=	Kilometres per hour (km/hr; kph)	X	0.621	=	Miles per hour (miles/hr; mph)

Fuel consumption*

	X	factor	=	unit	X	factor	=	unit
Miles per gallon, Imperial (mpg)	X	0.354	=	Kilometres per litre (km/l)	X	2.825	=	Miles per gallon, Imperial (mpg)
Miles per gallon, US (mpg)	X	0.425	=	Kilometres per litre (km/l)	X	2.352	=	Miles per gallon, US (mpg)

Temperature

Degrees Fahrenheit = (°C x 1.8) + 32

Degrees Celsius (Degrees Centigrade; °C) = (°F - 32) x 0.56

*It is common practice to convert from miles per gallon (mpg) to litres/100 kilometres (l/100km), where mpg (Imperial) x l/100 km = 282 and mpg (US) x l/100 km = 235

Index

HAYNES AUTOMOTIVE MANUALS

NOTE: New manuals are added to this list on a periodic basis. If you do not see a listing for your vehicle, consult your local Haynes dealer for the latest product information.

ACURA
*1776   **Integra & Legend** '86 thru '90

ALFA-ROMEO
531   **Alfa Romeo Sedan & Coupe** '73 thru '80

AMC
    Jeep CJ – see JEEP (412)
694   **Mid-size models,** Concord, Hornet, Gremlin & Spirit '70 thru '83
934   **(Renault) Alliance & Encore** all models '83 thru '87

AUDI
615   **4000** all models '80 thru '87
428   **5000** all models '77 thru '83
1117   **5000** all models '84 thru '88
207   **Fox** all models '73 thru '79

AUSTIN
    Healey Sprite – see MG Midget Roadster (265)

BLMC
527   **Mini** all models '59 thru '69
*646   **Mini** all models '69 thru '88

BMW
276   **320i** all 4 cyl models '75 thru '83
632   **528i & 530i** all models '75 thru '80
240   **1500 thru 2002** all models except Turbo '59 thru '77
348   **2500, 2800, 3.0 & Bavaria** '69 thru '76

BUICK
    Century (front wheel drive) – see GENERAL MOTORS A-Cars (829)
*1627   **Buick, Oldsmobile & Pontiac Full-size (Front wheel drive)** all models '85 thru '90 **Buick** Electra, LeSabre and Park Avenue; **Oldsmobile** Delta 88 Royale, Ninety Eight and Regency; **Pontiac** Bonneville
*1551   **Buick Oldsmobile & Pontiac Full-size (Rear wheel drive) Buick** Electra '70 thru '84, Estate '70 thru '90, LeSabre '70 thru '79 **Oldsmobile** Custom Cruiser '70 thru '90, Delta 88 '70 thru '85, Ninety-eight '70 thru '84 **Pontiac** Bonneville '70 thru '86, Catalina '70 thru '81, Grandville '70 thru '75, Parisienne '84 thru '86
627   **Mid-size** all rear-drive **Regal & Century** models with V6, V8 and Turbo '74 thru '87 **Regal** – see GENERAL MOTORS (1671) **Skyhawk** – see GENERAL MOTORS J-Cars (766)
552   **Skylark** all X-car models '80 thru '85

CADILLAC
*751   **Cadillac Rear Wheel Drive** all gasoline models '70 thru '90 **Cimarron** – see GENERAL MOTORS J-Cars (766)

CAPRI
296   **2000 MK I Coupe** all models '71 thru '75
205   **2600 & 2800 V6 Coupe** '71 thru '75
375   **2800 Mk II V6 Coupe** '75 thru '78 **Mercury Capri** – see FORD Mustang (654)

CHEVROLET
*1477   **Astro & GMC Safari Mini-vans** all models '85 thru '91
554   **Camaro** V8 all models '70 thru '81
*866   **Camaro** all models '82 thru '91 **Cavalier** – see GENERAL MOTORS J-Cars (766) **Celebrity** – see GENERAL MOTORS A-Cars (829)

625   **Chevelle, Malibu & El Camino** all V6 & V8 models '69 thru '87
449   **Chevette & Pontiac T1000** all models '76 thru '87
550   **Citation** all models '80 thru '85
*1628   **Corsica/Beretta** all models '87 thru '90
274   **Corvette** all V8 models '68 thru '82
*1336   **Corvette** all models '84 thru '91
704   **Full-size Sedans** Caprice, Impala, Biscayne, Bel Air & Wagons, all V6 & V8 models '69 thru '90 **Lumina** – see GENERAL MOTORS (1671)
319   **Luv Pick-up** all 2WD & 4WD models '72 thru '82
626   **Monte Carlo** all V6, V8 & Turbo models '70 thru '88
241   **Nova** all V8 models '69 thru '79
*1642   **Nova and Geo Prizm** all front wheel drive models, '85 thru '90
*420   **Pick-ups '67 thru '87** – Chevrolet & GMC, all full-size models '67 thru '87; Suburban, Blazer & Jimmy '67 thru '91
*1664   **Pick-ups '88 thru '90** – Chevrolet & GMC all full-size (C and K) models, '88 thru '92
*1727   **Sprint & Geo Metro** '85 thru '91
*831   **S-10 & GMC S-15 Pick-ups** all models '82 thru '92
*345   **Vans** – Chevrolet & GMC, V8 & in-line 6 cyl models '68 thru '92

CHRYSLER
*1337   **Chrysler & Plymouth Mid-size** front wheel drive '82 thru '89 **K-Cars** – see DODGE Aries (723) **Laser** – see DODGE Daytona (1140)

DATSUN
402   **200SX** all models '77 thru '79
647   **200SX** all models '80 thru '83
228   **B-210** all models '73 thru '78
525   **210** all models '78 thru '82
206   **240Z, 260Z & 280Z** Coupe & 2+2 '70 thru '78
563   **280ZX** Coupe & 2+2 '79 thru '83 **300ZX** – see NISSAN (1137)
679   **310** all models '78 thru '82
123   **510 & PL521 Pick-up** '68 thru '73
430   **510** all models '78 thru '81
372   **610** all models '72 thru '76
277   **620 Series Pick-up** all models '73 thru '79 **720 Series Pick-up** – see NISSAN Pick-ups (771)
376   **810/Maxima** all gasoline models '77 thru '84
124   **1200** all models '70 thru '73
368   **F10** all models '76 thru '79 **Pulsar** – see NISSAN (876) **Sentra** – see NISSAN (982) **Stanza** – see NISSAN (981)

DODGE
*723   **Aries & Plymouth Reliant** all models '81 thru '89
*1231   **Caravan & Plymouth Voyager Mini-Vans** all models '84 thru '90
699   **Challenger & Plymouth Saporro** all models '78 thru '83
236   **Colt** all models '71 thru '77
610   **Colt & Plymouth Champ (front wheel drive)** all models '78 thru '87
*556   **D50/Ram 50/Plymouth Arrow Pick-ups & Raider** '79 thru '91
*1668   **Dakota Pick-up** all models '87 thru '90
234   **Dart & Plymouth Valiant** all 6 cyl models '67 thru '76
*1140   **Daytona & Chrysler Laser** all models '84 thru '89
*545   **Omni & Plymouth Horizon** all models '78 thru '90
*912   **Pick-ups** all full-size models '74 thru '91
*1726   **Shadow & Plymouth Sundance** '87 thru '91
*1779   **Spirit & Plymouth Acclaim** '89 thru '92
*349   **Vans** – Dodge & Plymouth V8 & 6 cyl models '71 thru '91

FIAT
080   **124 Sedan & Wagon** all ohv & dohc models '66 thru '75
094   **124 Sport Coupe & Spider** '68 thru '78
479   **Strada** all models '79 thru '82
273   **X1/9** all models '74 thru '80

FORD
*1476   **Aerostar Mini-vans** all models '86 thru '92
788   **Bronco and Pick-ups** '73 thru '79
*880   **Bronco and Pick-ups** '80 thru '91
268   **Courier Pick-up** all models '72 thru '82
789   **Escort & Mercury Lynx** all models '81 thru '90
*2021   **Explorer & Mazda Navajo** '91 thru '92
560   **Fairmont & Mercury Zephyr** all in-line & V8 models '78 thru '83
334   **Fiesta** all models '77 thru '80
754   **Ford & Mercury Full-size,** Ford LTD & Mercury Marquis ('75 thru '82); Ford Custom 500, Country Squire, Crown Victoria & Mercury Colony Park ('75 thru '87); Ford LTD Crown Victoria & Mercury Gran Marquis ('83 thru '87)
359   **Granada & Mercury Monarch** all in-line, 6 cyl & V8 models '75 thru '80
773   **Ford & Mercury Mid-size,** Ford Thunderbird & Mercury Cougar ('75 thru '82); Ford LTD & Mercury Marquis ('83 thru '86); Ford Torino, Gran Torino, Elite, Ranchero pick-up, LTD II, Mercury Montego, Comet, XR-7 & Lincoln Versailles ('75 thru '86)
*654   **Mustang & Mercury Capri** all models including Turbo '79 thru '92
357   **Mustang** V8 all models '64-1/2 thru '73
231   **Mustang II** all 4 cyl, V6 & V8 models '74 thru '78
649   **Pinto & Mercury Bobcat** all models '75 thru '80
*1670   **Probe** all models '89 thru '92
*1026   **Ranger & Bronco II** all gasoline models '83 thru '92
*1421   **Taurus & Mercury Sable** '86 thru '91
*1418   **Tempo & Mercury Topaz** all gasoline models '84 thru '91
1338   **Thunderbird & Mercury Cougar/XR7** '83 thru '88
*1725   **Thunderbird & Mercury Cougar** '89 and '90
*344   **Vans** all V8 Econoline models '69 thru '91

GENERAL MOTORS
*829   **A-Cars** – Chevrolet Celebrity, Buick Century, Pontiac 6000 & Oldsmobile Cutlass Ciera all models '82 thru '90
*766   **J-Cars** – Chevrolet Cavalier, Pontiac J-2000, Oldsmobile Firenza, Buick Skyhawk & Cadillac Cimarron all models '82 thru '92
*1420   **N-Cars** – Buick Somerset '85 thru '87; Pontiac Grand Am and Oldsmobile Calais '85 thru '90; Buick Skylark '86 thru '90
*1671   **GM: Buick** Regal, **Chevrolet** Lumina, **Oldsmobile** Cutlass Supreme, **Pontiac** Grand Prix, all front wheel drive models '88 thru '90
*2035   **GM: Chevrolet** Lumina APV, **Oldsmobile** Silhouette, **Pontiac** Trans Sport '90 thru '92

GEO
    Metro – see CHEVROLET Sprint (1727)
    Prizm – see CHEVROLET Nova (1642)
    Tracker – see SUZUKI Samurai (1626)

GMC
    Safari – see CHEVROLET ASTRO (1477)
    Vans & Pick-ups – see CHEVROLET (420, 831, 345, 1664)

(continued on next page)

* Listings shown with an asterisk (*) indicate model coverage as of this printing. These titles will be periodically updated to include later model years – consult your Haynes dealer for more information.

Haynes North America, Inc., 861 Lawrence Drive, Newbury Park, CA 91320 • (805) 498-6703

NOTE: New manuals are added to this list on a periodic basis. If you do not see a listing for your vehicle, consult your local Haynes dealer for the latest product information.

HONDA
351	**Accord CVCC** all models '76 thru '83
*1221	**Accord** all models '84 thru '89
160	**Civic 1200** all models '73 thru '79
633	**Civic 1300 & 1500 CVCC** all models '80 thru '83
297	**Civic 1500 CVCC** all models '75 thru '79
*1227	**Civic** all models '84 thru '91
*601	**Prelude CVCC** all models '79 thru '89

HYUNDAI
*1552   **Excel** all models '86 thru '91

ISUZU
*1641   **Trooper & Pick-up,** all gasoline models '81 thru '91

JAGUAR
*242   **XJ6** all 6 cyl models '68 thru '86
*478   **XJ12 & XJS** all 12 cyl models '72 thru '85

JEEP
*1553   **Cherokee, Comanche & Wagoneer Limited** all models '84 thru '91
412   **CJ** all models '49 thru '86
*1777   **Wrangler** all models '87 thru '92

LADA
*413   **1200, 1300. 1500 & 1600** all models including Riva '74 thru '86

LAND ROVER
529   **Diesel** all models '58 thru '80

MAZDA
648	**626** Sedan & Coupe (rear wheel drive) all models '79 thru '82
*1082	**626 & MX-6 (front wheel drive)** all models '83 thru '90
*267	**B1600, B1800 & B2000 Pick-ups** '72 thru '90
370	**GLC Hatchback (rear wheel drive)** all models '77 thru '83
757	**GLC (front wheel drive)** all models '81 thru '86
460	**RX-7** all models '79 thru '85
*1419	**RX-7** all models '86 thru '91

MERCEDES-BENZ
*1643	**190 Series** all four-cylinder gasoline models, '84 thru '88
346	**230, 250 & 280** Sedan, Coupe & Roadster all 6 cyl sohc models '68 thru '72
983	**280 123 Series** all gasoline models '77 thru '81
698	**350 & 450** Sedan, Coupe & Roadster all models '71 thru '80
697	**Diesel 123 Series** 200D, 220D, 240D, 240TD, 300D, 300CD, 300TD, 4- & 5-cyl incl. Turbo '76 thru '85

MERCURY
See FORD Listing

MG
111   **MGB** Roadster & GT Coupe all models '62 thru '80
265   **MG Midget & Austin Healey Sprite** Roadster '58 thru '80

MITSUBISHI
*1669   **Cordia, Tredia, Galant, Precis & Mirage** '83 thru '90
*2022   **Pick-ups & Montero** '83 thru '91

MORRIS
074   **(Austin) Marina 1.8** all models '71 thru '80
024   **Minor 1000** sedan & wagon '56 thru '71

NISSAN
1137	**300ZX** all Turbo & non-Turbo models '84 thru '89
*1341	**Maxima** all models '85 thru '91
*771	**Pick-ups/Pathfinder** gas models '80 thru '91
*876	**Pulsar** all models '83 thru '86
*982	**Sentra** all models '82 thru '90
*981	**Stanza** all models '82 thru '90

OLDSMOBILE
Custom Cruiser – *see BUICK Full-size (1551)*
658   **Cutlass** all standard gasoline V6 & V8 models '74 thru '88
Cutlass Ciera – *see GENERAL MOTORS A-Cars (829)*
Cutlass Supreme – *see GENERAL MOTORS (1671)*
Firenza – *see GENERAL MOTORS J-Cars (766)*
Ninety-eight – *see BUICK Full-size (1551)*
Omega – *see PONTIAC Phoenix & Omega (551)*

PEUGEOT
663   **504** all diesel models '74 thru '83

PLYMOUTH
425   **Arrow** all models '76 thru '80
For all other PLYMOUTH titles, see DODGE listing.

PONTIAC
T1000 – *see CHEVROLET Chevette (449)*
J-2000 – *see GENERAL MOTORS J-Cars (766)*
6000 – *see GENERAL MOTORS A-Cars (829)*
1232   **Fiero** all models '84 thru '88
555   **Firebird** all V8 models except Turbo '70 thru '81
*867   **Firebird** all models '82 thru '91
Full-size Rear Wheel Drive – *see Buick, Oldsmobile, Pontiac Full-size (1551)*
Grand Prix – *see GENERAL MOTORS (1671)*
551   **Phoenix & Oldsmobile Omega** all X-car models '80 thru '84

PORSCHE
*264   **911** all Coupe & Targa models except Turbo & Carrera 4 '65 thru '89
239   **914** all 4 cyl models '69 thru '76
397   **924** all models including Turbo '76 thru '82
*1027   **944** all models including Turbo '83 thru '89

RENAULT
141   **5 Le Car** all models '76 thru '83
079   **8 & 10** all models with 58.4 cu in engines '62 thru '72
097   **12 Saloon & Estate** all models 1289 cc engines '70 thru '80
768   **15 & 17** all models '73 thru '79
081   **16** all models 89.7 cu in & 95.5 cu in engines '65 thru '72
Alliance & Encore – *see AMC (934)*
984   **Fuego** all models '82 thru '85

SAAB
247   **99** all models including Turbo '69 thru '80
*980   **900** all models including Turbo '79 thru '88

SUBARU
237   **1100, 1300, 1400 & 1600** all models '71 thru '79
*681   **1600 & 1800** 2WD & 4WD all models '80 thru '89

SUZUKI
*1626   **Samurai/Sidekick and Geo Tracker** all models '86 thru '91

TOYOTA
*1023	**Camry** all models '83 thru '91
150	**Carina Sedan** all models '71 thru '74
229	**Celica ST, GT & liftback** all models '71 thru '77
437	**Celica** all models '78 thru '81
*935	**Celica** all models except front-wheel drive and Supra '82 thru '85
680	**Celica Supra** all models '79 thru '81
1139	**Celica Supra** all in-line 6-cylinder models '82 thru '86
361	**Corolla** all models '75 thru '79
961	**Corolla** all models (rear wheel drive) '80 thru '87
*1025	**Corolla** all models (front wheel drive) '84 thru '91
*636	**Corolla Tercel** all models '80 thru '82
230	**Corona & MK II** all 4 cyl sohc models '69 thru '74
360	**Corona** all models '74 thru '82
*532	**Cressida** all models '78 thru '82
313	**Land Cruiser** all models '68 thru '82
200	**MK II** all 6 cyl models '72 thru '76
*1339	**MR2** all models '85 thru '87
304	**Pick-up** all models '69 thru '78
*656	**Pick-up** all models '79 thru '91

TRIUMPH
112   **GT6 & Vitesse** all models '62 thru '74
113   **Spitfire** all models '62 thru '81
028   **TR2, 3, 3A, & 4A** Roadsters '52 thru '67
031   **TR250 & 6** Roadsters '67 thru '76
322   **TR7** all models '75 thru '81

VW
159   **Beetle & Karmann Ghia** all models '54 thru '79
238   **Dasher** all gasoline models '74 thru '81
*884   **Rabbit, Jetta, Scirocco, & Pick-up** all gasoline models '74 thru '91 & **Convertible** '80 thru '91
451   **Rabbit, Jetta & Pick-up** all diesel models '77 thru '84
082   **Transporter 1600** all models '68 thru '79
226   **Transporter 1700, 1800 & 2000** all models '72 thru '79
084   **Type 3 1500 & 1600** all models '63 thru '73
1029   **Vanagon** all air-cooled models '80 thru '83

VOLVO
203   **120, 130 Series & 1800 Sports** '61 thru '73
129   **140 Series** all models '66 thru '74
244   **164** all models '68 thru '75
*270   **240 Series** all models '74 thru '90
400   **260 Series** all models '75 thru '82
*1550   **740 & 760 Series** all models '82 thru '88

SPECIAL MANUALS
1479	**Automotive Body Repair & Painting Manual**
1654	**Automotive Electrical Manual**
1480	**Automotive Heating & Air Conditioning Manual**
1762	**Chevrolet Engine Overhaul Manual**
1736	**Diesel Engine Repair Manual**
1667	**Emission Control Manual**
1763	**Ford Engine Overhaul Manual**
482	**Fuel Injection Manual**
1666	**Small Engine Repair Manual**
299	**SU Carburetors** thru '88
393	**Weber Carburetors** thru '79
300	**Zenith/Stromberg CD Carburetors** thru '76

See your dealer for other available titles

Over 100 Haynes motorcycle manuals also available

7-1-92

* *Listings shown with an asterisk (*) indicate model coverage as of this printing. These titles will be periodically updated to include later model years – consult your Haynes dealer for more information.*

Haynes North America, Inc., 861 Lawrence Drive, Newbury Park, CA 91320 • (805) 498-6703